What Americans Believe

ISBN-13: 9780578736037
ISBN-10: 0578736039

Layout: Lisa Daly | lisa@goodcographics.com

Published by
Sidgwick Press

Front cover photos clockwise from top left:
Martha C. Nussbaum, T. H. Green, Ralph Reed, and Edmund Burke.
Back cover photos clockwise from top left:
Adam Smith, David Hollenbach, S. J., John Rawls, and Peter Vallentyne.

What Americans Believe

A Dialogue on
American Political Ideas

by James DeHullu

DEDICATION

Frederick Copleston, S. J. wrote a well-known history of western philosophy. He wrote clearly and sympathetically in a style that students could understand. More important, Copleston had a rare gift. He could fairly and accurately describe the views of philosophers with whom he profoundly disagreed. For that reason, he has always been one of my heroes. This book is dedicated to him.

TABLE OF CONTENTS

PREFACE

My father, an elementary-school principal, was a devout Catholic with a scientific education. He didn't read much philosophy, but he did own one paperback volume by the medieval theologian Thomas Aquinas. I tried to read that volume when I was in high school, but I never really understood what it said. Trying to understand it, though, showed me that there had been people who had thought about the great questions of life at a very deep level.

A little later, I encountered Frederick Copleston's history of philosophy. Copleston's chapters focus on individual philosophers who wrote about God, knowledge, justice, politics, ethics, law, human rights, beauty, and so much more. I wanted to know what those men (they were all men) had thought. What was it they knew? Why did they disagree with each other? What were their questions? Did they or anyone else know the answers? I was hooked.

After college and graduate school, I dreamed of writing a long dialogue that covered all the important issues as seen by all the important groups in American politics. It would be an interconnected discussion of justice, poverty, class, race, gender, inequality, property, human rights, education, capitalism, and everything else. Written as an impossibly complex computerized hypertext with hundreds of links, it would allow the reader to choose topics, read arguments, and follow any trail at will. I imagined that a fictitious Professor Sidgwick facilitated the discussions and hoped that the real Professor Sidgwick, a 19th-century Cambridge don, would not have been offended. The project was grandiose, to say the least; but thinking about it convinced me that the dialogue form is uniquely suited for expressing a wide range of opposing views.

I wrote parts of that long dialogue, but as time went on, I became convinced that more was at stake than the issues themselves. I realized that Americans often misunderstand and talk past each other in their political discussions.

The art of serious political conversation is dying. For one thing, it requires a great deal of work to clarify one's own ideas while listening to what others say. It is far easier to regard others as ignorant, malevolent, or foolish.

To help revive that art, I decided that it could be helpful to write a shorter dialogue presenting the main ideas that frame our personal political conversations and public debates. In a time of increasing political polarization and increasingly bitter political argument, I wanted to encourage understanding and civility, realizing that agreement may not be possible. There may be no definitive answers to many contested issues. But we must try.

The result is *What Americans Believe*.

Jim DeHullu, Philadelphia, 2021

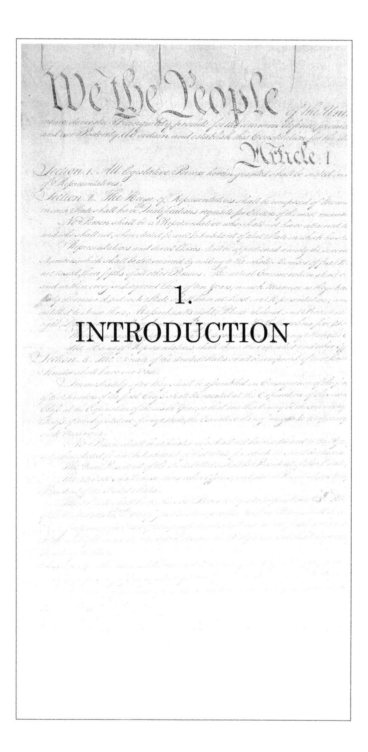

1.
INTRODUCTION

What Americans Believe is a dialogue among a group of American university students who are studying political philosophy, political science, and history. The focus of the dialogue is on the ideas that form the background for much of American political life. The dialogue is guided by a Professor Sidgwick, named after a Victorian philosopher at Cambridge University. All of the characters are fictitious.

The main participants include a Reagan conservative, an evangelical conservative, three social liberals, a right-libertarian, a left-libertarian, a liberal Catholic, and a conservative Catholic.

- Readers can follow the main argument of the dialogue by reading the speakers identified with the letters **m** **P** ("Main Path").

- Speakers who make comments on the main argument are identified with the letters **O** **P** ("Off Path"). Their comments are also shaded and italicized.

- Documentary source excerpts are identified with the letters **S** **E** ("Source Excerpt").

The dialogue includes four main parts, each of which presents a different framework of ideas. It begins with American conservatism and works its way through modern social liberalism, libertarianism, and Catholic social thought. In addition to those parts, there is a discussion of what philosophers refer to as political legitimacy, a short conclusion, and a postscript on Donald Trump and the Trump movement.

The dialogue does not attempt to reach final answers to the questions it raises. Nor does it cover every possible way to approach those questions. It does attempt to present several well-known political philosophies and to show that there is more than one plausible way to look at political philosophy and public policy. Taken together, the participants will present, defend, and criticize many of the ideas accepted by the American people. By doing so, their discussion may lead to a better understanding of several well-established points of view, less distrust of political opponents, and greater civility in the public square.

Readers who hope for final answers to hotly contested issues will be disappointed. As indicated, the goal is not to supply answers. It is rather to present and discuss several frameworks of ideas. The dialogue is intended to raise questions and to introduce concepts, claims, and arguments that are relevant to political philosophy and public policy. In addition, it will introduce authors and writings from different philosophical traditions that the reader may find intriguing and informative. In some cases, excerpts from primary sources are included. In many cases, leading writers are introduced so that the reader has options for further reading. If this book tempts the reader to read John Rawls, Robert Nozick, Martha C. Nussbaum, Frank Meyer, David Hollenbach, or any of the other authors referred to, it will have been successful. In the end, however, the reader alone must decide which concepts, which claims, and which arguments are compelling.

Professor Sidgwick Speaking

ⓜⓟ WELCOME

Good morning. I'm glad everyone could make it today. It's great to be here and to have a chance to exchange ideas.

This morning we are going to do something that is unusual even in a university setting. You are all students in different departments, but it is rare for students to come together in a structured way to carry on an extended dialogue on political ideas. That is our goal today.

I am asking each of you to bring your ideas together into a coherent political philosophy and present it to the group. I want Fred and Diego to put forward a broad, coherent statement of their conservatism. I want Ann, Vera, and John to present modern social liberalism. Dee and Elijah will present libertarianism. And finally, Ayesha will give us an overview of Catholic social thought. Since Fred is also a Catholic, I have asked him to add to what Ayesha says even though he is in the conservative group.

The United States includes people with many different views. I want us to try to lay out several of the main packages of ideas that form the background of our political culture. Try to imagine our group as a microcosm of the whole country. With luck, our discussion will simulate a national discussion. Try to think of yourselves not just as individuals with certain views, but as representatives of larger groups: conservatives, liberals, libertarians, Catholics, evangelicals, and so on.

I have asked Ayesha to talk with each of you and start us off with a short description of your beliefs.

Ayesha Speaking

🄼🄿 INTRODUCTIONS

I want to introduce everyone by giving a very short description of their overall political philosophy. Here goes.

Fred considers himself a typical American conservative in the Reagan tradition. He believes in constitutionally limited government at all levels, a less intrusive federal government, more power to state governments, lower taxes, and relatively free markets. Like me, he is a Catholic, but his interpretation of Catholic social thought is more conservative than mine.

Dee describes herself as a right-libertarian. She believes in strong individual rights, including strong property rights and freedom of contract. Governments exist to protect those rights and not a whole lot more. We should have minimal government that monopolizes the use of force, defends the nation, and enforces contracts. The modern welfare state is morally unacceptable.

John is not easy to classify, but he offers a description of an ideal society as a goal to be sought. In his ideal, everyone has the freedom and resources to develop his or her capacities and to pursue the good as they understand it. As a means to realizing that ideal, he supports a welfare state.

Ann accepts the ethical theory called utilitarianism, which tells us that actions, institutions, and policies should be chosen to maximize human welfare. Utilitarians have defined welfare in many ways, including pleasure, happiness, and the satisfaction of preferences. She tends to favor some form of welfare state and certain welfare rights.

Diego is an evangelical Christian. He bases his political views and his political philosophy on Christian principles found in the Bible. While he often agrees with Fred and other more secular conservatives, he sees the roots of our most serious social problems in moral decline. His emphasis is on strengthening the family and stopping the moral decline of our society.

Vera is a strong feminist and tends to be skeptical about traditional political philosophy. She rejects all so-called proofs for moral principles. Instead, she believes that moral principles are a human choice for which we are responsible. She also believes that women's interests and women's experiences should have more weight in political philosophy and political affairs.

Elijah describes himself as a left-libertarian. He agrees with Dee that individual people own themselves and have strong individual rights. Unlike Dee, he believes that all human beings begin with a right to use the earth's natural resources and that when some people take full individual ownership of resources, others are owed some form of compensation.

As for myself, I'm Ayesha and I'm a Catholic. I have been very impressed by Catholic social thought as expressed in both papal encyclicals and statements made by the American bishops. I reject both centralized socialism and free-market capitalism. I see Catholicism as a "third way" that avoids the problems of those two alternatives.

Professor Sidgwick Speaking

🅜🅟 SMALL GROUPS

Thank you, Ayesha. Now I'd like us to break up into small groups. Each group will work together and present a broad philosophical point of view for all of us to consider. You can also present the different opinions that are found within your group. Once again, here are the groups:

- **Conservative Group:** Fred and Diego
- **Liberal Group:** Ann, John, and Vera
- **Libertarian Group:** Dee and Elijah
- **Catholic Group:** Ayesha (with comments from Fred)

I am asking each group to organize its presentation to include the following elements:

- **Fundamental concepts**
- **Fundamental principles**
- **Background history, including key thinkers**
- **Major arguments supporting your principles**
- **Ideas about individual rights and property**

After each presentation, I will ask someone from a different group to give us an overall evaluation of what was said. I know it isn't easy to evaluate a political philosophy you don't agree with, but I want you to try. Feel free to be critical, but I also want you to try to find the value in the view you are evaluating. I would also like those who do the evaluations to identify one or two important questions that they feel have not been adequately addressed.

Professor Sidgwick Speaking

🄼🄿 ETHICAL TRADITIONS

Before we get started let me provide a little historical background that might be helpful. In the history of western moral philosophy there are several traditions that have all produced influential ideas on ethics and politics. We have at least the following traditions that you can dig into to help organize your political ideas. I'm going to mention a number of philosophers, some of whom we will hear more about later.

Natural law. This is an old tradition that includes both theistic and non-theistic variations. The main idea is that there is a moral law implied by human nature. Most natural law theorists assume that the moral law was established by God, but others do not. In either case, the law suits our nature and therefore it can be discerned by a study of our nature and our circumstances. Some of the medieval philosophers, Thomas Aquinas for example, believed in a natural moral law. The idea was later used by the English philosopher John Locke and is still defended by some Catholic moral philosophers. There are also libertarian anarchists, such as Murray Rothbard, who have worked in the natural law tradition.

Contractarianism or social contract theory. This tradition uses a hypothetical agreement as the foundation for rights, morals, or legitimate government. Locke was a contractarian and some very prominent 20th-century writers have been as well. For example, philosophers John Rawls, David Gauthier, and Jan Narveson are all contractarians.

Consequentialism. Here I would include any theory that defines good or right actions and institutions in terms of their consequences. The best-known form of consequentialism is called **utilitarianism,** a theory that has been popular for the last 200 years. The philosopher John Stuart Mill is probably the most famous 19th-century utilitarian. More recent advocates include Richard Brandt, R. M. Hare, and Peter Singer. Utilitarians argue that actions are morally good or right because they tend to maximize human welfare. In the 1950s and 1960s utilitarianism was the dominant ethical theory among secular moral philosophers in the United States.

Rationalism. Theories in this tradition place little or no stress on consequences when determining what is morally good or right. They may stress the analysis of moral concepts or some other approach that derives moral principles from reason. I would include the 18th-century philosopher Immanuel Kant and the 20th-century philosopher Alan Gewirth.

I don't mean to suggest that you are limited to working within these traditions. If you have other ideas, that's fine; but I think these are the main historical sources available for you to consider.

*Professor
Sidgwick
Speaking*

🅞🅟 COMMENT ON
ETHICAL TRADITIONS

Let me mention several more traditions that may be of help to you.

- *Scriptural exegesis. Many writers have based their moral and political principles on holy scripture. In the United States, that usually means the Christian Bible. Of course, Jews and Muslims can make arguments using their own scriptures.*

- *Intuitionism. Philosophers in this tradition believe that at least some moral judgements are in a sense self-evident. The best-known example is the 20th-century British philosopher W. D. Ross.*

- *Virtue ethics. This tradition is usually associated with the ethics of Aristotle. Rather than emphasizing aggregate consequences or rules that embody obligations and prohibitions, it stresses the importance of virtuous character. Living well or properly consists less in following rules or calculating consequences than in being a virtuous person and doing what a virtuous person would do.*

- **Care ethics.** *In recent years, more women have become involved in academic philosophy and some of them have developed what is called an ethics of caring. This approach stresses concrete relationships between individuals rather than impartiality and the search for universal principles. The best-known writer in this group is the philosopher Nel Noddings. This approach places greater emphasis on the experiences of women and the way many women approach moral thinking.*

Professor Sidgwick Speaking

Ⓜ Ⓟ LET'S GET STARTED

I think we are ready to begin the conversation. I have asked Fred and Diego to start us off by presenting an overview of conservatism. Let's get going.

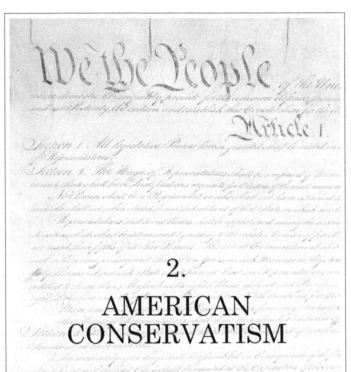

2.
AMERICAN CONSERVATISM

Presented by Fred and Diego

Conservative Group: Fred Speaking

🅜🅟 CONSERVATISM

American conservatism is complicated. It might be best to say that there is a family of conservatisms that resemble each other in various ways but also have important differences.

The best I can do is to pick out one package of ideas and attitudes from the various conservatisms. Of course, I'm going to focus on the conservatism that I believe in, but I think it is also a conservatism that many thoughtful Americans accept. In general terms, I would say that my conservatism consists of a generous dose of classical liberalism combined with a tablespoon of Edmund Burke. Here are some of the basic concepts:

American Conservatism: Basic Concepts

- **Constitutionally limited government**
- **Respect for tradition**
- **Cautious, organic reform**
- **The limited plasticity of human beings and society**
- **Religious faith, fixed moral principles, and natural rights**
- **Fiscal responsibility**
- **Equality before the law**
- **Property rights, free markets, and private enterprise**
- **The autonomy of the institutions that make up civil society**
- **Strong national defense**

Let me try to go further and formulate a set of principles and typical views held by conservatives.

American Conservatism: Principles and Beliefs

- The United States Constitution should be narrowly interpreted. That means that the powers of the federal government should be limited, the powers of the states should be greater than they are today, and the Supreme Court should not loosely interpret the Constitution.

- Conservatives have great respect for traditional institutions and values. Traditions that have developed slowly over a long period are assumed to fit the character of the people and to fulfill important functions in society.

- Abstract plans designed to radically improve society are regarded with skepticism. Change and reform should be carefully considered and implemented slowly. Gradual "organic" change is preferable, partly because it maintains stability and reduces conflict. The plasticity of individuals and institutions is limited, and the best plans often have unintended consequences that are highly undesirable.

- Many conservatives stress belief in God and fixed moral principles. Many deplore what they call the moral relativism of some secular intellectuals. Strictly speaking, I don't think it is necessary to believe in God in order to be a good conservative; but conservatives are often people of strong religious faith.

- The belief in individual rights is fundamental for most American conservatives. It is incorporated into our Declaration of Independence, the main body of our Constitution, and our Bill of Rights. The classical liberal rights to belief, expression, movement, and association are of great importance. For many conservatives, the most basic rights are also natural rights.

- Citizens are equal before the law. That means that all citizens have the same legal rights. It does not guarantee equal chances to succeed in life or equal outcomes in the competition that characterizes American life.

- Power should be dispersed in many ways: between the federal and state governments, among the branches of government, between public and private institutions, and between large and small enterprises.

- Fiscal responsibility implies low taxes, small deficits (if any), and a modest national debt.

- Private property and free markets are important not only because they allow the profit motive to spur economic progress, but because they balance and limit the power of government. Furthermore, many conservatives wonder whether other rights can survive without strong property rights. It follows that communism is to be opposed abroad and the regulatory welfare state in the US should be quite limited.

- Government should not control the institutions of civil society more than is necessary to maintain order and liberty.

Conservative Group: Fred Speaking

▣▣ COMMENT ON CONSERVATISM

I would like to explain what I said about civil society.

Conservatives emphasize the importance of the many groups that exist between the state and the individual. I'm thinking not only of the family, but of countless associations such as guilds, unions, churches, professional organizations, chess clubs, baseball teams, book clubs, corporations, non-profit organizations, discussion groups, philanthropic organizations, and many, many more. Sometimes social scientists refer to this whole layer of organized activity as "civil society."

Most of these associations are voluntary. That's part of their beauty. They are not the brainchild of government. They are fluid, dynamic, flexible, and endlessly creative.

The plea for limited government is, in one respect, a plea to leave these associations alone. Robert Nisbet, in his book Conservatism, wrote about the "triangular relationship of state, corporate group and individual." He refers to the ongoing concern of conservatives with the right "of the whole intermediate structure of the nation to survival against the tides of both individualism and nationalism" (Nisbet 1986, 21-22).

In my opinion, that intermediate structure is the secret of American dynamism and creativity.

*Conservative
Group:
Diego Speaking*

🄾🄿 COMMENT ON CONSERVATISM

As Fred indicated, there is no single definition of conservatism. In The Corrosion of Conservatism, *author Max Boot indicated that his conservatism included the following elements (Boot 2018, xix):*

- *"prudent and incremental policymaking"*
- *support for "American global leadership and American allies"*
- *"a strong defense"*
- *opposition to "the enemies of freedom"*
- *"respect for character, community, personal virtue, and family"*
- *"limited government and fiscal prudence"*
- *"freedom of opportunity rather than equality of outcome"*
- *A modest "social safety net"*
- *"individual liberty to the greatest extent possible consistent with public safety"*
- *"freedom of speech and of the press"*
- *"immigration and assimilation"*
- *"colorblindness and racial integration"*

I think that Boot is typical of many American conservatives today.

Professor Sidgwick Speaking

🅜🅟 RIGHTS

Fred just referred to individual rights and natural rights. Let me introduce a definition and a distinction. First, the definition of a right:

A person has a right to do or to have something if, and only if, others have a duty not to prevent that person from doing or having that thing. In some cases, we also say that a person has a right to have something if, and only if, someone or some institution has a duty to provide that person with that thing.

Of course, that's just a definition. Whether we have any rights, what rights we have, and why we have them are open questions.

Now, let me introduce a distinction. Political philosophers distinguish between non-interference rights and welfare rights. Non-interference rights are rights not to be prevented from doing what we want to do by institutions or other people. If I have a non-interference right to go to California, no one has the right to physically prevent me from doing so. In some cases, a non-interference right indicates that a specific party cannot interfere with my doing a certain thing. For example, the First Amendment indicates that "Congress" shall make no law "abridging the freedom of speech." We could also think of the classical liberal freedom of contract as a non-interference right.

Notice that my non-interference right to go to California does not guarantee me the money I need to go to California. Rights to resources go beyond rights to non-interference.

Welfare rights are usually thought of as rights to resources and services such as food, medical care, or housing. A welfare right could be a natural right or a statutory right. We can prove that a person has a statutory right to housing by pointing to certain provisions in the law. To establish a natural right to housing would require a completely different approach, perhaps one that introduced moral considerations. In the United States, we have a strong tradition of recognizing certain non-interference rights, but welfare rights remain controversial. Does everyone have a natural right to basic medical care? Should everyone have a statutory right to basic medical care? We are still arguing about that sort of issue.

Catholic
Group:
Ayesha Speaking

🅞🅟 COMMENT ON TERMINOLOGY FOR RIGHTS

Both Fred and Professor Sidgwick referred to natural rights. That's a technical term, and it makes me think that it might be useful to say a little more about the terminology philosophers use to discuss rights. I am going to suggest a few definitions, but I have to say up front that all of them are controversial. I'm simplifying a lot.

- *__Moral rights__ are established by appealing to moral principles indicating what is morally good or right or obligatory. They are not created by law or government.*

- *__Legal rights or positive rights__ are created by law. In the United States, legal rights include both constitutional and statutory rights. Of course, we might establish a legal right to do something because we believe that people have a moral right to do that thing (for example, to get married).*

- *__Human rights__ are rights that all people possess because of some feature or features of human beings. For example, we might argue that human beings have certain rights*

*Catholic
Group:
Ayesha Speaking*

because they are intelligent or sentient, because they have interests to defend, or because they can be harmed in various ways.

- *Natural rights are not created by government. Sometimes they are said to be "prior" to government. For example, some philosophers have said that in the "state of nature" people have a natural right to defend themselves or to acquire property. It is important to ask whether governments can modify natural rights or whether natural rights restrict what government can do.*

- *Absolute rights can never be justifiably abridged or overridden. Someone might claim that an innocent person has an absolute right not to be killed.*

- *Inalienable or unalienable rights can never be taken away or given away. Our Declaration of Independence refers to unalienable rights to life and liberty, among others.*

- *Prima facie rights are rights that we acknowledge under normal circumstances, but they can be overridden in some cases. We might, for example, acknowledge that a property owner has the right to keep people off her land, but also believe that this right can be overridden in cases of life and death. When deciding whether to override a prima facie right, it may be balanced against other prima facie rights or against other moral concerns.*

These are only some of the terms associated with rights, but I hope they will help our discussion.

*Liberal
Group:
Vera Speaking*

🄾🄿 COMMENT ON RIGHTS

I support many of the traditional liberal freedoms — especially freedom of belief, speech, movement, and association. But those are mainly negative or non-interference rights. No one is allowed to interfere with me if I choose to go to a doctor or to go to college or to move to North Dakota to find a new job. The problem is that doing these things requires resources, and many people do not have those resources.

What good is the freedom to do something if you do not have the resources necessary to do it?

The philosopher John Dewey spoke of "effective freedom." Effective freedom requires resources, and that is the kind of freedom I want people to have.

Conservative Group: Fred Speaking

🅜🅟 CONSERVATISM

I mentioned a family of conservatisms, so I want to give you an idea of what some of the family members are like. People often talk about conservatives and liberals as if all conservatives believe this and all liberals believe that. It doesn't work that way. I've already described my own conservatism. Now I want to introduce some of the other members of the family.

If this confuses you, you are not alone. Society doesn't break down into groups with neatly defined packages of ideas. These labels are just a crude way to divide people into categories that help us to organize our thinking.

- **Paleoconservatism.** The paleocons or "old" conservatives tend to stress the value of Christianity as the spiritual core of American culture and have a reverence for tradition and local culture. They oppose communism and the federal regulatory welfare state. They are skeptical about foreign military intervention, unrestricted free trade, and large-scale immigration. They lean toward isolationism and tend to oppose the neoconservative impulse to spread democracy and free markets around the world. Philosopher and historian Paul Gottfried and commentator Pat Buchanan are sometimes identified as paleoconservatives.

- **The conservative movement or conservative "fusion"** centered around the *National Review* magazine in the 1950s and 1960s. The leaders of the movement were William F. Buckley, Jr. and Frank Meyer. They sought to bring together several strands of conservative thought (and several conservative groups) into a unified movement. They strongly opposed communism abroad as well as the New Deal welfare state, the expansion of federal power, and economic regulation at home. In addition, their philosophy included a reverence for the past and a preference for the gradual, piecemeal change sometimes referred to as organic change.

- **Neoconservatism.** The early neocons or "new" conservatives were often former leftists who changed their views after disappointment with Soviet policy and the failures of the welfare state here in the US. They look to social science to support their criticisms of many liberal programs and stress the limits of our capacity to change people and society. Neocons recognize and value the achievements of a free economy but also accept the need for limited government intervention and a modest welfare state. They sometimes advocate the use of American military power to spread democracy and free markets throughout the world. Irving Kristol (now deceased) and his son Bill Kristol both qualify as neoconservatives.

- **New Conservatism.** In 1949 the poet and historian Peter Viereck called for a "New Conservatism" that was "evolutionary" and not "static." He spoke of the "organic" growth of "archetypal values" over a long period of time. In contrast to many conservatives, Viereck believed that American conservatism needed to assimilate, rather than reject, the best elements of the New Deal of the 1930s. He placed Franklin Roosevelt in a tradition of Tory socialist conservatives who were against unregulated capitalism. He criticized William F. Buckley, Barry Goldwater, and the *National Review* (Viereck 1962, 100, 126-128).

I recommend looking at Paul Gottfried's book *The Conservative Movement*. It may help you to get a clearer notion of what these labels mean.

*Conservative
Group:
Fred Speaking*

🄾🄿 COMMENT ON
JUDICIAL CONSERVATISM

Judicial conservatism is concerned with principles guiding court decisions. In general, it should be contrasted with the "living law" view which holds that both laws and the Constitution should be flexibly interpreted to adapt to new circumstances. In addition, it should not be confused with judicial restraint, which encourages judges to give considerable leeway to legislatures.

Judicial conservatism may require a very close reading of a law under review. The idea is that judges should apply and interpret law as written but not make new law. In other cases, judicial conservatism requires that judges adhere closely to precedent. Finally, judicial conservatism may require that judges should rely on what they believe to be the original understanding of constitutional or legal language.

One thing is for certain — we should understand that judicial conservativism is not the same as political, economic, or social conservatism.

Conservative Group: Diego Speaking

🅜🅟 CONSERVATISM

I generally agree with what Fred has said, but I'm a Christian first and a political-economic conservative second.

Secular conservatives tend to advocate a less intrusive federal government, more power to state governments, fiscal responsibility, lower taxes, freer markets, and less social engineering. I agree with all of that, but as a Christian I would add something else.

I believe that there has been an underlying moral decline in our country. Look around you. The divorce rate has risen enormously in the last 50 years. We have some of the highest crime rates in the developed world. Pornography has become more and more common, and now it is easily available on the Internet. Worse yet, a lot of it involves children. There is sex everywhere in movies and on television — and most of it is between people who are not married. In real life, sex has become the norm for people who are dating. More and more children are born to unmarried women. Abortion has become commonplace. Many fathers do little or nothing to support their children. Legalized gambling has spread to many states. Illegal drug use is everywhere. Marriage is no longer limited to one man and one woman. A sympathetic depiction of homosexuality permeates popular culture. There is more international traffic in women for sexual exploitation. And to top it off, a simple thing like prayer in public schools has been declared unconstitutional.

My point is that these are moral problems and they require moral solutions. We need to recover our values. At the base of our problems is a spreading moral relativism, which can only be stopped by a return to God as the source of moral principles. Meanwhile, all of these changes affect the family in negative ways. Gambling and drugs, for example, are tearing families apart.

I guess you could say that I'm a conservative with a twist. I want the things that Fred wants, but I also want to strengthen the religious basis of morality and society. If we cannot do that, the best economy and all the money in the world won't help us.

Conservative Group: Fred Speaking

🄼🄿 EDMUND BURKE

As a bit of historical background, one of the people I want to bring in is Edmund Burke (1730-1797). I mentioned him already, but I want to say more.

Burke was born in Dublin, Ireland and served in the British House of Commons for decades. He was a leading Whig statesman, known for his defense of the English Glorious Revolution of 1688, his efforts to compromise with the American rebels in the 1770s, and his intense opposition to the French Revolution in the years after 1789. Burke published many works, the most famous of which today is his 1790 *Reflections on the Revolution in France*. Another book, in which he explained and defended his own views as an "Old Whig," appeared in 1791. It was called *An Appeal from the New to the Old Whigs*. Historians often describe Burke as the founder of modern conservatism. Many American conservatives such as William F. Buckley, Jr. and Russell Kirk have taken inspiration from him. My point is not that modern American conservatives are all followers of Burke, but that there is a tone or attitude in his view of society and government that is still important to us.

Edmund Burke: Basic Ideas

- There are few abstract moral principles that apply to political policy. In particular, there are no universal rights of man as claimed by some of the French revolutionaries. There are, however, specific rights of Englishmen that have developed over centuries. These rights are established in law or custom.

- Liberty is an attribute of order. Without order, liberty becomes chaos.

- There is no single best form of government in the abstract. In the case of England, Burke favored a mixed or balanced government. Such a government distributes power among the monarch, the House of Lords, and the House of Commons. This balance prevents arbitrary and abusive government by any one party.

- The government of England is based on an ancient compact. The people have no right to change the nature of that government simply because they wish to do so. The Revolution of 1688 was justified by necessity and not by any abiding right that the people had to replace the king.

- Societies are highly complex systems that develop slowly over long periods of time. They are not to be tinkered with on the basis of abstract arguments. This does not imply that reform is always a mistake, but that it must be very carefully considered. Traditional values and institutions are to be treated with great respect.

- A natural aristocracy can develop that forms the "leading, guiding, and governing part" of a society or nation (Burke 1962, 105).

I don't agree with Burke on everything. Our Declaration of Independence asserts that people have "unalienable Rights," and I suspect that Burke would have been skeptical about that claim. It is also true that the United States is a republic rather than a mixed government such as Burke favored. Still, Burke's reverence for the past and his preference for organic change is shared by many modern conservatives.

🆂🅴 EXCERPTS FROM EDMUND BURKE
Reflections on the Revolution in France

The French Revolution began in 1789. Burke published his Reflections *in 1790. Although not a systematic presentation of political conservatism,* Reflections *is generally regarded as one of its seminal documents. The following excerpts give some idea of the value Burke placed on tradition as well as his skepticism about the value of liberty in the abstract. Burke preferred the rights of Englishmen, which had developed over centuries, to the abstract rights of man advocated by the French revolutionaries. The headings in brackets have been added.*

[On tradition]

All the pleasing illusions, which made power gentle, and obedience liberal, which harmonized the different shades of life, and which, by a bland assimilation, incorporated into politics the sentiments which beautify and soften private society, are to be dissolved by this new conquering empire of light and reason....

On the principles of this mechanic philosophy, our institutions can never be embodied, if I may use the expression, in persons; so as to create in us love, veneration, admiration, or attachment (Burke 1890, 85, 86).

But power, of some kind or other, will survive the shock in which manners and opinions perish; and it will find other and worse means for its support. The usurpation which, in order to subvert ancient institutions, has destroyed ancient principles, will hold power by arts similar to those by which it has acquired it....

When ancient opinions and rules of life are taken away, the loss cannot possibly be estimated. From that moment we have no compass to govern us; nor can we know distinctly to what port we steer (Burke 1890, 87).

[On abstract liberty]

The circumstances are what render every civil and political scheme beneficial or noxious to mankind. Abstractedly speaking, government, as well as liberty, is good....Is it because liberty in the abstract may be classed amongst the blessings of mankind, that I am seriously to felicitate a madman, who has escaped from the protecting restraint and wholesome darkness of his cell, on his restoration to the enjoyment of light and liberty?....

I should therefore suspend my congratulations on the new liberty of France, until I was informed how it had been combined with government; with public force; with the discipline and obedience of armies; with the collection of an effective and well-distributed revenue; with morality and religion; with the solidity of property; with peace and order; with civil and social manners. All these (in their way) are good things too; and, without them, liberty is not a benefit whilst it lasts, and is not likely to continue long (Burke 1890, 8).

Conservative Group: Diego Speaking

m P ADAM SMITH

Another 18th-century thinker we want to make you aware of is Adam Smith (1723-1790). Smith was one of a group of 18th-century writers called the Scottish Moralists, who were part of a larger movement called the Scottish Enlightenment. The group included Smith, Francis Hutcheson, Adam Ferguson, David Hume, John Millar, and Dugald Stewart. Most of these men were associated with the Scottish Universities. They helped create the way modern people view the world by promoting scientific explanations in psychology, sociology, history, and economics. Smith and Hume are still read today — Smith for his contributions to economics and Hume for his ethical theory and epistemology.

In 1776, Smith published *The Wealth of Nations*, a massive work that laid the foundations of liberal economics. He advocated what he referred to as the "system of natural liberty." In very broad terms, he argued that if people were left to pursue their own profit, it would result — overall and in the long run — in a vast increase in wealth for society as a whole. Smith was not a dogmatist about economic liberty. He believed that the government had an important role to play. At the same time, however, he stressed the benefits of liberty.

American conservatives, unlike some conservatives in other countries, have generally regarded Smith as an intellectual hero. Although the science of economics has evolved in many ways since 1776, they have accepted Smith's overall attitude toward liberty and the market. In general, they favor free markets and very limited government intervention in the economy.

Adam Smith: Basic Ideas

- At the broadest level, Smith believed that societies have a tendency to evolve through four stages which he referred to as the Age of Hunters, the Age of Shepherds, the Age of Agriculture, and the Age of Commerce. Evolution from stage to stage occurred as population increased. In the *Wealth of Nations* he was primarily concerned with the Age of Commerce.

- Production and productivity can be increased greatly by extending the division of labor among workers. In Smith's example, the production of pins can be increased greatly by having each worker attend to one small task rather than producing a finished pin by himself.

- The good of all or nearly all members of a society can be promoted even though each member does not aim at that result. Each individual typically aims at his own benefit, but the overall result is an improvement for all. The owner of a workshop may extend the division of labor among workers to increase his own profit, but the price of 100 pins, for example, would be reduced for everyone.

- Efforts by governments to limit trade between nations (or between mother countries and colonies) fail to maximize wealth for any of the nations or colonies involved. Freer trade was mutually beneficial because it made the international division of labor more productive.

*Conservative
Group:
Fred Speaking*

O|P COMMENT ON FREE MARKETS

The extent to which government can and should intervene in economic markets is a major bone of contention between American liberals and conservatives even today. Liberals often claim that government intervention can accelerate growth, lower unemployment, reduce poverty, moderate inflation, increase investment in blighted areas, limit racial and gender discrimination, help new industries, foster scientific research, and so on. In broad terms, American conservatives tend to be more skeptical about all those claims and to put their faith in market incentives that do not require government action.

S|E EXCERPTS FROM ADAM SMITH
The Wealth of Nations

In 1776 Adam Smith published An Inquiry into the Nature and Causes of the Wealth of Nations. *His book is arguably the finest piece of social science written in the 18th century. Smith's work helped to consolidate political economy as a field of study. It is widely respected by economists even today and truly revered by many American conservatives. The excerpts below give some idea of Smith's views.*

THE annual labour of every nation is the fund which originally supplies it with all the necessaries and conveniencies of life which it annually consumes, and which consist always either in the immediate produce of that labour, or in what is purchased with that produce from other nations (Smith 1822, Vol. I, 1).

The greatest improvement in the productive powers of labour, and the greater part of the skill, dexterity, and judgment with which it is any where directed, or applied, seem to have been the effects of the division of labour....The division of labour, however, so far as it can be introduced, occasions, in every art, a proportionable increase of the productive powers of labour. The separation of different trades and employments from one another seems to have taken place, in consequence of this advantage. This separation too is generally carried furthest in those countries which enjoy the highest degree of industry and improvement; what is the work of one man in a rude state of society, being generally that of several in an improved one....It is the great multiplication of the productions of all the different arts, in consequence of the division of labour, which occasions, in a well-governed society, that universal opulence which extends itself to the lowest ranks of the people (Smith 1822, Vol. I, 6, 9, 16).

This division of labour, from which so many advantages are derived, is not originally the effect of any human wisdom, which foresees and intends that general opulence to which it gives occasion (Smith 1822, Vol. I, 19).

Every individual is continually exerting himself to find out the most advantageous employment for whatever capital he can command. It is his own advantage, indeed, and not that of the society which he has in view. But the study of his own advantage naturally, or rather necessarily, leads him to prefer that employment which is most advantageous to the society (Smith 1822, Vol. II, 177).

Those systems, therefore, which preferring agriculture to all other employments, in order to promote it, impose restraints upon manufactures and foreign trade, act contrary to the very end which they propose, and indirectly discourage that very species of industry which they mean to promote. They are so far, perhaps, more inconsistent than even the mercantile system. That system, by encouraging manufactures and foreign trade more than agriculture, turns a certain portion of the capital of the society from supporting a more advantageous, to support a less advantageous species of industry. But still it really and in the end encourages that species of industry which it means to promote. Those agricultural systems, on the contrary, really and in the end discourage their own favourite species of industry.

It is thus that every system which endeavours, either, by extraordinary encouragements, to draw towards a particular species of industry a greater share of the capital of the society than what would naturally go to it; or, by extraordinary restraints, to force from a particular species of industry some share of the capital which would otherwise be employed in it; is in reality subversive of the great purpose which it means to promote....

All systems either of preference or of restraint, therefore, being thus completely taken away, the obvious and simple system of natural liberty establishes itself of its own accord. Every man, as long as he does not violate the laws of justice, is left perfectly free to pursue his own interest his own way, and to bring both his industry and capital into competition with those of any other man, or order of men....According to the system of natural liberty, the sovereign has only three duties to attend to... first, the duty of protecting the society from the violence and invasion of other independent societies; secondly, ... the duty of establishing an exact administration of justice; and, thirdly, the duty of erecting and maintaining certain public works and certain public institutions, which it can never be for the interest of any individual, or small number of individuals, to erect and maintain; because the profit could never repay the expense to any individual, or small number of individuals, though it may frequently do much more than repay it to a great society (Smith 1822, Vol. III, 41-43).

Conservative Group: Fred Speaking

🅼🅿 THOMAS JEFFERSON

Limited government is very much a part of the American conservative ideal, and no one embodies that ideal more than Thomas Jefferson. Jefferson was born into a landowning, slaveholding family in Virginia in 1843. He attended the College of William & Mary and went on to become one of the leaders in the movement for colonial independence. Jefferson wrote *A Summary View of the Rights of British America* in 1774 and later drafted the American Declaration of Independence. He published *Notes on the State of Virginia* in 1785. After the United States was established, Jefferson served as vice president under John Adams and president from 1801 to 1809. In 1819 he helped found the University of Virginia. He died on July 4, 1826.

Jefferson envisioned the United States as a predominantly agricultural republic based on a large number of small farmers. Among the founders, he is sometimes contrasted with Alexander Hamilton, who envisioned the nation as a commercial republic with a stronger central government. Jefferson hoped to avoid the development of a highly commercial society by acquiring more land in the west for farmers.

Thomas Jefferson: Basic Ideas

- Jefferson advocated small, constitutionally limited, republican government, especially at the federal level.

- He strongly advocated tolerance for a diversity of religious views.

- He criticized slavery and hoped that it would gradually disappear. Nevertheless, he owned slaves all his adult life and could not envision whites and blacks participating as equals in American life. Instead, he believed that freed slaves should be transported to the Caribbean or returned to Africa.

- He believed that the United States and its territories would be best off as an agricultural society of independent small farmers. Small farmers, he thought, would have the virtues required for successful republican government.

- He believed that the United States should be led by a natural aristocracy of refined, educated men with the character that allowed them to aim at the common good rather than be driven by narrow self-interest.

Jefferson has fascinated Americans with very different political perspectives. He was not only multifaceted, but in some ways he embodied contradictions (or at least tensions) between opposing values and ideas. Although he spoke eloquently against slavery and the slave trade, he owned slaves. A strong believer in constitutionally limited government, as president he presided over the Louisiana Purchase even though it was not clear that the Constitution gave the federal government the power to make such a purchase. Perhaps more than anyone else among the founders, Jefferson has allowed later Americans to choose what they wish to see in his life and ideas.

Conservative Group: Fred Speaking

🔲🔲 CLASSICAL LIBERALISM

In 2019, the conservative columnist George Will wrote that "American conservatives are the custodians of the classical liberal tradition" (Will 2019, xxiv). That sounds like a contradiction, but it's not. How can it be true?

The answer is that in the United States, conservatism has its own distinct history, and it has never been quite the same as European conservatism. Some European conservatives in the 19th century criticized the emerging industrial society for destroying the more personal relationships thought to have been characteristic of earlier times. In the United States, this criticism of an industrial and market-oriented society was muted.

Classical liberalism was a cluster of ideas and policies that grew up mainly in the United Kingdom and the United States. The emphasis was on small government, free markets, free trade, strong property rights, freedom of contract, an overall harmony of economic interests, and an electoral political system of some kind. Government should be limited, focusing on enforcing contracts and providing services that markets are poorly equipped to provide (such as defense, roads, canals, and postal service). It reached the peak of its popularity and influence in 19th-century America.

Classical liberal ideas and policies fitted conditions in the United States pretty well. We had no entrenched nobility and no powerful established religion. Land ownership was widespread among the white population, private enterprise was highly successful, and a free-wheeling sense of independence was common. Furthermore, our Constitution in theory (and often in practice) placed severe limits on the power of the federal government.

The point is that as we entered the 20th century and progressives sought to expand the power of the federal government, the historical reality to be conserved was in many ways a classical liberal reality.

I don't mean to suggest that 20th-century conservatism is exactly the same as classical liberalism, but there is an undeniable overlap.

*Professor
Sidgwick
Speaking*

**⬛P COMMENT ON
CLASSICAL LIBERALISM**

One of the fundamental issues separating 19th-century classical liberalism from 20th-century social liberalism concerns the relationship between government and civil society. Classical liberals tended to view government as the source of a wide range of problems, including war, privilege, political patronage, corruption, economic monopoly, and artificial hierarchy. Limited government and the free flowing, voluntary arrangements of civil society were seen as solutions to those problems. Modern social liberals, on the other hand, tend to see government as the solution to problems arising out of civil society, including racial discrimination, gender discrimination, extreme economic inequality, and poverty. American conservatives tend to accept the classical liberal view.

The classical liberal had faith in the overall consequences of voluntary action. The social liberal has faith in the consequences of rational design and centralized planning. In my opinion, there is a case to be made for both views. One of the recurring questions for Americans is how to best combine freedom and planning.

Liberal Group: John Speaking

🅜🅟 A REPLY TO FRED

I like your introductions to Burke, Smith, and Jefferson. From what I have read, Burke admired Smith's work in political economy and often agreed with his views. He argued against government economic intervention in agriculture and strongly supported freedom of contract. And Jefferson, well, as you said, nobody represents the idea of limited central government better than Jefferson. But I want to make a few comments before we go on.

John: First Thoughts on Conservatism

- I think that Burke and Smith may represent two different sets of ideas that do not fit together entirely without tension. In Burke, we see a great reverence for the past, for traditional values, and for institutions that have developed slowly over centuries. In Smith, we see a tendency to allow people to act freely according to their view of their own interests. Smith and his followers tended to favor free markets, but here's the rub: There are few things more dangerous for traditional ideas and institutions than free markets. A free market tends to transform customs, habits, and attitudes. We don't think of it as radical, but it is; and many European conservatives have seen it as such. I'm not saying that there is a formal contradiction between Burke and Smith, but I do think that there is a tension between respect for tradition and individual freedom in economic activity. I think we can still see that tension in 20th-century American conservative thought. I hope we get to that subject later.

- Respect for the past or for tradition sounds simple enough. At first glance it sounds like a guide that can help us make decisions, but I think that is deceptive. In the first place, the past may contain contradictions. In the United States, we have a past that valued individual freedom, but it also valued slavery. In that case, the past is no guide. Second, even when there is no contradiction, we all agree that ideas change over time and there are elements of the past that we no longer value and no longer want to preserve. Do we want to preserve all the 19th-century ideas about gender? Of course not. Again, the point is that a general admonition to respect the past is not very helpful as a guide. Each generation has to decide what to respect, what to accept, and what to discard from the past. I don't see how conservatives can avoid that.

- Smith's system of "natural liberty" also sounds good and in a great many cases I think it works very well. I am not at all against letting markets work their magic, but we also have to face the fact that some people do very poorly in a market-driven society. There are also cases in which free markets allow some people to pass costs on to others with impunity. Pollution and global warming are good examples of that kind of problem. I wonder how conservatives think we should deal with issues like those.

Conservative Group: Fred Speaking

🅜🅟 THE DECLINE OF LIMITED GOVERNMENT

I'm going to jump to the 20th century. I'm basically a Goldwater-Reagan conservative and I want to tell you where all that came from. In order to do that, I have to say something about the decline of constitutionally limited government.

Our original Constitution limited the federal government to a list of enumerated powers. In the first half of the 20th century there were major changes in the interpretation of the Constitution that essentially constituted a revolution in federal power.

The Decline of Limited Government

- The Progressive movement of the early 20th century advocated a long list of reforms, many of which required an expansion of government at the federal level. Here are just a few examples of the change. In 1906 Congress passed the Meat Inspection Act and the Pure Food and Drug Act. In 1913 the 16th amendment was adopted, allowing the federal government to levy an income tax. Congress also created the Federal Reserve System (1913) to regulate banking and the Federal Trade Commission (1914) to restrict unfair business practices. A further expansion of the federal government occurred in the 1930s with President Franklin Roosevelt's New Deal. The New Deal attempted to plan agricultural production and to encourage the unionization of workers. It increased the regulation of banks, provided insurance for bank deposits, regulated the stock market, and established a minimum wage in some industries. It accelerated the development of the modern welfare state by creating the social security system for the elderly, a food stamp program for the poor, and a program to aid poor families with children.

• Initially, several New Deal programs were declared unconstitutional by the Supreme Court. By the end of the 1930s, however, the court was inclined to reinterpret the Constitution to allow for a more powerful federal government. Traditional property rights, the authority of the states, and freedom of contract were increasingly restricted. The Court opened the door for an almost unlimited expansion of federal power over the next 50 years.

*Conservative
Group:
Diego Speaking*

**O P COMMENT ON
CHANGES IN DOMINANT IDEAS**

Let me add a little to what Fred said. There were also changes in the academic world that disturbed conservatives.

• *The economics of John Maynard Keynes became dominant in many of the leading universities. Economist Paul Samuelson's textbook on economics, which incorporated Keynes's ideas, became a standard text for undergraduates. A whole generation of students used it. Free-market ideas were shoved aside and sometimes ridiculed.*

• *Leading anthropologists like Melville Herskovits taught what they called "cultural relativism." Herskovits argued that moral ideas were only binding within a single culture and that there was no rational method for choosing between the moral systems of different cultures. Many students at some of the best schools in the country came to doubt the possibility of objective moral standards.*

*Liberal
Group:
Vera Speaking*

▣▣ COMMENT ON
LIMITED GOVERNMENT

Everything Fred says is true. The power of the federal government was transformed in the 20ᵗʰ century. But many of the things you mention needed to happen. Jobs programs, bank insurance, regulation of the stock market, aid to poor families, social security for the aged, all of it. Some conservatives are basically stuck in the past saying that the government either should or can do nothing about the problems those programs addressed. That is just not true and most of the American people know it. Furthermore, only the federal government could address those problems on a national scale.

Conservative Group: Fred Speaking

🅜🅟 THE CONSERVATIVE REVIVAL

There were intellectuals, politicians, journalists, and organizations that never accepted the ideas and institutions associated with the New Deal. But for at least twenty years, those people were marginalized. The newer ideas about the role of the federal government and Keynesian economic theory took over. There's no question about it.

But critics continued to exist even if they were poorly organized and sometimes ridiculed. In the mid-1950s, William F. Buckley, Jr. (1925-2008) founded the *National Review* magazine. In it he brought together several strands of thought and numerous people (many of whom were former leftists) in an attempt to create a coherent, unified conservative point of view. Buckley not only edited the *National Review*, but gave hundreds of speeches, wrote dozens of books, and hosted one of the longest-running programs in the history of television. His first book, *God and Man at Yale*, appeared in 1951. *Up from Liberalism* followed in 1959. He was one of the great political publicists of the 20th century.

Buckley worked closely with others, especially Frank Meyer, to create a "fusion" of several conservative traditions. He provided the glue that held together different points of view that were not always friendly to one another.

The Conservative Revival: Basic Ideas

- Unqualified anti-communism

- A reaffirmation of constitutionally limited government combined with strong opposition to the expanding regulatory welfare state and the increasing power of the Supreme Court to reinterpret the Constitution

- A Burkean respect for the past, a distrust of abstract designs for social change, and a preference for organic reform

- A belief in an objective basis for moral principles and a rejection of moral relativism

- A respect for individual liberty, including free markets and property rights

- A rejection of utopian goals

I would also like to add that Buckley denounced several streams of thought that are sometimes included in the American conservative tradition. He rejected antisemitism and he rejected the conspiratorial views of the John Birch Society.

*Conservative
Group:
Fred Speaking*

**◻◻ COMMENT ON
THE CONSERVATIVE REVIVAL**

Another component of the conservative revival was the foundation of Young Americans for Freedom (YAF) in 1960. YAF was created by a group of young conservatives at a meeting at Buckley's home in Sharon, Connecticut. The group approved a statement of principles that came to be called the Sharon Statement.

The Sharon Statement affirmed certain "eternal truths" including the "God-given free will" of each individual and the subsequent right to be free from "arbitrary force." It declared that "liberty is indivisible," that political freedom requires economic freedom, and that the purpose of government is to "protect those freedoms."

Conservative
Group:
Fred Speaking

The Constitution of the United States was praised as the "best arrangement yet devised for empowering government to fulfill its proper role" and preventing the "concentration and abuse" of power. The statement also affirmed that a "market economy, allocating resources by the free play of supply and demand, is the single economic system compatible with the requirements of personal freedom and constitutional government" as well as "the most productive supplier of human needs."

In 1962, future president Ronald Reagan joined the YAF National Advisory Board and later became its Honorary National Chairman.

SE THE *NATIONAL REVIEW*
"Our Mission Statement," 1955

The following short excerpts are taken from the National Review *mission statement written by William F. Buckley, Jr.*

On the proper role of government: "It is the job of centralized government (in peacetime) to protect its citizens' lives, liberty and property. All other activities of government tend to diminish freedom and hamper progress."

On social planning: "The profound crisis of our era is, in essence, the conflict between the Social Engineers, who seek to adjust mankind to conform with scientific utopias, and the disciples of Truth, who defend the organic moral order."

On communism: "The century's most blatant force of satanic utopianism is communism....[W]e find ourselves irrevocably at war with communism and shall oppose any substitute for victory."

On intellectual conformity: "The largest cultural menace in America is the conformity of the intellectual cliques which... are out to impose upon the nation their modish fads and fallacies, and have nearly succeeded in doing so."

On the two major political parties: "[A]n identifiable team of Fabian operators is bent on controlling both our major political parties.... [W]e shall advocate the restoration of the two-party system at all costs."

On free markets: "The competitive price system is indispensable to liberty and material progress." As a result, *NATIONAL REVIEW* will explore and oppose the inroads upon the market economy caused by monopolies in general, and politically oriented unionism in particular; and it will tell the violated businessman's side of the story."

On world government: "No superstition has more effectively bewitched America's Liberal elite than the fashionable concepts of world government, the United Nations, internationalism, international atomic pools, etc." On the contrary, "It would make greater sense to grant independence to each of our 50 states than to surrender U.S. sovereignty to a world organization" (*National Review*, November 19, 1955 brackets added).

Conservative Group: Diego Speaking

🅜🅟 THE CONSERVATIVE REVIVAL

Frank Meyer (1909-1972) was one of the leading thinkers of the conservative revival of the 1950s. Several writers associated with the *National Review* had been leftists, and Meyer himself had once been a member of the Communist Party. In the 1950s, however, he articulated a staunchly anti-communist conservative political philosophy. He attempted to develop a synthesis of two different strands of American political thought: the traditionalist or Burkean strand and the libertarian or classical liberal strand. The resulting philosophy was sometimes called fusionism. In 1962 he published *In Defense of Freedom: A Conservative Credo*.

Meyer did not deny the tension that existed between his views and those of some others who considered themselves conservatives. He criticized Russell Kirk, Robert Nesbitt, Peter Viereck, and all those whom he regarded as deferring too much to tradition or community and failing to realize the importance of individualism, failing to acknowledge the role of reason, or conceding too much to the "collectivist Liberalism" of the post-New Deal period.

Frank Meyer : Basic Ideas

- There is an "objective moral order based upon ontological foundations" (Meyer 1996, 192). That order serves as the basis for respecting the freedom of the individual. It is objectively true; therefore, moral relativism must be rejected.

- The individual is rational, volitional, and autonomous. The individual possesses "innate freedom" (Meyer 1996, 47).

- All value resides in the individual rather than in institutions or in society as a whole (Meyer 1996, 8).

- The proper end for man is the development of moral virtue. Freedom is the necessary condition for that development.

- The proper end to be sought in the political realm is freedom.

- Communism is a "monstrous, atavistic attack upon the survival of the very concepts of moral order and individual freedom" (Meyer 1996, 39).

- The separation of political power from other kinds of power, especially economic power, is crucial in order to preserve freedom (Meyer 1996, 8).

- The utopian ideas of collectivist liberalism are to be rejected. This implies a rejection of the American welfare state.

- "The fundamental political issue today is that between, on the one hand, collectivism and statism which merge gradually into totalitarianism and, on the other, what used to be called liberalism...." The latter includes "the principles of the primacy of the individual, the division of power, the limitation of government, the freedom of the economy" (Meyer 1996, 5).

Meyer opposed many of the dominant ideas of mid-20th-century America. In his view, the liberal collectivist dogma was "relativist, pragmatic, positivist, scornful of absolute criteria, of all strictly theoretical thought, of all enquiry not amenable to the methods of the natural sciences" (Meyer 1996, 57).

Conservative Group: Diego Speaking

🄾🄿 COMMENT ON FRANK MEYER

Meyer was aware that there were different groups of people with different ideas who were all opposed to modern liberalism. He believed that bringing these people together could be politically effective and that a logically consistent synthesis of at least some of their ideas was possible. He argued that both traditionalist and libertarian ideas were part of the same western tradition. They might seem incompatible, but at a deeper level they depended on each other.

The split was between "those who abstract from the corpus of Western belief its stress upon freedom and upon the innate importance of the individual person" and "those who, drawing upon the same source, stress value and virtue and order...." The first group could be called "libertarian" and the second could be called "traditionalist." Western civilization was "distinguished by its ability to hold these apparently opposed ends in balance and tension." This was due to the fact that both positions "accept, to a large degree, the ends of the other." The libertarian tradition needed "an absolute ground of value," while at the same time, traditionalists understood that "the belief in virtue as the end of men's being implicitly recognizes the necessity of freedom to choose that end; otherwise, virtue could be no more than a conditioned tropism" (Meyer 1996, 16).

Not everyone accepted Meyer's proposed synthesis. There were tensions between different types of conservatives. For example, Meyer himself criticized Russell Kirk's Burkean conservatism and Kirk criticized libertarians. Even so, a conservative movement held together and supported Barry Goldwater in 1964 and Ronald Reagan in 1980. Perhaps the strongest forces holding the movement together were its enemies: the regulatory welfare state at home and international communism abroad.

5⃞3⃞ EXCERPTS FROM FRANK MEYER
"Conservatism"

In his 1967 essay "Conservatism," Meyer identified the following elements in a conservative political philosophy:

- "Conservatism assumes the existence of an objective moral order based upon ontological foundations."

- "Within the limits of an objective moral order, the primary reference of conservative political and social thought and action is to the individual person."

- "The cast of American conservative thought is profoundly anti-utopian."

- "Conservatives may vary on the degree to which the power of the state should be limited, but they are agreed upon the principle of limitation...." They are firmly opposed to the "Liberal concept of the state as the engine for the fixing of ideological blueprints upon the citizenry."

- "Similarly, American conservatives are opposed to state control of the economy, in all its Liberal manifestations, whether direct or indirect."

- "American conservatism derives from these positions its firm support of the Constitution of the United States as originally conceived — to achieve the protection of individual liberty in an ordered society by limiting the power of government."

- "In their devotion to Western civilization and their unashamed...American patriotism, conservatives see Communism as an armed and messianic threat to the very existence of Western civilization and the United States" (Meyer 1996, 192-195).

*Liberal
Group:
Vera Speaking*

🄾🄿 COMMENT ON THE REVIVAL

The leaders of the conservative revival, people like Buckley, Meyer, and Goldwater, hoped to restore the federal government to what it was before the Roosevelt years. They believed that the Supreme Court decided wrongly when it failed to strike down certain New Deal programs as unconstitutional.

In my opinion, the only way to deal with the large-scale problems of the 20th century was to expand the role of the federal government. In theory, that could have been done by amendments to the Constitution. We did that in order to extend the franchise to women. But the reality is that the amendment process is extremely difficult and cumbersome. It's entirely impractical. Instead, we found a simpler way to solve the problem. The Supreme Court became, in effect, a committee for reinterpreting and amending the Constitution. I know that Fred will disagree, but I think that was a very practical solution to the problems we faced.

Conservative Group: Fred Speaking

🅜🅟 ORGANIC CHANGE

Conservatives often talk about organic change. I'm going to try to explain what that means by quoting L. Brent Bozell. In 1966 Bozell wrote *The Warren Revolution*. He distinguished what he called the "fixed" from the "fluid" elements of our Constitution. He associated the latter with organic change.

Bozell on Organic Change

The fixed elements are adopted by "*formal*" procedures. The fluid elements develop through "*informal*" procedures. The fluid elements "are fashioned gradually, subtly, often imperceptibly, by the society's organic process. There is no moment — no 'time and place' — at which the provision may be said to have been framed and adopted...."

The fluid elements are the result of "an *accumulation* of actions taken over a period of years by various public authorities, as well as by private citizens and groups...." All these actions, from many different sources, "may eventually produce a broad synthesis."

But Bozell also pointed out that "the establishment of this kind of constitutional consensus does not preclude divergences from the fluid provision's principal thrust...." In fact, it is "in the very nature of a fluid provision...that it contemplates some front-runners, some laggards, even some die-hards who try still to move in the opposite direction" (Bozell "The Unwritten Constitution" in Buckley 1970, 57-59).

I think this describes what many conservatives believe. The idea of organic change derives from the Burkean tradition, and it was important to the conservative revival. It is also important to me. I'm not against reform and progress, but I think that if we move forward slowly and organically, we can avoid the kind of intense conflict that we have experienced over issues like abortion and racial integration. One reason we have lost the tradition of organic reform is because the Supreme Court has moved in and abruptly reinterpreted the Constitution. That's a recipe for social conflict.

*Liberal
Group:
Vera Speaking*

◻◻◻ COMMENT ON ORGANIC CHANGE

Historians of sociology sometimes divide sociologists into those who take a consensus view of society and those who take a conflict view. Conservative talk about organic change strongly favors the consensus view even in cases when it shouldn't. Does anyone think that as racial segregation developed in the American South in the late 19th and early 20th centuries it was the result of a developing consensus? Bozell talked about an evolving consensus on race in the South and the US generally that was disrupted by the Supreme Court's 1954 Brown decision. But there was no consensus. Do you honestly think that black people in the South were part of a consensus that denied them the right to vote? Of course not. Instead, there was conflict of interest and group domination, pure and simple. In my opinion, the conservative emphasis on organic change refuses to recognize domination in our own society and therefore cannot supply a model for resolution in cases of fundamental conflict.

Liberal Group: Vera Speaking

m p ORGANIC CHANGE

I have to say something about the idea of organic change. First, I agree that there are cases in which organic change does occur and sometimes it helps to solve problems. But I question whether it works to solve problems that are fundamental, or problems about which feelings are strong and interests are sharply divided.

Second, I think that there are many cases in which conservative rhetoric about organic change is really just a cover for doing nothing. Let me give you an example. In the 1950s the United States was faced with serious racial problems and increasing conflict. In the southern states a system of segregation existed. Blacks and whites had separate public schools, separate restaurants, separate hotels, and separate restrooms. Blacks were not hired for most of the better jobs and were usually not allowed to register to vote. Something had to be done. Perhaps the most important single issue was the right to vote. What did the advocates of organic change say? Well, in 1957 *National Review* gave us the following editorial advice:

s e *National Review* on Race Relations

"The central question that emerges ... is whether the White community in the South is entitled to take such measures as are necessary to prevail, politically and culturally, in areas in which it does not predominate numerically? The sobering answer is Yes...."

If we ask why that was true, the answer from *National Review* was that "the White community is so entitled

because, for the time being, it is the advanced race."
Furthermore, "The question, as far as the White
community is concerned, is whether the claims of
civilization supersede those of universal suffrage."

The author added that "It is more important for any
community, anywhere in the world, to affirm and live by
civilized standards, than to bow to the demands of the
numerical majority" (Buckley 1957).

In short, white people are the bearers of "civilized standards" and black
people are not.

I have to give whoever wrote that editorial (probably Buckley) credit for
honesty if nothing else. But it does not speak well for the *National Review* or
the advocates of organic change in the 1950s.

It is one thing for the advocates of organic change to recognize a problem
and put forward a plan that will, in a reasonable length of time, solve it
through a series of small steps. But that is not what we have here. What we
have here is simply an argument in favor of the existing situation. If that is
what organic change implies, then I question its value.

*Conservative
Group:
Fred Speaking*

🄾🄿 COMMENT ON RACE

*OK, Vera. You are absolutely right about Buckley's
1957 editorial on race. He took a similarly
conservative view in his 1959 book* Up from
Liberalism. *Buckley was content to allow the
southern states to deny African Americans the
right to vote. He was wrong to say what he did. It
was deplorable and racist. And, by the way, from
what I have read, not everyone at* National Review
agreed with his views.

*But don't try to pin those racist views on me or
other conservatives today. Things have changed
and thank goodness for that.*

Conservative Group: Fred Speaking

🅼🅿 BARRY GOLDWATER

I know we are concerned mainly with political ideas, but I would like to say something about a conservative politician who ran for president: Barry Goldwater (1909-1998). Goldwater represented the more conservative wing of the Republican Party and was the party's presidential candidate in 1964. He lost the election to Lyndon Johnson. But perhaps more important, Goldwater represented a victory for the conservative revival we have been talking about. His nomination indicated the growing power of conservatives within the Republican Party.

Goldwater served in the Army Air Force in World War II and was senator from Arizona from 1953 to 1965 and again from 1969 to 1987. He embodied many of the ideas characteristic of the conservative revival of the 1950s. In his 1960 book *The Conscience of a Conservative* (probably ghost written by L. Brent Bozell), he rejected many of the ideas and programs of the New Deal and strongly advocated victory over what he called the "Soviet Menace." In general, he criticized the expansion of federal power and advocated more limited government. He rejected the basic idea that the federal government should do what was needed rather than be limited to the powers given to it on a narrow reading of the Constitution. He advocated returning more power to state governments and rejected the idea that government should guide social and cultural change. Goldwater opposed the progressive income tax. He largely rejected the federal welfare state along with any federal role in education. As a senator, he voted against the Civil Rights Act of 1964 because it expanded federal power.

In *The Conscience of a Conservative* he wrote that "The government must begin to withdraw from a whole series of programs that are outside its constitutional mandate — from social welfare programs, education, public power, agriculture, public housing, urban renewal and all the other activities that can be better performed by lower levels of government or by private institutions or by individuals" (Goldwater 1961, 68, 88-91). Goldwater may have been the last presidential candidate to run against the New Deal.

In later years, Goldwater sometimes endeared himself to social liberals. In the early 1980s, he supported Sandra Day O'Connor as the first woman nominated to serve on the Supreme Court. In the 1990s, he criticized the ban on gay people serving in the armed forces, remarking that gays had served in the military since the time of Julius Caesar.

Liberal Group: John Speaking

🅼🅿 LET'S MOVE ON

Fred, you have given us some sense of the ideas that were part of the conservative revival in the 1950s and 1960s. You have told us what Buckley, Meyer, and Bozell believed about communism, the welfare state, organic change, and fusion. But hasn't conservatism changed since then?

As I see it, in the 1970s and 1980s the cultural issues related to women, abortion, and gay rights became much more important. Evangelical Christians and conservative Catholics began to organize politically. Ronald Reagan was elected president in 1980. In 1991, the Soviet Union collapsed, and world communism ceased to be the threat that it had been for more than half a century. In 1995, the Republican Party took over the House of Representatives and the Senate.

It seems to me that the conservative program shifted to the fiscal and cultural issues, and it has stayed there ever since. These days conservatives don't talk about communism. They talk about lower taxes and abortion. What happened?

Conservative Group: Diego Speaking

🔲🔲 MORAL ISSUES

Let me talk about this. John is right. I agree with a lot of what Fred says but I care more about the cultural and moral issues than the issues that concerned Buckley and Meyer. If I had been around in 1964, I probably would have voted for Barry Goldwater — but the Goldwater program was about anti-communism, rolling back the New Deal, reducing the size of the federal government, and lowering taxes. It wasn't about moral decline and cultural change.

For a long time evangelical Christians stayed away from politics. Their leadership believed that their role was to reach out to individuals and bring them to Jesus Christ. To the extent that the world would be transformed, it would be transformed because individuals had been transformed rather than because politicians had passed another law or created a new federal program. But in the 60s and 70s evangelical thinking changed. Many evangelicals came to believe that the whole culture had drifted away from them and they had to fight back. For example, in 1962 and 1963, the Supreme Court decided two cases that outlawed prayer in public schools. For many Christians that was a devastating blow. Then in 1973 the Court legalized abortion. Between 1969 and 1983 almost every state established no-fault divorce. And that's just a sample of the legal changes. In the culture at large, sex became more and more common as part of dating. Pornography was everywhere. Even presidential candidate Jimmy Carter did an interview with *Playboy* magazine in 1976. Drug use became so common in the 70s that President Nixon declared war on drugs.

My point is that the law and the culture were changing, and conservative Christians decided it was time to get into politics and try to reverse the trends. Several important Christian leaders and organizations emerged. Well-known people included Jerry Falwell, Pat Robertson, Richard Viguerie, Paul Weyrich, and, later, Ralph Reed. Those people and organizations have been very much involved in electoral politics, usually supporting Republican candidates and culturally conservative positions.

In the early 1990s, the Republican Party published its *Contract with America* as a legislative program. The Christian Coalition published its *Contract with the American Family* as a companion piece. Fred and I will give you some idea of what those programs involved in a minute. They show us the small-government, free-market conservatives and the Christian conservatives working together on a practical program.

All of these developments were very different from the conservative revival of the 1950s and 60s. They involved a new set of ideas entering into American conservatism. For some people, including me, they produced a new synthesis of political and religious ideas. For me, American conservatism isn't just a mixture of classical liberalism and Edmund Burke. It combines classical liberalism, Edmund Burke, and evangelical Christianity.

*Catholic
Group:
Ayesha Speaking*

O P **COMMENT ON
THE CHRISTIAN COALITION**

Hold on, Diego. I need to correct a possible misunderstanding concerning what you are saying. For an organization to name itself the Christian Coalition can be misleading.

There are a lot of seriously religious people, including lots of Christians, who do not agree with the Christian Coalition or with conservative evangelicals in general on political issues. That includes liberal evangelicals plus many Catholics and members of the mainline Protestant churches. All those groups disagree with the conservative evangelicals on a lot of points. The relationship between being liberal or being conservative on the one hand, and being religious or being secular on the other, is complicated.

My point is that the conservative evangelicals represent only a minority of Christians in the United States. Let's keep that in mind as we discuss their political ideas and the policies they support.

Conservative Group: Diego Speaking

🅜🅟 JERRY FALWELL

The three most important evangelical political leaders of the period from 1970 to 1995 were Jerry Falwell, Pat Robertson, and Ralph Reed. They guided the larger group of evangelicals into the political arena and focused their efforts on specific candidates and policies. I'm going to say a little about Falwell and Reed.

Jerry Falwell (1933-2007) was a Southern Baptist minister based in Lynchburg, Virginia. Beginning in the 1950s, Falwell appeared on the Old Time Gospel Hour, a nationally known radio and television program. He founded or cofounded many organizations, including the Moral Majority, Inc. in 1979 and Liberty University, one of the largest Christian schools in the world. In his 1980 book *Listen, America!* he described himself as a "fundamental, independent, separatist Baptist," who hoped to build a broad coalition of Americans to support morally conservative policies and legislation (Falwell 1981, 224). Falwell and the Moral Majority supported Ronald Reagan in the 1980 election.

Falwell took conservative positions on the cultural issues of his day, including feminism, abortion rights, and gay rights. He believed that America had entered a period of potentially fatal moral decline. "Pro-moral" people were a "sleeping giant," but "Liberal forces such as the abortionists, the homosexuals, the pornographers, secular humanists, and Marxists have made significant inroads in the giant's house." A return to a biblically based morality was essential in order to reverse current trends (Falwell 1981, Prologue).

Conservative
Group:
Diego Speaking

🅞🅟 COMMENT ON JERRY FALWELL

Falwell was more of an old-time preacher than Reed. He often sounded like an Old Testament prophet warning our nation of its sins and the coming justice of God.

Here he is calling out to the country: "Listen, America! Our nation is on a perilous path in regard to her political, economic, and military positions. If America continues down the path she is traveling, she will one day find that she is no longer a free nation. Our nation's internal problems are direct results of her spiritual condition. America is desperately in need of a divine healing, which can only come if God's people will humble themselves, pray, seek His face, and turn from their wicked ways. It is now time that moral Americans awake to the fact that our future depends upon how we stand on moral issues. God has no reason to spare us if we continue to reject Him."

For Falwell, the key was to restore "biblical morality." The problems were great, but recovery was still possible. "I am seeking to rally together the people of this country who still believe in decency, the home, the family, morality, the free-enterprise system, and all the great ideals that are the cornerstone of this nation. Against the growing tide of permissiveness and moral decay that is crushing our society, we must make

> a sacred commitment to God Almighty to turn this nation around
> immediately....We are late, but I do not believe that we are too late.
> It is time to put our lives on the line for this great nation of ours"
> (Falwell 1981, 213-214).
>
> I belong to a different generation than Falwell. I wouldn't use the same
> biblical rhetoric, but I still believe that moral decay is at the root of our
> problems and that we can turn that around if we choose to do so.

Conservative Group: Diego Speaking

🄼🄿 RALPH REED

Ralph Reed (1961-present) was born in Portsmouth, Virginia. He graduated from the University of Georgia and earned a PhD in history from Emory University. Reed has been a member of many conservative political organizations and served as the first Executive Director of the Christian Coalition from 1989 to 1997. In 2009 he founded the Faith and Freedom Coalition and is currently its chairman.

The Faith and Freedom Coalition has put forward several principles, including respect for life, family, and marriage, limited government, lower taxes, fiscal responsibility, educational reform, help for the poor, free markets, and "victory in the struggle with terrorism." The Coalition is anti-abortion, pro-Israel, and supports tax cuts for families. It has sought to eliminate limitations on the political speech of clergy that are part of the US tax code. It has also conducted extensive voter education campaigns in order to increase the conservative Christian vote.

In 1996 Reed published *Active Faith*, a record of his own political history, a statement of his views on the impact of moral decline in the United States, and an outline for a pro-family political agenda designed to reverse that decline.

Conservative Group: Diego Speaking

🅞🅟 COMMENT ON RALPH REED

I would like to give you a better idea of what Reed believes using his own words. I like him a lot. He's smart, well educated, and articulate. To be honest, I think that some liberals believe that evangelicals are all poorly educated people. They're wrong, and Reed proves it.

He knows American history, and he knows that evangelicals like me didn't really want to be involved in politics. "They are reluctant political actors....They look out upon a society they see as torn asunder by explicit sex and violence on television, rampant divorce, skyrocketing illegitimacy, epidemics of crime and drugs, and a million teen pregnancies every year. Their way of life and their values are under assault. For these activists, the most important issue in the nation is not 'the economy, stupid,' as the sign in the Clinton campaign headquarters proclaimed. It is the culture, the family, a loss of values, a decline in civility, and the destruction of our children" (Reed 1996, 5).

*Conservative
Group:
Diego Speaking*

Reed believes, and I believe, that a combination of evangelicals, conservative Catholics, and other conservatives can turn this country around. "Their goal: to limit government, reinvigorate the family, and restore the culture's Judeo-Christian principles. Their hierarchy of loyalties is uncompromisingly simple: They are people of faith first, Americans second, and Republicans or Democrats third. And they are proving yet again that man does not live by bread alone. The real battle for the soul of our nation is not fought primarily over the gross national product and the prime interest rate, but over virtues, values, and the culture" (Reed 1996, 8).

The Contract with the American Family provided focus. "Some of the issues were simple enough: a religious freedom amendment, ending taxpayer funding of abortion, family tax relief, and ending the tax funding of pornography through the National Endowment for the Arts....We believed that the First Amendment rights of people of faith were at stake, and that the entire culture had suffered from the treating of religious expression as a danger to be censored and silenced" (Reed 1996, 200).

I think that Reed is spot on. He sees the real, underlying problems that we face as a nation.

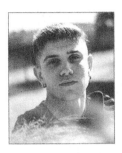

Conservative Group: Fred Speaking

ⓜ ⓟ RONALD REAGAN

We have been talking about the entry of evangelical Christians and other cultural conservatives into politics. Ronald Reagan profited from that development. He pulled evangelical votes from his Democratic opponent, the self-proclaimed evangelical Jimmy Carter.

Reagan (1911-2004) was a Hollywood actor from the late 1930s until the early 1960s. He served in an Armed Forces film unit during World War II. Politically, he was a Democrat for many years, but became a Republican in the early 1960s. In 1964 he delivered his famous "A Time for Choosing" speech in support of Goldwater's presidential campaign. He was elected governor of California in 1966 and 1970 and was well known for his opposition to political protestors at the state universities. He unsuccessfully sought the Republican presidential nomination in 1976, but went on to receive it in 1980. He won both the popular and the electoral college vote (receiving over 90% of the latter). Reagan was reelected in a landslide in 1984.

Unlike Goldwater, Reagan did not campaign to overturn the New Deal, although he did criticize the Great Society programs of President Lyndon Johnson. He also advocated strong anticommunism, a less powerful federal government, increases in the defense budget, decreases in domestic spending, lower federal income taxes, more power for state governments, less economic regulation, more limited environmental protection, and less aggressive enforcement of civil rights laws.

The years between Goldwater's loss in 1964 and Reagan's victory in 1980 saw the emergence of the religious and cultural conservatives who supported Reagan. They gave him many of the votes that Goldwater lacked.

*Conservative
Group:
Fred Speaking*

🄾🄿 COMMENT ON REAGAN'S POLICIES

Reagan's election in 1980 is generally thought of as part of a conservative shift in American politics. In Reagan's rhetoric, government was not the solution to the nation's problems, it was the problem. As of early 1981, the Republican Party controlled the Presidency and the Senate, although not the House of Representatives. Nevertheless, they drew enough support from conservative House Democrats to carry out what has been called the Reagan Revolution.

The 'revolution' included a sizable cut in the federal income tax and the elimination of many federal regulations on business. It was hoped that lower taxes and lower costs for business would lead to more investment and the creation of more jobs. At the same time, the military budget was increased. Deficits continued because domestic spending cuts balancing the tax cuts and military increases could not be enacted. The national debt rose substantially during Reagan's two terms in office, but the price inflation of the 1970s and early 80s was brought under control.

Reagan appointed four justices to the Supreme Court and made Justice William Rehnquist the Chief Justice. One of Reagan's appointees, Antonin Scalia, interpreted the Constitution as an "originalist" and became exceptionally well-known for his views. Reagan also appointed Sandra Day O'Connor, the first woman to sit on the Court. In addition, he appointed hundreds of judges to lower courts.

Conservative Group: Diego Speaking

🅜🅟 THE 1990s

Fred and I want to give you some idea of the kind of thing that conservatives were advocating in the 1990s, well after Reagan left office. Republicans won big in the 1994 election, taking control of both the House and the Senate. I have already mentioned that they published a legislative program called the *Contract with America* and the Christian Coalition put out the *Contract with the American Family*. We think those two programs show what conservatism meant at the legislative level.

The Contract with America

The *Contract with America* promised that Republicans would propose a set of procedural reforms on the first day of the new Congress. The reforms were to include requiring that all laws apply to Congress itself, conducting an audit of Congressional spending, limiting the terms of committee chairs, banning proxy voting, opening meetings to the public, requiring a 3/5 majority to pass a tax increase, and implementing zero base budgeting. These first-day reforms were to be followed by a raft of legislation to be introduced in the first 100 days of the new session. We can only give you a taste of these new bills. They included legislation to introduce a balanced budget amendment and the line-item veto, an anti-crime bill, restrictions on welfare payments, child support enforcement, a $500 tax credit for children, an increase in the Social Security earnings limit, incentives to small businesses, limits on punitive damages in law suits, and term limits for members of Congress.

The Contract with the American Family

The *Contract with the American Family* advocated adopting a constitutional amendment to protect religious liberty, transferring federal funds for education to families and local school boards, expanding parental choice of schools, defeating the United Nations convention on the rights of children, reducing the tax burden on families, taking measures to reduce the number of abortions, incentivizing contributions to private charities, protecting children from exposure to pornography, converting several federal programs that fund the arts into private, voluntary organizations, and requiring convicts to work or study and to pay restitution to their victims.

We think it is fair to say that although these reforms were proposed in the 1990s, they represent the kind of change that conservatives like Fred and I have continued to advocate. The biggest change in the early 2000s was the rise of the neoconservatives and the fight against terrorism. Fred and I don't think of ourselves as neoconservatives, and we are going to leave neoconservatism for another discussion.

Conservative Group: Fred Speaking

🅜🅟 GEORGE WILL

There is one more writer I would like to say something about. He has been a well-known conservative for a long time. He even worked at the *National Review* in the 1970s. I'm thinking of George Will (1941-present). I think it's fair to say that he is the dean of conservative public intellectuals, and it would be a shame to leave him out of our presentation.

Will has an unusual background. His father was a philosophy professor and George himself went to graduate school at Princeton University and earned a doctorate in political philosophy. Since then he has taught at several universities, written hundreds of newspaper and magazine articles, and published 15 books. His latest work, *The Conservative Sensibility*, was published in 2019.

Will's conservatism is based on a belief that there are important fixed elements in human nature. Because of those fixed elements, it is possible to determine a natural moral law and certain natural rights. Because those rights do not derive from government, government must be appropriately limited. In Will's view, progressives in the early 20th century rejected all those ideas. They replaced them with faith in science, expertise, and active government. While the men who drafted our Constitution hoped to design government to prevent the harm that human nature might produce, modern liberals hope to use government to mold human nature and social institutions for the better.

The reason I have brought up Will's work is that I think he raises tough questions for all of us to consider. Here's a sample of the questions he discusses:

Questions for All of Us

- Is there a natural moral law? Are there natural rights? How can we know? If there are no natural rights, where do moral rights come from?

- To what extent are individuals and social institutions amenable to intentional modification? To what extent are there fixed elements in human nature and how much do they matter for political action?

- Does modern conservatism require a belief in God? After all, Jefferson said that all men are "endowed by their Creator" with certain rights. Was he right? Will doesn't think so. He calls himself a "low-voltage" atheist (Will 2019, 479).

- Does modern genetic science undermine the idea of the self or the person required by a liberal democratic society? Does that society assume a kind of personal autonomy that does not exist?

- Does that same science undermine our belief in human agency as well as moral and legal responsibility? Does it undermine our ideas about human dignity and value?

- To what extent can modern social science tell us how to solve social problems?

These are all basic issues, and Will brings them back into our political discussions. You may not agree with his answers, but these are questions for all of us. If we are going to think seriously about our political ideas, we need to find answers.

I know we can't answer these questions today, so I'm suggesting that we all take them home and think about them.

Liberal Group: John Speaking

🅜🅟 CONSERVATISM

I just want to make a couple of comments on the kind of conservatism that Fred and Diego have been advocating.

John's Criticisms of Conservatism

- Fred, I notice that you place emphasis on natural rights, and I see that George Will also stressed their importance. But I am not at all sure where natural rights come from. According to Will, they are knowable because they foster human "flourishing" (Will 2019, 8-11). I think that conservatives need to say more about the basis of those rights.

- The kind of limited-government conservatism you describe may have been adequate at some time in the past, but I have my doubts that it will work for the problems we have today. Could it solve the problems of the Great Recession of 2007-2009 or the COVID-19 pandemic in 2020-2021? Can it deal with problems like pollution, global warming, persistent poverty, and racism? In my opinion, a strong, active federal government is needed to deal with those issues. I don't see any other way.

- I also have concerns about the difficult amendment process built into our Constitution. Vera said that she sees the Supreme Court as a standing committee for reinterpreting the Constitution. I know you can't possibly agree with that, but what's the alternative?

- Diego, I'm worried about the entry of so many conservative Christians into our electoral politics. I know that Pat Robertson sought the Republican nomination for president back in 1988. I tend to think of the United States government as a secular government. When a religious leader like Robertson runs for office, it makes we wonder just what role religious leaders and religious ideas should play in our political system.

Liberal Group: Ann Speaking

ⓜ ⓟ RELIGION AND POLITICS

I want to pick up on the last thing that John said. I have concerns about the large number of conservative Christians entering electoral politics. I don't want to sound like a bigot, but I think these are legitimate concerns.

- If we bring all sorts of religious ideas into our politics, I'm afraid that reasonable debate will be impossible. We'll just end up yelling at each other. I think we will be much better off if we begin from some common ground, some shared assumptions, and work from there. Leave our personal religious convictions out of it.

- Some religious people rely on theological assumptions that others reject. Not only that, they may rely on sources and authorities that others don't accept.

- What is to prevent someone like Jerry Falwell from advocating a law against gay sex or pre-marital sex if he thinks that those things are against God's law? In my opinion, those things do no harm at all. What is to prevent him from supporting his case by citing passages in the Bible? What is to prevent Congress from passing such a law if they can rely on religious arguments and scripture for a justification? It's a dangerous road to go down. I don't want any religious group to use the government to impose its moral views on the rest of us.

- Like John, I have always thought of the US as a secular state. Our Constitution does not allow an established religion. Not only that, but we all remember Jefferson advocating a "wall between church and state." That's our tradition and I want to keep it that way.

Catholic Group: Ayesha Speaking

🅜🅟 RELIGION AND POLITICS

Ann, I have to disagree with part of what you say; and I'm pretty sure Diego disagrees too.

My religious convictions are part of who I am, and I can't just set them aside when I talk about important political issues. I don't even want to. Of course, other people can bring in their own convictions, and they have every right to disagree with me.

Besides, the only way I can answer some basic questions is to go back to my Catholic faith. For example, my faith tells me that God created human beings in His image and created the earth for the benefit of all. When we get to talking about human rights, welfare rights, racial equality, or environmental stewardship, those things matter. I need to go back to those ideas to think through the issues.

The bottom line is that I think you're wrong on this. It would be nice to be able to start from common ground and reason together toward solutions to our problems, but it can't always be done. Many of us hold different views on some very basic issues. That's just a fact.

Catholic Group: Ayesha Speaking

🅞🅟 COMMENT ON RELIGION AND POLITICS

In The Naked Public Square *Richard John Neuhaus wrote about the role of religious ideas and traditions in politics. He understood that religion and politics must interact. The question is "whether we can devise forms for that interaction which can revive rather than destroy the liberal democracy that is required by a society that would be pluralistic and free" (Neuhaus 1984, 9).*

Notice the words "pluralistic and free." I think that some people are too quick to assume that if religion gets involved in politics, pluralism and freedom go out the door. That doesn't have to be true. I don't want any religion, including my own, to dominate this country and impose its moral and theological doctrines. But I do agree with Neuhaus that religion has been pushed out of the "public square." For the American people, with their strong religious traditions and motivations, that is an absurd situation. We need to "restore the role of religion in helping to give moral definition and direction to American public life and policy" (Neuhaus 1984, 59). Perhaps we need to develop a "public ethic" that will help us to discuss "ultimate truths that serve as points of reference in guiding our agreements and disagreements" (Neuhaus 1984, 37).

I want you to think about what Neuhaus is saying. I think he's on to something.

Libertarian Group: Elijah Speaking

🅼🅿 RELIGION AND POLITICS

I agree with Ann. In a modern democracy, it seems to me that government should pursue secular ends — ends that are not defined in religious terms. For example, government should pursue peace, prosperity, national security, low crime rates, better education, low unemployment, access to medical care, and the reduction of poverty. Look at the Preamble to our Constitution. It tells us that the Constitution is being adopted in order to promote union, justice, tranquility, defense, the general welfare, and liberty. Those are goals we all agree on, and they are all secular.

Furthermore, I think that the assumptions that legislators make when they pass laws should be secular. We have values and principles like free speech, equality before the law, the right to vote, non-discrimination, and lots of others. They are the proper basis for debating law and policy, and they are secular too.

If we assume that government is limited to secular goals and assumptions, then none of us should urge it to make something illegal solely because we believe that it is sinful. A preacher like Jerry Falwell may believe that gay sex or sex between unmarried people is a sin, but it isn't a concern for government. It's a private matter.

Let me also say this: Dee and I believe in self-ownership, and self-ownership implies strong individual rights. As long as people act within their rights, they will not violate the rights of others and government has no business limiting what they do. Keep government to a minimum and there will be no problem concerning religion and politics.

*Conservative
Group:
Diego Speaking*

◻◻ COMMENT ON RELIGION AND POLITICS

Let me remind you of a little history. Everyone agrees that Americans have often based their political positions on their religious beliefs. The abolitionist movement, the temperance movement, the Social Gospel movement, the civil rights movement, and the Vietnam anti-war movement were all partly inspired by religious ideas and supported by religious arguments. Modern liberals were fine when black ministers urged their congregations to protest segregation or to vote (when they could) a certain way. They were fine when the Catholic archbishop of New Orleans said that racial segregation was morally wrong and excommunicated some Catholics who supported it. It wasn't until evangelicals began to oppose the liberal position (on abortion, women's rights, and gay rights) that liberals began to say that religious ideas should be kept out of politics. It's more than a little hypocritical if you ask me.

Some liberal writers, such as the philosopher John Rawls, say that they want everyone to base political arguments about basic issues on a set of agreed-upon political values and principles. But I think they are doing something more than that. I think they are trying to give their own agnostic humanist philosophy a privileged position in political arguments. They are trying to force everyone to formulate their arguments in the terms that secular liberals accept rather than the terms that express their most fundamental views.

> *They are trying to push religious concepts and convictions out of the public debate.*
>
> *All I want is a level playing field. You can formulate your arguments in whatever terms you choose. You can base your arguments on whatever principles are most important to you. Just let me do the same.*

Conservative Group: Diego Speaking

🄼🄿 RELIGION AND POLITICS

As an evangelical Christian, I would be the first to admit that evangelicals base some of their political positions on their moral values and that their moral values are rooted in their religion. I don't try to hide that fact. I'm proud of it. Not only that, but I also think that Christians should feel free to include their religious convictions in public political debate.

Don't get me wrong. I expect secular people and people on the political left to do the same thing. We all have to get our values from somewhere. Some Christians are social liberals and base their liberalism on scripture. Some people on the left attempt to base their values on reason alone. That's fine. Let them do that. Just don't ask me to keep my religion out of my politics. If you do that, you are asking me to ignore the most important part of myself when I take a political position. How could anyone do that? It's psychologically impossible.

Liberals wouldn't dream of asking African Americans or women or gay people to set aside their life experience or their sense of identity when they enter politics. It's the same for evangelicals. We have our own sense of identity. Our religious convictions make us who we are. It is unfair to ask us to set them aside.

Conservative Group: Diego Speaking

🅜🅟 RELIGION AND POLITICS

I think that Ann and Elijah are assuming that the United States government is a completely secular state. Have you asked yourself what that means and why you think it is true? Of course, the federal Constitution prohibits an established religion. We all accept that. But is that enough to exclude the whole Judeo-Christian tradition from major political debates and decisions? Most Americans draw their moral inspiration from that tradition. Doesn't that matter?

I think that it is perfectly proper for government to pursue the ideals valued by its people. Both Christians and non-Christians have moral and social ideals. They have ideas about what is good for human beings, and we need to bring those ideas into our political debates. Otherwise, we will not be able to resolve basic issues.

Liberal Group: Ann Speaking

🅜🅟 RELIGION AND POLITICS

OK, Diego. You have a right to base your public political arguments on your religious beliefs. But that leaves us with lots of questions and problems. We can still ask whether you *should* base your political positions on your religious beliefs. Is it the best thing to do in a diverse society like ours? Or does it paralyze the political system by making debate impossible?

Keep in mind that not everyone shares your religious beliefs. Furthermore, not everyone accepts your method of determining the truth or your sources of knowledge.

For example, you might claim that gay sex or gay marriage is immoral and that it ought to be illegal because God has condemned it. You might support those claims by referring to the writings of the Apostle Paul. But some Americans don't believe in God. Some don't believe that God inspired Paul's epistles. Some people believe that the Jewish or the Islamic or the Mormon scriptures tell us more about God's will than the New Testament. Some people agree that the New Testament is sacred, but they interpret it much more liberally than you do.

My point is this: *We cannot reason together if we do not begin with some common premises.* If everyone constructs political arguments based on their religious beliefs, how can we ever resolve anything? There is too much variation among us. That's why I think we would be better off to stick to a core set of secular political principles that we all accept. Then we can use those principles to answer the tough political questions that we have to deal with.

Liberal Group: John Speaking

🅼🅿 A COMPROMISE?

I want to propose a possible compromise between Ann's view and the view taken by Diego and Ayesha. Let me introduce you to Michael Perry, the author of *Love and Power*. Perry wants to find a more prominent place for religious conviction in politics. He proposes what he calls "ecumenical dialogue." My question for Ann, Diego, and Ayesha is whether they can accept Perry's ecumenical dialogue as a compromise?

Michael Perry: Ecumenical Political Dialogue

Perry is concerned not only with the role of religious conviction in public political debate, but with a broader question concerning the role of differing ideas of the human good in politics. Some of those ideas are based on religious conviction, but others are not.

- He proposes that we engage in what he calls "ecumenical political dialogue." Such a dialogue would allow citizens to introduce values, principles, and ideas of the human good that are based on their religious or secular convictions. In doing so, however, they should defend their views in ways that are neither "sectarian" nor "authoritarian." These limitations are significant, but Perry believes that they would still allow our public dialogue to be open to powerful religious influences (Perry 1991, chapter six, especially 106).

- If a religiously based value or principle is neither sectarian nor authoritarian, it can be introduced into public dialogue even if it is not shared by all others in the dialogue (Perry 1991, 119). This applies as well to secular convictions.

*Liberal
Group:
John Speaking*

🄾🄿 COMMENT ON PERRY'S VIEWS

I said that Perry believes that public political arguments made by religious people should not be "sectarian" or "authoritarian." Let me explain.

An argument is sectarian "if (and to the extent) it relies on experiences or premises that have little if any authority beyond the confines of one's own moral or religious community." An argument is authoritarian "if it relies on persons or institutions that have little if any authority beyond the confines of one's own community" (Perry 1991, 106).

Perry believes that even though a moral or political view is based on religious conviction it can sometimes be put forward in a way that does not assume that the audience shares that conviction. For example, a Christian may be moved by the story of the Good Samaritan. The story is inspired by religious conviction and derived from a religious scripture, but it still has meaning for people who are not Christian.

Perry refers to statements and arguments that are non-sectarian and non-authoritarian as publicly accessible. He believes that publicly accessible statements and arguments, religious or secular, should be allowed in the public square (Perry 1991, 111).

Conservative Group: Diego Speaking

ⓜⓟ A COMPROMISE?

I agree with Perry on some points, but not on everything. I don't think a compromise based on his ideas is sufficient.

For example, I agree with Perry that the secular political values and principles we all share are not enough to resolve some of our most serious political problems. To answer some questions, people need to go back to their basic convictions (religious or secular) and their ideas about what constitutes the good for human beings. For me, that means going back to my evangelical faith. For Ayesha, it means going back to Catholic doctrine. I don't see any alternative. We can't always work from shared assumptions like Ann wants us to.

But, to tell you the truth, I don't think Perry goes far enough. Instead of pussyfooting around by trying to use secular arguments or avoiding sectarian appeals, I don't see why citizens shouldn't come straight out and say that their political position on some issues (such as gay marriage or human rights or abortion) is based on their religious faith. If that turns out to be what Perry calls "sectarian" or "authoritarian," why is that such a big problem?

I think that religious ideas are part of the core of every great culture. I don't see why they should be left out of politics just because there are some people who reject them. After all, there will be some people who reject any assumption we make.

Professor Sidgwick Speaking

🅜🅟 WRAPPING UP

I think we have to bring this to a close, but you are raising some great questions that we should come back to. Here are a few issues to think about:

- What is the proper role of religious belief in public political debate? Should conservative Christians like Diego develop their political opinions based on their religious views and base their public arguments on those views? Or should religious belief be kept in a private sphere, away from politics and public political debates?

- Is it possible to define a set of core political values and principles that nearly all Americans agree upon and use only those values and principles as the basis of political debate and as a rationale for legislation? If so, would those core principles have to be secular?

Right now, I'm going to ask Fred and Diego to make their final pitch for American conservatism. I have also asked Ayesha to offer a final evaluation of what they have presented to us.

Conservative Group Fred Speaking

🅜🅟 FINAL STATEMENT

Diego and I are going to try to sum up the essence of American conservatism. Not every conservative thinker or politician will agree with us, but this is our considered opinion.

We believe that history has shown that the principles we offer here are the best guarantee of prosperity and freedom.

A Final Statement of Principles

- **Strong individual rights**. That includes freedom of belief, expression, and association. We want to include here strong property rights because we believe that if property rights are weakened, other rights will be weakened as well.

- **Constitutionally limited government**. This applies especially to the federal government, which has grown in wealth and power to a level way beyond what the drafters of our Constitution envisioned. The Constitution should be narrowly interpreted in order to limit federal power.

- **Fiscal responsibility**. This implies lower taxes, modest deficits, and a much smaller national debt.

- **Dispersal of power**. Power should be dispersed in many ways: between the federal and state governments, among the branches of government, between public and private institutions, and between large and small enterprises. Government should not control the institutions of civil society more than is necessary to maintain order and liberty.

- **Equality before the law**. This means that all citizens have the same legal rights. It does not guarantee equal chances to succeed or equal outcomes in life.

- **Strong support for private enterprise and free markets**. These are important not only because they promote economic progress, but because they balance and limit the power of government with private power.

- **Respect for traditional values, traditional religion, and traditional social institutions**. This applies to many institutions, but especially to the family. Government should act to strengthen families and traditional morality because they are the foundations of any stable society.

- **Skepticism regarding government programs to reform people and social institutions**. When government measures are appropriate, we have a strong preference for careful planning and a minimalist approach. We recognize the inevitability of unintended consequences and the importance of minimizing unintended harm.

- **A strong national defense**. We recognize that the world is a dangerous place, and that the best way to deter war is to be well prepared to fight.

*Liberal
Group:
John Speaking*

🅞🅟 COMMENT ON
FEDERAL AND STATE POWER

I want to pick up on something that Fred and Diego have mentioned. Our country was founded as a federal republic. The states were to be independent in many ways and not simply appendages of the national government. Yet states have tended to lose independence over time, especially in the 20th century. Modern liberals (including me) have often supported that tendency.

But we need to ask ourselves what is the proper division of power between the federal and state governments? Today, liberals are pleased that some states, such as Colorado, have legalized marijuana and Oregon has legalized assisted suicide. On the other hand, they do not want different states to have different laws on gay marriage. The question is whether there is a principle at work here?

It seems to me that both liberals and conservatives often ignore principle and simply go to the level of government or the branch of government where they think they can get the most favorable response.

My point is this: First, liberals should realize that state autonomy has real value. Colorado and Oregon have proven that. Second, all of us need to ask ourselves what principle should govern the division of power between the state and federal governments. We should not simply go shopping for the way to get the most of what we want.

Catholic Group: Ayesha Speaking

🅜🅟 AN EVALUATION

I'm going to try to provide a fair evaluation of American conservatism. I don't want to focus on what I think is wrong. I believe in trying to find the value in what other people say, although I will also try to point out some limitations and suggest some questions that I would like to see answered.

Ayesha's Evaluation of Conservatism

- Limited-government, free-market conservatism represents a deeply-rooted American tradition. It helped to make the United States a wealthy country with freedoms that are envied around the world. It deserves our respect. Free markets are creative and productive. That's a good thing. On the other hand, markets are sometimes imperfect. John pointed out that they allow some people to pass on large costs to others. That's especially true in cases of environmental damage. They can also allow enormous concentrations of economic and political power. As a result, regulation can also be good.

- The best kind of American conservatism is a form of humanism. It should not be equated with racism, militarism, and xenophobic attitudes and policies. All those problems exist as part of our culture, but it is unfair to speak of them as if they were inherent elements of American conservatism. I know that Fred would agree with me on that.

- Conservatives have repeatedly reminded us that government actions have unintended consequences, sometimes the opposite of what they were intended to achieve. I think they are correct on that point. Social liberals have not paid enough attention to that problem. Our ability to predict and control human behavior is more limited than they like to think. Liberals sometimes put too much faith in the claims of experts and social scientists. Conservatives are correct to underscore their limitations. They are also correct to point out that many social problems are more intractable than liberals think.

- Conservatives usually support some form of federalism. They are correct that the federal government has grown enormously in scope and power. I think that John has raised a good question: What is the best division of power between the federal government and the states? I'm not sure any of us has a principled answer to that question.

- One of the problems with American conservatism is that a preference for small government and slow organic change can become a tendency to do very little about some very serious problems. Vera pointed this out and I think it is sometimes true.

- Modern liberalism, on the other hand, finds it easy to justify government's attempts to solve problems, but difficult to place principled limits on what government can do. Conservatives are correct to point that out. It seems to me that we need a political philosophy that will allow government to act effectively in the modern world but will also place principled limits on that action. I don't think that either conservatism or modern liberalism offers us that philosophy.

- My big question for conservatives is this: How can the limited government they favor solve the major problems we face today as a society? I'm thinking of pollution, racism, increasing inequality, widespread gun violence, global warming, future pandemics, and more.

- Let me add another question. I think that if conservatives wish to rely on natural rights, it is fair to ask them to supply a solid basis for those rights. What is that basis? I don't think Fred has said enough about that.

OK. That's my evaluation. I've tried to be fair, but I'll leave it to the rest of you to decide whether I was successful.

Professor Sidgwick Speaking

🄼🄿 A DIGRESSION

Thank you, Ayesha. Now I want to go back to something that came up when the group was talking about religion and politics. It wasn't clear that we had enough shared values and principles to resolve some of our basic political disputes. That leads to questions about what political philosophers call legitimacy.

I want us to talk a little about legitimacy, so I'm going to ask that we digress for a few minutes before we hear from Ann, Vera, and John on social liberalism.

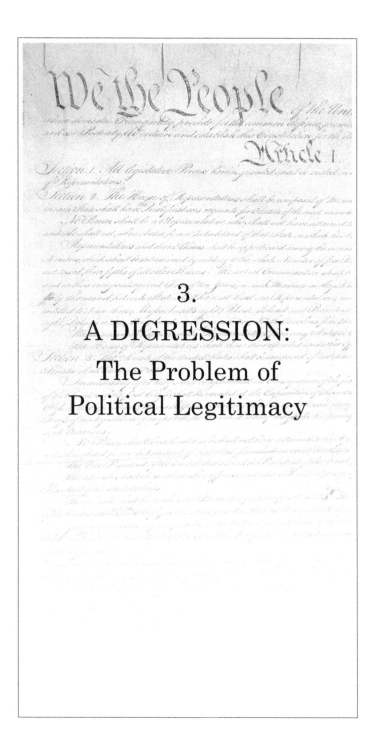

3.

A DIGRESSION:
The Problem of
Political Legitimacy

Professor Sidgwick Speaking

🅜🅟 LEGITIMACY

I want to introduce a new concept that is especially relevant today because of the polarization in our national politics. That concept is what political philosophers call legitimacy.

The word 'legitimacy' has been used by journalists a lot in the last year or two. It is somewhat ambiguous. Sometimes, when we speak of legitimate government, we mean a government that people trust or in which people have faith or confidence. The philosophical concept is different, and like many things in philosophy it is controversial. It's the philosophical concept that I want to discuss for a moment.

For many philosophers, a legitimate government is one that is justified in exercising coercion to enforce its laws. Furthermore, citizens normally have a moral obligation to abide by those laws.

That leads us to the big question: Under what conditions is a government philosophically legitimate? Another way to put it would be to ask "What are the criteria for legitimate government?"

*Professor
Sidgwick
Speaking*

🄾🄿 COMMENT ON LEGITIMACY

Once we have the concept of legitimacy, we can distinguish between several different questions about laws and policies. For example:

- *Is a given law or policy correct or incorrect, reasonable or unreasonable, just or unjust?*

- *Is a given law or policy promulgated by a legitimate or an illegitimate government? Is it legitimate law?*

It is important to realize that an unreasonable or unjust law may be enacted by a legitimate government. When that happens, citizens normally have a moral obligation to abide by the law. Of course, they may disagree with the law, criticize it, protest against it, and work to change it. But they are normally obligated to abide by the law until it is changed.

*Libertarian
Group:
Elijah Speaking*

🔲🔳 COMMENT ON LEGITIMACY

I know from my own reading that many different principles of legitimacy have been historically important. Some people have argued that governments are legitimate if they are based on an ancient compact between the people and their king. Others have argued that it is the ruler's relationship to God that makes his or her rule legitimate. John Locke famously argued that legitimate government must be based on some form of consent. Some have believed that the ruler's special powers make him a legitimate ruler.

Every society requires some principle of legitimacy. Without it, there is a danger of slipping into chaos.

Professor Sidgwick Speaking

🅜🅟 RAWLS ON LEGITIMACY

Ann is going to introduce the philosopher John Rawls when the liberal group does its presentation. She is going to talk about Rawls's theory of justice. I want to say something here about his view of legitimacy.

Rawls's problem was to find a rationale for legitimate government in a modern democracy containing a wide range of what he called reasonable but incompatible "comprehensive doctrines." Some people like Diego are evangelical Christians. Others are agnostic humanists. Some are Marxists. Ayesha is a Catholic. They all have different comprehensive doctrines or world views that try to answer the great questions of life: Is there a God? Does life have a purpose? What is justice? Is there an afterlife? What are the basic moral principles by which we should live? What is the good for human beings? And so on.

Rawls asked how it was possible to have a legitimate government in a society with such profound differences. As an answer, he proposed what he called the liberal principle of legitimacy. That principle essentially requires that legitimate government should be based on an "overlapping consensus" of political values and principles. Those values would include, for example, some type of liberty, equality, and stability.

Given that principle, Rawls concluded that public debate or "public reason" on fundamental issues should be based on shared political values and principles. Decisions should be based on those same values and principles. That was the key to legitimate government.

*Professor
Sidgwick
Speaking*

🔲🔲 COMMENT ON RAWLS'S VIEW

Rawls asked several important questions. "How is it possible that there may exist over time a stable and just society of free and equal citizens profoundly divided by reasonable though incompatible religious, philosophical, and moral doctrines?" (Rawls 1996, xx). How is legitimate government possible in such a diverse society? What should be the content of public political discussion or "public reason"? Should the partisans of each comprehensive doctrine bring any or all of their ideas explicitly into the discussion, or should some of those ideas be excluded?

I have already said that Rawls offered what he called the liberal principle of legitimacy. The "exercise of political power is proper and hence justifiable only when it is exercised in accordance with a constitution the essentials of which all citizens may reasonably be expected to endorse in the light of principles and ideals acceptable to them as reasonable and rational" (Rawls 1996, 217). To put it differently, on "constitutional essentials" and matters of "basic justice" (including some basic legislative issues), it is ideal to "appeal only to principles and values each citizen can endorse." In short, we must "try for an agreed basis" when deciding fundamental issues (Rawls 2001, 41). Rawls referred to that agreed-upon basis as an overlapping consensus among reasonable comprehensive doctrines.

The citizens who accepted each reasonable comprehensive doctrine could, for different reasons, agree on that core set of political values and principles. They would agree not because it was expedient to do so, but because they could find reasons within their doctrine for doing so.

Initially, Rawls held that public political debate with regard to questions of "constitutional essentials and matters of basic justice" should be conducted using only the core political values and principles of the overlapping consensus. Those values and principles were a "reasonable public basis of justification on fundamental political questions" (Rawls 1996, xxi). Later, he took what he called the "wide view" of public reason. On that view, citizens could introduce arguments based on their own comprehensive doctrine as long as "in due course" public reasons based on shared values and principles were introduced to support their political position (Rawls 1996, li).

Professor Sidgwick Speaking

🅜🅟 LEGITIMACY

All of this leads to new questions that have to do with legitimate government.

I am going to assume that something similar to Rawls's liberal principle of legitimacy is the best principle for a diverse, modern democracy like the United States. Given that assumption, consider these questions:

Questions About Legitimacy

- Can we find enough shared political values and principles to satisfy the Rawlsian principle of legitimacy?

- In our current political situation, which seems to be increasingly polarized, are we losing the shared ground we need to provide a rationale for legitimate government and to support faith in that government?

- If we are losing that shared ground, are there ways to rebuild it?

I said a few minutes ago that questions about legitimacy were especially important today because of the polarization in our national politics. Now I think you can see what I meant. It is possible that increasing polarization is leading us to a crisis of legitimacy. We need to understand legitimacy in order to confront that crisis.

Professor Sidgwick Speaking

🄾🄿 COMMENT ON RAWLS'S VIEW

I simplified Rawls's view and I want to explain some of what I left out. Rawls did not believe that everyone who accepted a reasonable comprehensive doctrine would agree on exactly the same set of common political values and principles. He believed that there were several forms or varieties of what he called political liberalism. Each form specified a set of rights or liberties, identified their priority, and also guaranteed the means required to make "intelligent and effective use" of those liberties (Rawls 1996, xlviii). Rawls hoped that the people who accept each reasonable comprehensive doctrine would also be able to accept one of the forms of political liberalism. Since the forms might differ, for example, in the priorities they identified among liberties, there would continue to be vigorous debate among their advocates. Citizens could accept one form as the most reasonable while still regarding the others as reasonable. Rawls appeared to believe that this satisfied what he called the criterion of reciprocity and the requirements of legitimacy.

Conservative Group: Diego Speaking

🅜🅟 RAWLS'S VIEW

I would like to respond to Rawls with a couple of points.

First, I think that his scheme is unrealistic. If he is only saying that it might be possible to come up with a core set of shared political values and principles that we could use to solve fundamental political problems, I would say "OK. It's possible in theory." In practice, I don't think there is much chance of it happening. We are too diverse in our ideas. Rawls himself said that there was no guarantee that we could reach an overlapping consensus that supported his own conception of justice "or any reasonable conception for a democratic regime" (Rawls 2001, 37). Furthermore, he rejected the notion that his overlapping consensus was a mere "modus vivendi" based on self-interest. But in some cases, that may be all there is to be had.

I don't doubt that there are some core political values and principles like freedom of speech and universal suffrage on which we can agree. That's good as far as it goes. But can those core values and principles serve as a basis on which we can resolve the most fundamental issues? I doubt it. In fact, I think any such core principles will be woefully inadequate. I don't think we have any alternative except for each of us to go back to our personal beliefs (what Rawls calls our comprehensive doctrines) to get the necessary values and principles to work with. In my case, that means going back to my Christian faith.

Second, I think that what secular liberals are trying to do is push religious ideas out of the public square completely. They want to privilege their own epistemology, their own methodology, and their own naturalistic metaphysics. I'm not buying it. I think law professor Stephen Carter put it well:

"What is needed is not a requirement that the religiously devout choose a form of dialogue that liberalism accepts, but that liberalism develop a politics that accepts whatever form of dialogue a member of the public offers. Epistemic diversity, like diversity of other kinds, should be cherished, not ignored, and certainly not abolished" (Carter 1994, 230).

Catholic Group: Ayesha Speaking

🅜🅟 RELIGIOUS BELIEFS

I agree with Diego that the core political values and principles we agree upon are insufficient to decide some very important questions. Abortion might be one of them. I'm sure there are others, especially questions having to do with human rights, civil rights, property, and welfare rights. My faith tells me that human beings were created in the image of God. That gives me a basis for thinking about those issues.

I'm not arguing for or against a right to have an abortion. My point is that I don't see how citizens can ignore their religious convictions when deciding some basic issues. If the agreed-upon values and principles cannot provide a solution, then more is needed. For the same reason, I don't see how they can keep their convictions out of public debate. Rawls's idea that we can bring our various personal convictions into the public debate for a while and then, "in due course," replace them with arguments based on our shared values and principles doesn't work.

I think that Rawls admits that there are cases in which we will not be able to reach a resolution based on an overlapping consensus, and he suggests that in those cases citizens may simply have to take a vote and accept the result (Rawls 1996, lv). He is probably right about that.

Liberal Group: John Speaking

🅜🅟 LEGITIMACY

I'm not as pessimistic as some of you. Maybe we don't meet the requirements of Rawls's principle of legitimacy today, but maybe we can work towards it.

Earlier on I mentioned Perry's idea of ecumenical dialogue. That dialogue is well-informed and respectful. It involves listening as well as speaking. I'm wondering whether that sort of dialogue can help us to gradually expand our common ground and build up the conditions required for legitimacy.

At the very least, consider this: To some extent, what appears to be disagreement on values and principles is due to misunderstanding each other. To some extent, it is due to deliberate exaggeration by politicians and people in the media. I think that the kind of ecumenical dialogue Perry advocates could help us in at least those cases.

My point is that the common ground we share is not fixed. It changes over time, and we can create more of it. There's no magic bullet, but we can try.

Liberal Group: Vera Speaking

🅜🅟 COMMON GROUND

I think that we may be interpreting Rawls too narrowly. I want to suggest a way to interpret him that will expand our common ground and give us a basis for legitimate government despite our disagreements. I don't know whether Rawls would agree with me, but here's what I think.

We have been saying that we can't always reason from agreed-upon moral and political values and principles. We have said that our common ground isn't sufficient to allow us to settle some of our fundamental disagreements. Furthermore, it may not be sufficient to provide a basis for legitimate government. I think that may be true if we focus entirely on substantive values like free speech and principles like equal rights for all. It may not be true if we can agree on some procedural rules and include them in our common ground. Procedural rules include things like periodic elections, majority rule, or supermajority rule.

For example, we may never agree on whether abortion or gay marriage is moral or immoral, but maybe we can accept the legalization of abortion or gay marriage as legitimate law if the proper procedures have been followed.

I guess what I'm saying is that one part of the common ground we have may consist of substantive political values and principles while another part may consist of procedural rules. In a country as diverse as the United States, agreement on rules of procedure may be the best we can do sometimes. The combination of both parts may provide enough common ground to allow us to develop law or policy on some very controversial issues and also give us a basis for legitimate government. We then have a reason to abide by the law until it changes even when we disagree.

Professor Sidgwick Speaking

🅼🅿 LEGITIMACY

I'm going to break this off now, but I want us to return to the problem of legitimacy later.

I believe that the United States may be entering a legitimacy crisis. The crisis has two aspects. First, at the popular level, there is widespread loss of faith and trust in our federal government. Tens of millions of people in our country believe that the government is corrupt, incompetent, or manipulated by conspiratorial forces. Large groups of people believe that elections have been stolen, voting machines hacked, or voters suppressed. Second, we may be slowly losing the shared values and principles necessary for philosophical legitimacy.

If I am correct, there are two problems to address: how to restore faith and confidence at the popular level and how to rebuild the common ground required for legitimacy at the philosophical level.

I would like us to talk more about this later. Right now, it's time for Ann, Vera, and John to give us their presentation on social liberalism.

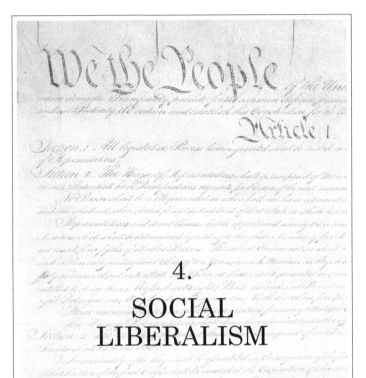

4.
SOCIAL LIBERALISM

Presented by Ann, Vera, and John

Liberal Group: Ann Speaking

🅜🅟 SOCIAL LIBERALISM

We are going to try to present a version of 20th-century liberalism. It won't be easy because there have been lots of philosophers and politicians involved in developing liberalism over the last century and a half. There are also many issues about which liberals disagree among themselves.

The first thing to understand is that modern liberalism or social liberalism developed out of the classical liberalism of the 19th century. Fred has already told us that 20th-century American conservatism has tried to combine elements of classical liberalism with some of the ideas of Edmund Burke. The liberalism of the 20th century can be thought of as an attempt to combine elements of classical liberalism with ideas taken from socialism. The goal was to preserve the valuable elements in classical liberalism and add some socialistic elements to the mix.

Let's start with some concepts that are characteristic of social liberalism. Here's our list:

Social Liberalism: Basic Concepts

- **Individual development**
- **Effective freedom**
- **Living law and a living Constitution**
- **Active government**
- **Equality before the law**
- **Traditional non-interference rights plus welfare rights**
- **Regulated property and regulated markets**

- **Protection for those with less market power**
- **Racial and gender equality**
- **Restitution for past injustice**

Liberal Group: Vera Speaking

🄼🄿 SOCIAL LIBERALISM

Now that Ann has given us some basic concepts, let me try to give you some principles and other views.

Social Liberalism: Principles and Beliefs

- Individual development is one of the key values and goals of modern liberalism. The idea is to guarantee each individual the resources required to develop his or her capacities. Ideally, the chance of success in life should be about the same for everyone with the same native ability.

- For the idea of freedom as non-interference, modern liberals substitute the concept of effective freedom. Effective freedom requires resources. Welfare rights are needed to guarantee the resources required for effective freedom. That includes, for example, guaranteeing that basic needs are met and creating the opportunity to work if necessary.

- Modern liberals point out that the conditions under which we live change rapidly. They conclude that the interpretation of the law and the Constitution must constantly evolve in order to adjust to new conditions. This is sometimes called the "living law" view.

- The older belief that the uncontrolled operation of markets works out in the interest of all (or nearly all) needs to be qualified. The modern liberal believes that there are many cases in which markets perform poorly and regulation is needed to achieve good or fair results.

- Modern liberals reject the notion that free contracts between employers and employees are always just and fair. They emphasize the great difference between the market power of employers and the individuals seeking employment. They favor labor unions and active government in order to equalize that power.

- Modern liberals believe that the limited government proposed by classical liberals and modern conservatives is insufficient to achieve racial equality and equality for women. In general, they believe that the proper role of government must include creating the conditions required for equality and fair treatment.

- Modern liberals sometimes advocate restitution for past injustice. They point out that racial and ethnic minorities, as well as women, have often been unjustly discriminated against. They reject the notion that an unfettered marketplace will stop that discrimination or repair the damage it has done.

Libertarian
Group:
Elijah Speaking

◻◻ COMMENT ON SOCIAL LIBERALISM

I think it is also true that social liberals take a narrower view of personal responsibility than conservatives like Fred. When they attempt to explain individual or group behavior they are more likely to stress the conditions in which people live rather than their personal characteristics and choices. This difference comes up over and over when we try to explain poverty, crime, family structure, educational achievement, and lots of other things.

*Liberal
Group:
Ann Speaking*

🄾🄿 COMMENT ON SOCIAL LIBERALISM

I don't want you to get the wrong impression about the nature of 20th-century liberalism. All of the important political 'isms' come in many different varieties. That is true for conservatism, socialism, feminism, liberalism, communism — all of them. There is no core of concepts or principles that all of the varieties of liberalism (and only the varieties of liberalism) share. That's true for the other 'isms' as well.

In our description of liberalism, we have tried to identify features that many of the varieties share, but that's all we can do. I think that Fred did the same thing for conservatism.

Liberal Group: John Speaking

🄼🄿 SOCIAL LIBERALISM

For me, modern liberalism has always been organized around a certain vision of an ideal society. That ideal society is one in which every individual is able to develop his or her capacities as much as possible in pursuit of their vision of a good life (within moral limits, of course). That's a bit of a mouthful, I know.

A society that fosters that sort of universal individual development has to be organized in certain ways. The major institutions, including government, education, and property, have to be set up to create the conditions in which people can experience that development.

That's a shift from the older classical liberalism. Development of capacity and achievement of a good life replace freedom from interference as the fundamental values. The right to the conditions required for personal development replaces the right to non-interference as the core individual right. One of the roles of government is to create or maintain those conditions.

In my opinion, in order to maintain the conditions of development, individuals must have welfare rights that classical liberalism did not recognize. Furthermore, to maintain those conditions, property rights, markets, and freedom of contract must be redefined and restricted in ways that classical liberalism would not allow.

Conservative Group: Fred Speaking

🄼🄿 SOCIAL LIBERALISM

I think of myself as an American conservative. I want a constitutionally limited federal government, strong property rights, relatively free markets, and the rule of law. A lot of my ideas come from classical liberalism, the same liberalism that 20th-century welfare state liberalism has tried to replace.

Sometimes modern liberals talk as though their form of liberalism is simply a logical extension of classical liberalism. They may say that their liberalism is the application of the same principles to new areas. I don't think that's true at all.

The 20th-century liberalism you are describing is not based on the same concepts and principles as classical liberalism. Vera has already admitted that its concept of freedom, for example, is entirely different from the classical liberal concept of freedom. So is the concept of property. In my opinion, you have used the language of classical liberalism (lots of talk about rights and individual freedom, for example) while changing the meaning behind the language.

Liberal Group: John Speaking

🅜🅟 T. H. GREEN

We want to proceed historically by talking a little about several of the key liberal thinkers of the last 150 years. I'm going to start off with Thomas Hill Green.

Green was born in 1836 in Yorkshire, England. He entered Balliol College at Oxford University in 1855 and studied Kant, Hegel, and other German philosophers along with British empiricists such as John Locke and David Hume. Ultimately, he was highly critical of the empiricist tradition. He did not believe that the empiricist approach to philosophy could account for our knowledge of the natural world. Nature, he believed, was constituted in part by relationships that the empiricist philosophers could not explain. The existence of those relationships could only be accounted for by presupposing the existence of a mind or consciousness. Thus, Green falls into the late 19th-century British idealist tradition that stressed the fundamentality of mind or spirit in the formation of the world as we know it. On the basis of his idealist metaphysics, Green developed a view of ethics and political philosophy that included a new kind of liberalism involving a more active state. He also provided a new philosophical foundation for Christianity. He died in 1882.

T. H. Green: Basic Ideas

- The distinguishing feature of human beings and the fundamental value to be protected and developed is the moral capacity to conceptualize a common good and to contribute to that good. Individual rights are established to protect that fundamental moral capacity.

- In a famous lecture on "Liberal Legislation and Freedom of Contract," delivered in 1881, Green argued for a new liberalism. To do so, he redefined freedom, property, and the proper role of government. Freedom was no longer "freedom from restraint or compulsion." It was not "merely freedom to do as we like irrespectively of what it is that we like." Instead, freedom was "a positive power or capacity of doing or enjoying something worth doing or enjoying, and that, too, something that we do or enjoy in common with others." Freedom was the power of individuals to "make the best of themselves" (Green 1888, 370, 371-372).

- In his lectures on political obligation, Green defined a right as "a power of acting for his own ends, — for what he conceives to be his good, — secured to an individual by the community, on the supposition that its exercise contributes to the good of the community" (Green 1895, 207).

- Individuals have a right to the conditions required to develop and maintain their moral capacity to contribute to the common good.

- Property is "only justifiable as a means to the free exercise of the social capacities of all" (Green 1888, 372).

- The state is justified in acting to maintain the conditions under which the individual's fundamental moral capacity is developed and maintained. In other words, the state was to "maintain the conditions without which a free exercise of the human faculties is impossible." This meant, among other things, that the state could limit the classical liberal freedom of contract (Green 1888, 374).

We can see that Green changed the concepts of freedom, rights, and property. He also assigned a new role to the state. I don't agree with Green's idealist metaphysics, but I accept his view that the state should be more active in guaranteeing the conditions required for personal development. For him, that development was moral development. I would expand that to include the general development of individual capacities.

*Liberal
Group:
Vera Speaking*

🄾🄿 **COMMENT ON
SOCIAL LIBERALISM**

We can't cover everybody, but we can pick out a few of the most important people. In addition to Green, we are going to say something about the English philosopher-sociologist L. T. Hobhouse, the American journalist Herbert Croly, the American philosopher John Dewey, and the British economist John Maynard Keynes. They were all influential historical figures, but they are not part of what you might call contemporary political thinking. So, after we talk about them, we are going to go on and talk a little about John Rawls and Martha C. Nussbaum, two philosophers whose work is part of current debates.

Libertarian Group: Dee Speaking

🄼🄿 **T. H. GREEN**

I'm not sure what Green is saying, but I'm scared already.

In the first place, I don't think that he can prove the existence of an eternal consciousness or mind. Most British philosophers rejected that sort of idealism in the early 20th century, and it has attracted very few followers since then. To me personally, British idealism is pretty much incomprehensible.

But that's not the part that scares me. I have read up a little on Green and it appears that he was prone to talking about a higher and a lower self, as well as some sort of real freedom or true freedom as opposed to the everyday freedom to do what we want to do.

Green's higher self is the self that manifests the eternal consciousness. Real freedom, or true freedom, is the freedom to act in accordance with that higher self — to act in accordance with our true essence. It isn't the freedom to do what we want to do.

John has already told us that in his lecture on the freedom of contract, Green made it clear that freedom "did not mean merely freedom from restraint or compulsion." He went on to say that "the mere removal of compulsion, the mere enabling a man to do as he likes, is in itself no contribution to true freedom" (Green 1888, 370, 371).

Frankly, as a libertarian, when I hear that kind of talk I say grab your wallet and head for the nearest exit. There is no telling where a political thinker is headed when they disregard what people actually want to do (and the freedom to do it) and start talking about true freedom and the inclinations of a higher self. The intellectual historian Isaiah Berlin warned us about this kind of thinking in his famous essay "Two Concepts of Liberty." Berlin acknowledged that Green's intentions were good. His sympathies with the working people of his time were humane, and he had no desire to contribute to the making of a totalitarian society. Still, Berlin warned us that talk about a true self or a higher self and the true freedom that is tied to it can lead to a complete disregard for what people actually want and their freedom to pursue it.

Liberal Group: Ann Speaking

🅜🅟 L. T. HOBHOUSE

Green was a metaphysician, and his work is difficult to understand. I think we can all agree on that. Let me introduce Leonard Trelawny Hobhouse, a British philosopher, sociologist, and journalist. He was born in the UK in 1864, attended Oxford University, and held the first chair in sociology at the University of London. He published his *Theory of Knowledge* in 1896, *Liberalism* as well as *Social Evolution and Political Theory* in 1911, and *The Elements of Social Justice* in 1922. According to historian Peter Weiler, Hobhouse was the "last of the nineteenth century system builders" (Weiler 1982, 136). He died in 1929.

Although influenced by Green, Hobhouse developed his own version of the social liberalism that emerged in the UK in the early 20th century. He rejected Green's metaphysics and his notion of an eternal consciousness. Nevertheless, he believed that a study of history showed a pattern of progress in the development of mind and morals. That notion of progress, according to Weiler, was fundamental to his political philosophy.

In *Liberalism*, Hobhouse criticized the theory of natural rights and the principle of utility, both of which had been used to justify the older British liberalism. He explicitly rejected the theory of the relationship between the individual and the state advocated by the Manchester school of liberals. The Manchesterites had stressed free trade, freedom of contract, and the right of the individual not to be interfered with by others. For them, the role of government was to protect the individual from interference and allow him or her to follow their own inclinations.

In his own theory, Hobhouse put forward the development of "personality" as the goal to be sought. In his words: "The good is something attained by the development of the basal factors of personality, a development proceeding by the widening of ideas, the awakening of the imagination, the play of affection and passion, the strengthening and extension of rational control" (Hobhouse 1919, 132).

Hobhouse hoped to combine the best elements in classical liberalism with the best elements of socialism in a new social liberalism or liberal socialism.

L. T. Hobhouse: Basic Ideas

- The good of each individual consists in "realizing his capacities of feeling, of loving, of mental and physical energy..." (Hobhouse 1919, 128).

- Liberty is required, because without it the individual cannot develop his or her capacities.

- The individual good and the common good are closely connected. The common good consists entirely of the good of those individuals in society. It "postulates free scope for the development of personality in each member of the community." In realizing his capacities, the individual "finds his own good in the common good" (Hobhouse 1919, 130, 128).

- Individuals have rights. Those rights are based on the common good and cannot conflict with the common good. We can think of them as based on the judgment of an "impartial observer" who considers the good of all. Each individual has a right to the conditions required for the development of his or her capacities. Those conditions include extensive liberties (Hobhouse 1919, 126).

- The proper role of the state is to guarantee that each individual has the conditions or resources required to develop his or her capacities.

According to Weiler, Hobhouse's thinking "shifted from the traditional Liberal emphasis on establishing a sphere of liberty in opposition to an authoritarian state to a concern for the harmonious development of the individual within society." He was mainly concerned with "the kind of society that would fulfill men's needs for both individual freedom and a sense of community" (Weiler 1982, 148).

*Liberal
Group:
Vera Speaking*

🄞🄟 COMMENT ON L. T. HOBHOUSE

I want to add something about Hobhouse. I believe that he not only changed our concept of freedom and our idea of the role of government. He also offered a new concept of property.

He argued that wealth "has a social as well as a personal basis." In his view, the "ground problem in economics is not to destroy property, but to restore the social conception of property to its right place under conditions suitable to modern needs....It is to be done by distinguishing the social from the individual factors in wealth, by bringing the elements of social wealth into the public coffers, and by holding it at the disposal of society to administer to the prime needs of its members" (Hobhouse 1919, 187-189). The value of a piece of land in London was not due entirely to the efforts of its owner, nor was the value of some item on which the owner was granted a monopoly. In these and other cases, the element of value that was due to the actions of society could be justly taken for public purposes.

What he said has huge implications if you think about it.

Liberal Group: Ann Speaking

🅜🅟 **HERBERT CROLY**

Now I want to switch to the United States and say something about a political writer who is seldom mentioned these days, but who was one of the most popular liberal or progressive writers of the early 20ᵗʰ century: Herbert Croly.

The late 19ᵗʰ and early 20ᵗʰ century is often called the Progressive Era. It was a time when some American writers and politicians were breaking away from the older liberalism and advocating a more active federal government to mitigate social problems. They were especially concerned with economic concentration, political corruption, party bosses and machines in cities, business regulation, women's suffrage, and the abuse of alcohol.

Croly was an American journalist and public intellectual. He was born in New York City in 1869 and attended both the City College of New York and Harvard College, although he dropped out of Harvard without a degree. Croly published *The Promise of American Life* in 1909 and cofounded *The New Republic* magazine in 1914. He died in 1930.

The Promise was well-known and influential among progressive thinkers. It was not primarily a philosophical work. Instead, its main argument was based on an interpretation of American history. Croly defined the promise as a gradually increasing standard of living and assumed it to be the proper goal of American society and politics. He looked at history to tell us how the promise had been achieved in the past and how it could be achieved in the future. Here's my summary of his views.

Herbert Croly: Basic Ideas

- American history has always been characterized by a tension between the Jeffersonian democratic and the Hamiltonian national ideas. The Jeffersonian ideal stressed very limited central government and non-interference with individual actions. The Hamiltonian ideal favored a stronger, more active federal or national government.

- The promise of American life has consisted in "an improving popular economic condition, guaranteed by democratic political institutions, and resulting in moral and social amelioration" (Croly 2013, 17). Concretely, for the wage-earner, the promise required a "constantly higher standard of living" (Croly 2013, 141).

- In the early and middle 19th century, the promise was achieved automatically. In other words, it was achieved without conscious planning or determined effort by any central body.

- In the late 19th and early 20th centuries, conditions changed. The diminished supply of inexpensive farm land, occupational specialization, increased inequality and poverty, urbanization, the rise of the experienced expert, and the emergence of both very large business enterprises and militant unions now made it impossible for the promise to be fulfilled automatically.

- Both new political ideas and new institutions will be needed to continue to fulfill the promise. The Jeffersonian ideal of non-interference must give way to a more active Hamiltonian state if the promise is to be fulfilled. If the promise cannot be fulfilled, the United States will cease to be a democracy (Croly 2013, 141).

Liberal Group: John Speaking

🅼🅿 TEDDY ROOSEVELT

Fred talked about how some ideas from the conservative revival entered politics dramatically with the nomination of Barry Goldwater for president. I think that was a good thing to do. It shows how ideas connect with the real world. I want to do something like that for the ideas of modern liberalism.

The ideas of modern liberalism overlap with the ideas of the Progressive movement of the late 19th and early 20th centuries. The progressives thought the classical liberal view of government was far too limiting. In general, they advocated more powerful and active government at all levels. One of the politicians representing that view was Theodore Roosevelt.

Roosevelt (1858-1919) was born in New York City. He attended Harvard College and Columbia Law School (although he dropped out of the latter). He served in the New York State Assembly and was later governor of New York. In 1900, Roosevelt ran successfully for vice president under William McKinley on the Republican ticket. When McKinley was assassinated in 1901, Roosevelt became president. In 1904, he ran for president in his own right and won handily. In 1912, he ran for president as the candidate of the Progressive Party and was defeated. Roosevelt was familiar with Croly's book *The Promise of American Life* and Croly actively supported him in his 1912 campaign.

As president, Roosevelt was a moderate progressive. He accepted the idea of a strong president leading a strong federal government with an active role in solving economic and other problems. He took a cautious approach to breaking up the large business trusts, but did bring suit in dozens of anti-trust cases. He also advocated greater regulation of business, especially in his second term. For example, he supported the Hepburn Act (1906) that expanded the authority of the Interstate Commerce Commission, allowing it to set some maximum rates for railroads. In addition, he supported the Meat inspection Act and the Pure Food and Drug Act, both passed in 1906.

Roosevelt may be most famous today for his interest in conservation. He worked to establish wildlife refuges, national parks, national monuments, and national forests.

I think it is fair to say that with Teddy Roosevelt we see a major step forward in the creation of modern regulatory government and the decline of a more limited view of what the federal government is constitutionally empowered to do. We also see a new kind of charismatic president. I personally think that Roosevelt did some good things, but I know that limited-government conservatives may disagree.

Liberal Group: John Speaking

🄾🄿 COMMENT ON PROGRESSIVES

I want to give you a better idea of the kinds of reforms that progressives typically advocated. Of course, they differed in their views; but they often advocated the initiative, the referendum, the direct primary to elect party candidates, the recall, the popular election of senators, more efficient city government, greater use of expertise to define and solve problems, regulation of very large corporations, limitations on child labor, special protections for women at work, work safety regulations, limits on the length of the work day, temperance, and more. At the municipal level, they sometimes advocated that cities form gas and electric companies.

🆂🅴 EXCERPTS FROM THEODORE ROOSEVELT
Speech on the "New Nationalism"

In 1910, Roosevelt gave a speech at Osawatomie, Kansas in which he outlined his view of the "New Nationalism." In that speech we can see a shift toward a modern liberalism that advocates a much more powerful federal government that regulates property and the terms of labor for the sake of the common good. The following excerpts give the flavor of his views.

Roosevelt made it clear that he opposed the special interests "who twist the methods of free government into machinery for defeating the popular will." The proper goal is to "equalize opportunity, destroy privilege, and give to the life and citizenship of every individual the highest possible value both to himself and to the commonwealth." If there is such equality, then "every man will have a fair chance to make of himself all that in him lies; to reach the highest point to which his capacities ... can carry him...."

Roosevelt's comments on the role of the government in the economy expressed the new attitude. "The effort at prohibiting all [business] combination has substantially failed. The way out lies, not in attempting to prevent such combinations, but in completely controlling them in the interest of the public welfare." People should be allowed to gain a fortune, but "only so long as the gaining represents benefit to the community." He added quickly that this "implies a policy of a far more active governmental interference with social and economic conditions in this country than we have yet had, but I think we have got to face the fact that such an increase in governmental control is now necessary." We must acknowledge that "every man holds his property subject to the general right of the community to regulate its use to whatever degree the public welfare may require it." Furthermore, we must recognize not only the "right to regulate the use of wealth in the public interest," but "the right to regulate the terms and conditions of labor...in the interest of the common good."

Finally, he indicated that "The betterment which we seek must be accomplished, I believe, mainly through the National Government" (Roosevelt 1910 brackets added).

Liberal Group: Ann Speaking

m P JOHN DEWEY

I want to go back to the philosophers and add someone to our list of early 20th-century liberals: John Dewey.

Dewey was an American philosopher in the pragmatist and naturalist traditions. He was born in 1859 in Burlington, Vermont, attended the University of Vermont as an undergraduate, and earned his PhD from Johns Hopkins University. He taught at the University of Michigan, the University of Chicago, and Columbia University. Although initially influenced by philosophic idealism (including the ideas of T. H. Green), Dewey went on to develop a philosophy referred to as instrumentalism, which stressed the use of scientific methods in all areas of inquiry, including morals. He published many works including *Democracy and Education* (1916) and *Reconstruction in Philosophy* (1920). He is probably best remembered for his views on education, but he also formulated his version of social liberalism in *Liberalism and Social Action* and "The Future of Liberalism," both published in 1935. He died in 1952.

Dewey allowed that the older liberalism had done "valiant service," but its ideas were historically tied to conditions that had changed. He offered a criticism that cut deep at the conceptual level. He rejected the older idea of freedom as formal freedom from constraint. He questioned the older liberalism's idea of human nature as fixed. He focused on the importance of developing individual capacities and the creation of institutions that foster the "growth" of individuals. The main problems to overcome were the obstacles left in place by the older liberalism (Dewey 1935).

I'm going to try to summarize Dewey's version of social liberalism.

John Dewey: Basic Ideas on Liberalism

- The good to be sought is the development of individual capacities — the "liberation of individuals so that realization of their capacities may be the law of their life" (Dewey 1963, 56).

- Liberty is to be understood as "actual" or "effective" liberty or freedom as opposed to formal or legal liberty. Effective freedom allows and fosters individual development of capacity. To achieve this, "organized society must use its powers to establish the conditions under which the mass of individuals can possess actual as distinct from merely legal liberty" (Dewey 1963, 27, 34).

- The key to social progress is the application of scientific methods to moral and social subjects. This application must rely not on the individual use of intelligence but on "intelligence as a social method" understood as "organized cooperative inquiry" (Dewey 1963, 69, 71). This intelligence must be used to determine which reforms in social institutions will provide effective freedom and thus facilitate individual development. This requires "continuous reconstruction of the ideas of individuality and of liberty" in relation to changing social conditions (Dewey 1935).

- Because of the power of concentrated private control of the means of production, the necessary reforms must "socialize the forces of production" in order to establish effective liberty. This reorganization will put "the results of the mechanism of abundance at the free disposal of individuals" (Dewey 1963, 88-89).

*Conservative
Group:
Fred Speaking*

🄾🄿 COMMENT ON JOHN DEWEY

I think that what you have said about Dewey proves the point I made before. I said that modern liberalism was fundamentally different from classical liberalism. Dewey and others changed some of the basic concepts.

I have a lot of problems with Dewey's ideas and I want to refer you to George Will's book The Conservative Sensibility *for a recent conservative criticism of his work. In Will's view, Dewey threw out much of what the Founding Fathers believed. He argued, in effect, that because society is constantly changing, we should constantly reassess our moral and political concepts and principles. Conservatives are not so sure about that.*

Liberal Group: Vera Speaking

🄼🄿 J. M. KEYNES

There is one more person that I would like to bring in, and that is the British economist John Maynard Keynes. He was not a philosopher, but his ideas had a major impact on the development of 20th-century social liberalism. Keynes was born in Cambridge, England in 1883. He attended Cambridge University where he studied mathematics and developed an interest in the ethical theories of the philosopher G. E. Moore. Although he had very little formal education in economics, he wrote extensively on the subject and became the most influential economist of his time. His most famous work, *The General Theory of Employment, Interest, and Money*, was published in 1936. Keynes was very much involved in public affairs and often wrote on current issues and events. He died in 1946.

I don't know enough to properly describe the theoretical innovations that Keynes brought to economics. It is my understanding that he developed new concepts, including aggregate supply and aggregate demand, that helped to create what we now call macroeconomics. Instead of looking at the economy from the point of view of the individual or the firm, these concepts provide a way of looking at it as a whole – from 30,000 feet in the air, so to speak.

At the practical level, Keynes proposed that the cycles of the economy could be smoothed out by judicious government action. Instead of cutting government expenditures when the economy went into recession, Keynes advised just the opposite. If aggregate demand was too low to maintain employment, he believed that government expenditure should be increased. If government revenue was down, deficit spending should be used in its place. In articles written in the early 1930s (at the time of the Great Depression) he urged increased government expenditure at all levels to boost aggregate demand, prices, and employment. In short, Keynes provided a theoretical rationale for a government that was much more involved in the economy. His approach was quite the opposite of that of many earlier economists.

Many people, especially modern liberals, accepted Keynes's view. For several decades, his ideas dominated schools in the United States and were a standard part of liberal political economic thinking.

Conservative Group: Fred Speaking

ⓜⓟ ON KEYNES

Keynes was a brilliant man and an extremely influential economist. I admit that, but that doesn't mean he was right in his theoretical views or in the policies he advocated.

There has been a long line of economists and other critics who disagreed with Keynes. I will mention only Henry Hazlitt, Friedrich Hayek, and Milton Friedman.

At the popular level, Hazlitt stands out. His best-known work was *Economics in One Lesson*, published in 1946. He also published *The Failure of the 'New Economics': An Analysis of the Keynesian Fallacies* in 1959. In both books he disagreed with the Keynesian view.

Hayek believed that Keynes was fundamentally wrong and strongly disagreed with the typical Keynesian explanation of persistent unemployment and its cure. In his Nobel prize lecture in 1974, he made it clear that he believed that the economic theory guiding recent policy was the result of "a mistaken conception of the proper scientific procedure." The theory asserts that "there exists a simple positive correlation between total employment and the size of the aggregate demand for goods and services" and therefore leads us to believe that "we can permanently assure full employment by maintaining total money expenditure at an appropriate level." There was some evidence to support the theory, but Hayek regarded it as "fundamentally false, and to act upon it, as we now experience, as very harmful." As is often the case, acting on the dominant theory can have consequences that are exactly the opposite of those intended. Doing so was "a cause of a very extensive misallocation of resources which is likely to make later large-scale unemployment inevitable" (Hayek 1974).

Friedman was a one of the great figures of the monetarist school of economics. He believed that monetary policy (adjustments in the money supply) could be used to control inflation and smooth out the peaks and valleys of the business cycle. Keynesians do not ignore monetary policy but tend to stress government fiscal policy (taxation and spending).

Obviously, we can't settle the many disputes between Keynes and his critics. I just want to make it clear that there were plenty of smart, well-informed people who disagreed with what he said. Modern liberals may have loved him, but there were others who didn't.

🄢🄔 EXCERPTS FROM JOHN MAYNARD KEYNES
Open Letter to Franklin Roosevelt

Keynes wrote many short pieces for non-economists. Some of these are contained his Essays in Persuasion. *He also published* The Means to Prosperity *in 1933. The following excerpts are taken from an open letter that he wrote to President Franklin Roosevelt late in 1933 on how to combat the Great Depression.*

You are engaged on a double task, Recovery and Reform; --recovery from the slump and the passage of those business and social reforms which are long overdue....

[A]n increase of output cannot occur unless by the operation of one or other of three factors. Individuals must be induced to spend more out of their existing incomes; or the business world must be induced, either by increased confidence in the prospects or by a lower rate of interest, to create additional current incomes in the hands of their employees, which is what happens when either the working or the fixed capital of the country is being increased; or public authority must be called in aid to create additional current incomes through the expenditure of borrowed or printed money. In bad times the first factor cannot be expected to work on a sufficient scale. The second factor will come in as the second wave of attack on the slump after the tide has been turned by the expenditures of public authority. It is, therefore, only from the third factor that we can expect the initial major impulse....

The stimulation of output by increasing aggregate purchasing power is the right way to get prices up, and not the other way round.

Thus as the prime mover in the first stage of the technique of recovery I lay overwhelming emphasis on the increase of national purchasing power resulting from governmental expenditure which is financed by Loans and not by taxing present incomes. Nothing else counts in comparison with this. In a boom inflation can be caused by allowing unlimited credit to support the excited enthusiasm of business speculators. But in a slump governmental Loan expenditure is the only sure means of securing quickly a rising output at rising prices. That is why a war has always caused intense industrial activity. In the past orthodox finance has regarded a war as the only legitimate excuse for creating employment by governmental expenditure. You, Mr. President, having cast off such fetters, are free to engage in the interests of peace and prosperity the technique which hitherto has only been allowed to serve the purposes of war and destruction....

In the field of domestic policy, I put in the forefront, for the reasons given above, a large volume of Loan-expenditures under Government auspices. It is beyond my province to choose particular objects of expenditure. But preference should be given to those which can be made to mature quickly on a large scale, as for example the rehabilitation of the physical condition of the railroads. The object is to start the ball rolling. The United States is ready to roll towards prosperity, if a good hard shove can be given in the next six months....

I put in the second place the maintenance of cheap and abundant credit and in particular the reduction of the long-term rates of interest....

With these adaptations or enlargements of your existing policies, I should expect a successful outcome with great confidence. How much that would mean, not only to the material prosperity of the United States and the whole World, but in comfort to men's minds through a restoration of their faith in the wisdom and the power of Government! (Keynes 1933 brackets added).

Liberal Group: Ann Speaking

🅜🅟 WHERE WE AGREE

John, Vera, and I want to give you some idea of where we stand in relation to the historical figures we have presented. We don't agree with everything that Green, Croly, and the others believed, but they helped form modern liberalism and we do accept some of their ideas. Here's what we think:

Liberal Group Agreement

- We reject Green's idealist metaphysics and his notion of a higher self, but we agree with him that there are reasons to change the classical liberal view of freedom, property, and the right of contract.

- We accept the emphasis that Hobhouse and Dewey placed on the value of developing individual capacities. We agree that welfare rights are needed to foster that development. Basically, we accept Dewey's notion of effective freedom and the idea that an expanded role for government is required to foster that freedom.

- We accept Croly's idea that the promise of American life includes a gradually increasing standard of living for all. We also accept his view that the promise will not be fulfilled automatically. It will require deliberate government action. This is especially true if the promise is to be fulfilled for marginalized groups.

- We agree with Keynes that government should have a major role in fighting recession and depression. Both fiscal and monetary policy should be used.

Professor Sidgwick Speaking

🅜🅟 RECENT THINKERS

I think it's very instructive for you to give us background on some historical figures. It helps us to understand how the ideas that make up 20th-century liberalism developed. It also helps us to see the differences between modern liberalism and the classical liberalism of the 19th century.

But most of the people you have mentioned are not part of recent debates. Most liberals today have never heard of Green or Croly or Hobhouse. What about the more recent philosophers, the people who have been discussed over the last 30 years or so?

For example, what about John Rawls? He's probably the best-known liberal philosopher of the last 50 years.

Liberal Group: Ann Speaking

🅜🅟 JOHN RAWLS

We have been planning to say something about recent writers. John Rawls (1921-2002) was probably the best known and most influential American political philosopher of the late 20th century. He attended Princeton University and later taught political philosophy at Harvard. People can disagree with him on any number of points, but his importance cannot be denied. Rawls published *A Theory of Justice* in 1971. It was followed in 1993 by *Political Liberalism*. He also published several shorter books and dozens of philosophical papers.

For decades before Rawls, there was a tendency for Anglo-American moral philosophy to focus on the meaning of moral concepts and the logical relationships between those concepts. Normative ethics, the kind of ethics that tells us what we *ought* to do, was downplayed. With Rawls, all that changed. *A Theory of Justice* was not an attempt to understand the concept of justice and its logical relationships to other moral concepts. It was an unabashed attempt to argue that we *ought* to construct basic social institutions in a certain way.

John Rawls: Basic Ideas

Rawls severely criticized utilitarianism. (As a utilitarian, I'm not too happy about that.) In its place, he sought to revive and refine social contract theory as an approach to basic questions about justice.

He proposed a thought experiment in which rational parties were situated behind a "veil of ignorance" and required to select principles that could be used to assess the justice of basic social institutions. The parties can be thought of as representing larger groups in a society. The veil of ignorance prevents the parties from knowing their own class, race, sex, natural abilities, and some other characteristics. Nor do they know the characteristics of the people they represent or the specific features of their society. Rawls argued that the parties would select the following two principles in preference to a few specific alternatives:

First, everyone should be guaranteed a set of basic liberties. Second, inequalities should be arranged so that they provide the greatest benefit for the least advantaged group and should be attached to positions open to all under conditions that he called "fair equality of opportunity."

This is a very brief and very rough statement of Rawls's principles, but I think it gives you some idea of his theory.

*Liberal
Group:
John Speaking*

🔲🅿 COMMENT ON RAWLS

Rawls was the most influential American political philosopher of the last 50 years, so I think it's worth saying a little more about his views. I'm going to try to summarize the main argument from A Theory of Justice. *For an overview of his entire philosophy, I recommend looking at* Justice as Fairness: A Restatement *published in 2001.*

John Rawls: A Theory of Justice

- *Rawls's main question in* A Theory of Justice *was this: How ought we to construct the basic structure of society if it is to be just? Another way to put it would be to ask what principles should guide us in evaluating basic institutions and what method should we use to find those principles?*

- *He argued that just institutions are those that comply with principles that would be selected by rational, self-interested parties in*

*Liberal
Group:
John Speaking*

a hypothetical "original position" with certain features. If chosen freely in that position, the principles are, for that very reason, reasonable and fair. The parties can be thought of as representatives of larger groups of people. They seek to secure the fundamental interests of themselves and the people they represent.

• Rawls did not suggest that the parties in his original position would consider all possible principles of justice. He did argue that the parties would prefer the two principles he proposed when compared to a few leading alternatives, including utilitarianism.

• A crucial feature of the original position is a "veil of ignorance" that prevents the parties from knowing the position that they or the people they represent occupy in society, their sex, race, age, natural endowments, and many other personal characteristics. In his later work, Rawls stressed that the parties do not know the "comprehensive doctrine" to which the people they represent adhere.

• The parties in the original position are not moved by envy, spite, or an extreme aversion to risk.

• The parties in the original position would seek to optimize the worst possible outcome for those they represent. In other words, they would attempt to make the worst possible outcome as good as possible.

• Briefly, Rawls argued that the parties in the original position would select the following two principles from a short list of alternatives.

- *"Each person is to have an equal right to the most extensive total system of equal basic liberties compatible with a similar system of liberty for all."*

- *"Social and economic inequalities are to be arranged so that they are both: (a) to the greatest benefit of the least advantaged, consistent with the just savings principle, and (b) attached to offices and positions open to all under conditions of fair equality of opportunity" (Rawls 1971, 302). (The requirement that inequalities be to the greatest benefit of the least advantaged is referred to as the difference principle. The just savings principle is concerned with savings for future generations.)*

• *In addition to these two principles, Rawls proposed what he called priority rules. For example, he stipulated that "liberty can be restricted only for the sake of liberty."*

• *The principles selected in the original position are reasonable and fair because they are chosen by people acting freely behind a veil of ignorance that eliminates bargaining advantages and excludes morally irrelevant factors like race and class from consideration. In effect, the veil imposes restrictions that are already widely accepted in American culture. All reflective Americans believe, for example, that race, class, and gender are not relevant to basic questions about justice.*

Rawls also discussed what he called "reflective equilibrium," an intellectual state in which a person or persons have developed a consistent set of specific moral judgments and more general moral principles. He believed that such an equilibrium would lend additional support to his principles of justice.

*Libertarian
Group:
Elijah Speaking*

🆗🅿 COMMENT ON RAWLS

Rawls was an important philosopher. I get that. But I want to make it clear that lots of people criticized his ideas. Here are just a few of the criticisms made by other philosophers:

A Sample of Rawls Criticism

- *Robert Nozick criticized Rawls from a libertarian perspective. He questioned whether there was any problem of distribution when people produced and freely exchanged goods and services. He argued that maintaining any ideal pattern of income distribution would require continuous interference with people's lives. He also advocated strong individual property rights that would be violated by attempting to make all inequalities benefit the least advantaged group (Nozick 1974, 163, 185-186, 194).*

- *R. M. Hare criticized Rawls from a utilitarian perspective. He argued that Rawls relied far too much on his own moral intuitions and that he offered very little analysis of moral concepts to support his theory. Hare also believed that Rawls's veil of ignorance was only one of several possible veils that could guarantee impartiality but would lead to different principles of justice being chosen. (Daniels 1989, 81-107).*

- *Michael Sandel criticized Rawls from what is often called a communitarian perspective. In particular, he criticized Rawls's notion of the self. In Sandel's view, Rawls posited an autonomous self that was always separate from and prior to the values and ends it chose. The self's values and ends were never constituent parts of itself. Sandel argued that Rawls's concept of the self could not support his theory and could not account for certain human capacities (Sandel 1998, chapter 1, especially p. 65).*

- *Charles W. Mills suggested that Rawls and most other academic philosophers made a fatal mistake by choosing to create "ideal theory" instead of a philosophy that dealt directly with the actual world with all its moral flaws. Mills claimed that ideal theory was a body of ideas, beliefs, and values that reflected the interests of the white middle and upper-middle class males who dominate academic philosophy (Mills 2005, 172).*

Dee is going to say more about Robert Nozick later. My point is simply that Rawls had lots of critics.

5E EXCERPTS FROM JOHN RAWLS
A Theory of Justice

John Rawls presented his views on justice first in several papers and then more comprehensively in A Theory of Justice *(1971). He summarized his views as follows:*

Many different kinds of things are said to be just and unjust: not only laws, institutions, and social systems, but also particular actions of many kinds, including decisions, judgments, and imputations.... Our topic, however, is that of social justice. For us the primary subject of justice is the basic structure of society, or more exactly, the way in which the major social institutions distribute fundamental rights and duties and determine the division of advantages from social cooperation. By major institutions I understand the political constitution and the principal economic and social arrangements (Rawls 1971, 7).

My aim is to present a conception of justice which generalizes and carries to a higher level of abstraction the familiar theory of the social contract as found, say, in Locke, Rousseau, and Kant. In order to do this we are not to think of the original contract as one to enter a particular society or to set up a particular form of government. Rather, the guiding idea is that the principles of justice for the basic structure of society are the object of the original agreement. They are the principles that free and rational persons concerned to further their own interests would accept in an initial position of equality as defining the fundamental terms of their association. These principles are to regulate all further agreements; they specify the kinds of social cooperation that can be entered into and the forms of government that can be established. This way of regarding the principles of justice I shall call justice as fairness.

Thus, we are to imagine that those who engage in social cooperation choose together, in one joint act, the principles which are to assign basic rights and duties and to determine the division of social benefits. Men are to decide in advance how they are to regulate their claims against one another and what is to be the foundation charter of their society. Just as each person must decide by rational reflection what constitutes his good, that is, the system of ends which it is rational for him to pursue, so a group of persons must decide once and for all what is to count among them as just and unjust (Rawls 1971, 11).

In justice as fairness the original position of equality corresponds to the state of nature in the traditional theory of the social contract. This original position is not, of course, thought of as an actual historical state of affairs, much less as a primitive condition of culture. It is understood as a purely hypothetical situation characterized so as to lead to a certain conception of justice. Among the essential features of this situation is that no one knows his place in society, his class position or social status, nor does anyone know his fortune in the distribution of natural assets and abilities, his intelligence, strength, and the like. I shall even assume that the parties do not know their conceptions of the good or their special psychological propensities. The principles of justice are chosen behind a veil of ignorance. This ensures that no one is advantaged or disadvantaged in the choice of principles by the outcome of natural chance or the contingency of social circumstances (Rawls 1971, 12).

[In contrast to certain alternatives] I shall maintain instead that the persons in the initial situation would choose two rather different principles: the first requires equality in the assignment of basic rights and duties, while the second holds that social and economic inequalities, for example inequalities of wealth and authority, are just only if they result in compensating benefits for everyone, and in particular for the least advantaged members of society (Rawls 1971, 14 brackets added).

Liberal
Group:
Ann Speaking

⊡⊡ COMMENT ON RAWLS

Rawls was important. There's no getting around that. The communitarian philosopher Michael Sandel criticized Rawls's theory of justice at length in his book Liberalism and the Limits of Justice. *At the same time, however, he acknowledged Rawls's impact. In his view, Rawls gave rise to three debates among political philosophers.*

First was the debate "between utilitarians and rights-oriented liberals." Second was the debate among rights-oriented liberals over which rights people have and whether and when they can be overridden. Of special importance here were the rights of property. Finally, Rawls stimulated debate on whether government should be neutral with regard to "competing conceptions of the good life" (Sandel 1998, 184-185).

Liberal Group: Vera Speaking

🅼🅿 MARTHA C. NUSSBAUM

It's always up to me to say something about philosophers who are women. What is it with you people? I'm going to bring in Martha C. Nussbaum, a woman who has written about justice for decades. She is one of the people shaping modern liberalism today.

Nussbaum (1947-present) was born in New York City. She earned a BA from New York University in 1969 and a doctorate from Harvard University in 1975. She has taught at Harvard, Brown, and the University of Chicago. In addition, she has written numerous books and scholarly articles in classics, philosophy, and law. They include *Women and Human Development* (2000), *Sex & Social Justice* (2000), *Frontiers of Justice* (2006), and *Creating Capabilities* (2011). Along with the economist Amartya Sen, she has developed the "capabilities approach" to social justice.

Martha C. Nussbaum: The Capabilities Approach

In *Frontiers of Justice*, Nussbaum discusses both utilitarianism and the social contract tradition. After offering fundamental criticisms of utilitarianism, she argues that the contract tradition has problems dealing with justice for those who are handicapped, for non-human animals, and for international relations. Even so, she believes that Rawlsian contractarianism and the capabilities approach are "allies across a wide space of the terrain of justice" and that the capabilities approach can help to "extend the Rawlsian approach" to the areas in which it encounters problems (Nussbaum 2006, 81).

- In place of the utilitarian and traditional social contract approaches, she offers the capabilities approach to justice. The capabilities approach begins "with a conception of the dignity of the human being, and of a life that is worthy of that dignity...." It includes a set of central capabilities "implicit" in the idea of such a life, or, in other words, capabilities that are "central requirements of a life with dignity" (Nussbaum 2006, 74, 70, 75). The central capabilities can be thought of as opportunities to function in certain ways.

- Each and every person is entitled to a threshold level of each of these central capabilities. Each person is also free to choose to what extent and in what way to make use of each capability in his or her life.

- The capabilities approach may be seen as "one species of a human rights approach." Nussbaum makes it clear that "the central human capabilities are not simply desirable social goals, but urgent entitlements grounded in justice." In fact, "in some form all are held to be part of a minimum account of social justice..." (Nussbaum 2006, 78, 290, 75).

Let me add that Nussbaum also believes that the central capabilities she identifies can be the object of a Rawlsian overlapping consensus. They can be formulated as a list that is "free of any specific metaphysical grounding" and can be approved by people who have "very different comprehensive conceptions of the good" (Nussbaum 2006, 70).

*Liberal
Group:
Vera Speaking*

⬛🅿 COMMENT ON NUSSBAUM

Nussbaum's list of central capabilities has evolved over the years. Here is a summary of the list given in Frontiers of Justice. *Keep in mind that the list is intended to be open-ended and flexible, not fixed and dogmatic. Also remember, I'm just giving you the main headings here. Each of these is elaborated more fully in her work (Nussbaum 2006, 76-77).*

- *"Life." This includes "Being able to live to the end of a human life of normal length...."*

- *"Bodily Health."*

- *"Bodily Integrity."*

*Liberal
Group:
Vera Speaking*

- *"Senses, Imagination, and Thought."*

- *"Emotions." This includes "Being able to have attachments to things and people outside ourselves...."*

- *"Practical Reason." This involves "Being able to form a conception of the good and to engage in critical reflection about the planning of one's life."*

- *"Affiliation." This includes "Being able to live with and toward others...." It also includes "Having the social bases of self-respect and non-humiliation...."*

- *"Other species." This includes "Being able to live with concern for and in relation to animals, plants, and the world of nature."*

- *"Play."*

- *"Control over One's Environment." This includes "Being able to participate effectively in political choices that govern one's life...." It also includes "Being able to hold property...."*

🆂🅴 EXCERPTS FROM MARTHA C. NUSSBAUM
Frontiers of Justice

Nussbaum respects and values the social contract tradition. Nevertheless, she criticizes some of its fundamental assumptions and believes that there are several areas in which it cannot provide a rationale for justice. Those areas deal with persons with serious disabilities, international relations, and non-human animals. For Nussbaum, a set of basic "entitlements" can be based on the central capabilities that she has identified. She writes as follows:

The deepest difference between the capabilities approach and Rawlsian contractarianism lies in its basic theoretical structure. Rawls's approach, like most social contract doctrines, is a procedural approach to justice. In other words, it does not go directly to outcomes and examine these for hallmarks of moral adequacy. Instead it designs a procedure that models certain key features of fairness and impartiality, and relies on these procedures to generate an adequately just outcome. Given an adequate design of the original situation, whatever principles emerge will be by definition just (Nussbaum 2006, 81).

The capabilities approach is like the criminal trial. That is, it starts from the outcome: with an intuitive grasp of a particular content, as having a necessary connection to a life worthy of human dignity. It then seeks political procedures (a constitution, various allocations of powers, a certain type of economic system) that will achieve that result as nearly as possible....Justice is in the outcome, and the procedure is a good one to the extent that it promotes this outcome (Nussbaum 2006, 82).

[S]ome deep moral intuitions and considered judgments about human dignity do play a fundamental role in the theory, although they are never immune from criticism in the light of other elements of the theory (Nussbaum 2006, 83 brackets added).

The capabilities approach insists from the start that the elements of a life with human dignity are plural and not single, and thus that the core social entitlements are also plural (Nussbaum 2006, 84).

It is the whole set of such entitlements, suitably defined, that is held to be required by justice, and no entitlement can substitute for any other. The approach does not invite, and positively forbids, trade-offs and balancing when we are dealing with the threshold level of each of these requirements (Nussbaum 2006, 85).

Libertarian Group: Dee Speaking

🄼🄿 ON NUSSBAUM

Fred and I have to say something about Nussbaum's capabilities approach. One of her major goals in developing her thinking on capabilities was to find a way to assess and compare the levels of well-being achieved by different groups (for example, different nations). We agree that her list of capabilities might be used in just that way and that it is superior to more traditional methods of comparison. We don't object to that at all.

On the other hand, it seems that Nussbaum is claiming that there is a very close connection between her central capabilities and human rights. Vera already told us that for Nussbaum the central human capabilities are "not simply desirable social goals, but urgent entitlements grounded in justice." What Fred and I do not understand is how to get from the fact that such capabilities are desirable to their status as entitlements or rights.

For our part, we agree that in an ideal world people would have the central capabilities that Nussbaum talks about, but we deny that wanting or needing those capabilities entails that people have rights to have them guaranteed. We would agree that people have a right to not be assaulted, enslaved, and interfered with in certain ways, but what Nussbaum wants goes way beyond that. She seems to be claiming that people have a right to the conditions and resources that are required in order to have and to use all of the central capabilities she lists. We question that claim.

This goes back to a perennial argument between libertarians (along with many American conservatives) and social liberals. Do basic needs entail rights to have those needs met? Do the requirements of a good life entail rights to have those requirements supplied or guaranteed? Those are the questions we want to ask. Nussbaum appears to be answering "yes," and we are saying "no."

Liberal
Group:
Ann Speaking

🅞🅟 COMMENT ON NUSSBAUM

As a utilitarian, I also have concerns about Nussbaum's capabilities approach to justice and entitlements.

The best-known utilitarian philosopher today is Peter Singer. He believes that Nussbaum's theory seems to require that "if a society has only one member below the minimum entitlement level, it should spend all its resources on bringing that member above the entitlement level" even if those resources could be of great benefit to others (Singer 2002). He also believes that Nussbaum has not offered a clear criterion for determining which capabilities are important and good. Without that criterion, it is not clear which capabilities should be fostered.

I think these criticisms have real value, and I would have to know a lot more about Nussbaum's theory before I could accept it.

Professor Sidgwick Speaking

🅼🅿 THE GOOD AND THE RIGHT

I would like to interrupt for a moment and introduce a distinction that may help us to understand and evaluate different political philosophies. In everyday life we have at least two ways of talking about morality. We can talk about what is good or bad and we can talk about what is right or wrong. In talking about the right, we sometimes talk about the rights that people have. These are different ways of describing and evaluating actions. They are different conceptual schemes, and the connection between them is controversial.

The Good and the Right

- Good and bad are ordinal concepts. In other words, we can speak of actions not only as good or bad but as better or worse. They are on a continuum.

- Right and wrong are categorical rather than ordinal. We seldom if ever describe an action as "more right" or "more wrong" than some other action.

- The good is usually connected with consequences. We typically describe an action as morally good because it benefits people. We typically describe actions as bad because of the harm they do.

- The right is more closely connected with abiding by moral rules and performing duties. An action is the right thing to do because it complies with the applicable rules.

- Because of these differences, it may be right to do something (because it abides by the appropriate rules), but it may not be good to do it (because of its harmful consequences). On the other hand, it may be good to do something (because of its consequences), but it may not be right (because it violates the appropriate rules).

Let me give some examples of how these two approaches may differ (and sometimes conflict) in practice. Telling the truth may be right (because it abides by the applicable rules), but it may be bad (because it has harmful consequences). Torturing an innocent person may be wrong (because it violates the applicable rules), but it may have enormously beneficial consequences. (What if we must torture an innocent person to find out where a time bomb is hidden in the middle of New York City?)

The case of rights is in some ways similar. It is not necessarily a contradiction to say that a woman has a right to have an abortion but it would not be good for her to do so. On the other hand, it may not be a contradiction to say that it would be good for her to have an abortion, but she does not have a right to do so. On a less serious level, we could say that John has a right to skip his mother's birthday party, but it would be bad for him to do so because it would upset her. In a legal context, we might say that someone has a right to burn the American flag but that it would be bad to do so. There are other cases in which we believe that an action is good, but we have no right to do it.

Philosophers differ in their views on the relationship between the good and the right. They may ask which is more fundamental or whether one can be defined in terms of the other. For example, if the good is defined as happiness, a utilitarian might define the right action to be done as the one that maximizes happiness.

*Professor
Sidgwick
Speaking*

🄾🄿 COMMENT ON
THE GOOD AND THE RIGHT

In political philosophy we can ask whether government should begin with an ideal of the good, with rules for right and wrong, or with a set of rights. Many political philosophies can be divided into those that give priority to the good and those that give priority to rights or the right. By "the good" I mean a definition of what constitutes the good for human beings. We have already seen that Michael Perry hopes to bring different ideas of the human good into political discussions. One of the oldest ethical and political philosophies on record, that of Aristotle, begins by determining the good for human beings.

Utilitarians give priority to the good. Libertarians usually give priority to rights. In some cases, however, it is difficult to say whether the good or the right has priority. Nussbaum, for example, has indicated that in her capabilities approach they are "thoroughly intertwined" (Nussbaum 2006, 162).

Professor Sidgwick Speaking

🄼🄿 REQUEST FOR COMMENTS

I have asked Fred and Dee to make a few general comments about modern social liberalism before we move on.

Conservative Group: Fred Speaking

🅜🅟 ON LIBERALISM

I strongly disagree with what you liberals are saying. I know we have been over a lot of this before, but what you are saying raises the same problems again and again. I have to criticize it.

Fred's Criticisms of Modern Liberalism

- First of all, modern liberalism has almost completely abandoned the idea of constitutionally limited government. According to its way of thinking, if something is good for someone, then the federal government is justified in doing it. That not only disregards constitutional limits on the federal government, but it also disregards Professor Sidgwick's distinction between the good and the right. I would argue that there are lots of things that are good, but it is not always right for the federal government to do them.

- In addition, I think that what you are saying, or implying, is just bad economics. Croly thought that without a very active federal government the standard of living would not continue to rise. In other words, "the promise of American life" would not be fulfilled. I believe he was mistaken about that. The standard of living was rising back in the early 20th century when he wrote his book, and it didn't require a hyperactive central government to make it happen then or now.

- Modern liberals overestimate the extent to which people and institutions can be molded by government. They also overestimate the ability of social scientists and other experts to predict the results of government policy and to mitigate social problems.

- Liberal policies tend to build up large government deficits and a huge national debt. The new Biden administration has proposed massive expenditures on health, infrastructure, education, family leave, and child care. Where does it end?

- Many of the things that active governments do fail to produce the results they promise to provide. Furthermore, they have unintended consequences that are sometimes the very opposite of what they promise. At the very least, they end up producing a bloated, costly bureaucracy.

- In a more philosophical vein, I don't believe that you have provided much in the way of foundations for active government and welfare rights. Furthermore, I don't see what principle you can offer to limit what active governments can and cannot do.

Libertarian
Group:
Dee Speaking

OP COMMENT ON LIBERALISM

Let me add a little to what Fred just said.

- *In part, what you liberals are saying is just another demand for welfare rights with very little justification. It is just another way for one group to use the government to make a different group turn over to them the product of its labor. The beauty of non-interference rights is that they do not allow one group to exploit another in that way. That's why I support them.*

- *Everyone agrees that modern liberalism has promoted more and more government regulation of what used to be private life. Some of those regulations do a certain amount of good, but a lot of them are just ways for some people to line their pockets.*

- *Anyone can offer a social ideal for others to consider. That's fine. As a matter of fact, I like John's ideal of a society in which everyone develops his or her capacities. But how do we get to that ideal? That's where we differ.*

*Conservative
Group:
Diego Speaking*

🄾🄿 COMMENT ON LIBERALISM

I agree with most of what Fred has said, but as an evangelical Christian I have something to add. My position is more like that of Ralph Reed, the former director of the Christian Coalition. In his book Active Faith, *Reed made a powerful case against modern liberalism.*

Reed points out that liberalism in the late 19th and early 20th centuries was often based on religious faith. Think of the temperance movement, the Protestant Social Gospel movement, and socially oriented Catholicism. In the mid-20th century, the civil rights movement still had, for many, a religious foundation. But more recently liberalism has lost its religious basis and become an entirely secular philosophy. In Reed's words, it has been "cut loose from its spiritual moorings" (Reed 1996, 84).

On a purely political level, modern liberalism has lost the moral high ground by rejecting traditional morality. When it defends abortion, for example, it is no longer defending the weak against the strong as it did in the case of working people and southern blacks. Instead, it has degenerated into a political coalition that simply defends the interests of its supporters. The "purpose of government, for liberalism, became less to guarantee equality than to solidify the political support of the special interest constituency that benefited" (Reed 1996, 76). It has "traded moral suasion for interest-group politics" (Reed 1996, 91).

By giving up its basis in religious faith, liberalism has lost its soul philosophically and also lost the support of the American people.

Libertarian Group: Elijah Speaking

AN ALTERNATIVE

As a left-libertarian, I want to propose an alternative to social liberalism that includes some of its attractive features but also includes a basis for strong individual rights. My alternative includes the following two elements:

A Left-Libertarian Alternative

- **Self-ownership**. Every individual owns himself or herself fully or to a very large extent. This self-ownership implies strong individual rights. Practically speaking, this guarantees the traditional rights of belief, expression, association, movement, and so forth. It also limits regulation by a paternalistic state.
- **Universal benefits from natural resources**. Every individual has a right to a share of the benefits we derive from the use and ownership of natural resources. Those who own valuable natural resources should pay into a fund that benefits others. A basic income or programs to satisfy basic needs could be financed by that fund.

I think that left-libertarianism gives us the best of both worlds, and I will say more about it later. It recognizes strong individual rights, but it also recognizes what philosopher Peter Vallentyne calls the "egalitarian sharing of the value of natural resources" (Vallentyne 2009b). Together, this includes the intuitive moral core of libertarianism and social liberalism.

Professor Sidgwick Speaking

🔲🔲 FOUNDATIONS

Fred asked Ann, John, and Vera to supply a basic moral justification for modern social liberalism. What are its ethical foundations, so to speak? That's a fair question.

Questions for Social Liberals

- Why should anyone accept your philosophy?
- What sort of ethical foundations can you offer?

I have asked Ann, John, and Vera to each give us what they think of as the foundation of their own version of modern liberalism.

Liberal Group: Vera Speaking

🔲🔲 FOUNDATIONS

OK. It's fair to ask us for foundations for our philosophy. We each have our own ideas about that.

Let me say right off that we reject some of the ways in which philosophers have tried to put a foundation under their ethics or their political philosophy.

We are not going to try to derive ethics from pure reason, and we are not going to try to base modern liberalism on theology or natural law. We are skeptical about all three of those approaches.

In general, Ann takes a utilitarian approach, John is a contractarian, and I make use of John Rawls's idea of a reflective equilibrium.

Let me make one point clear. Finding solid philosophical foundations is not just a problem for modern liberalism. It's a problem for all political philosophies, and that includes conservatism, libertarianism, and Catholic social thought.

Liberal Group: Ann Speaking

🅼🅿 UTILITARIANISM

I'll start. You all know that I am a utilitarian. I believe that actions and policies are good and right because they maximize human welfare. I think modern social liberalism can be justified on that basis. Here's a sketch of my argument:

Foundations: Utilitarianism

- The ultimate good to be pursued is human welfare. Welfare consists of the satisfaction of rational human preferences. Those preferences include, for example, health, happiness, and the development of individual capacities.

- Therefore, we should evaluate social institutions and policies according to their tendency to promote human welfare.

- When evaluating institutions and policies, certain restrictions should be observed. First, we must consider the welfare of all those affected by the institutions and policies. Second, we must be impartial among individuals. In other words, the welfare of each person is to be given the same weight or value as that of any other.

- Every individual strives to maximize his or her own welfare. Since we must be impartial among individuals, we must also believe that it is equally important to maximize the welfare of everyone affected by what we do and the policies we adopt.

- We must then ask the key empirical question: Which institutions and policies will maximize the welfare of the population in question?

- I claim that the traditional rights of belief, religious practice, expression, association, movement, and political participation combined with strong but regulated property rights and a set of welfare rights that guarantee certain goods and services for all will maximize welfare.

- Those welfare rights should include rights to safety, shelter, food, medical care, education, and the opportunity to work.

Libertarian Group: Dee Speaking

🅜🅟 UTILITARIANISM

Utilitarianism has been around in various forms for over 200 years. In the mid-20th century it was fairly popular in the United States. Today it is represented by philosopher Peter Singer. Even so, it has been subjected to a lot of criticism. Philosophers as different as John Rawls on the left and Robert Nozick on the right have strongly criticized it. To be honest, I feel that I am beating a dead horse here, but I will offer several standard criticisms of the utilitarian theory.

Dee's Criticisms of Utilitarianism

- Utilitarianism requires us to maximize human welfare, but it pays no attention to the distribution of that welfare. In my view that is a fatal flaw. Rawls was correct when he said that utilitarianism does not take seriously the distinction between persons. In principle, utilitarianism opens up the possibility of exploiting one group of people for the benefit of another group as long as aggregate welfare is maximized.

- I think there is at least one major logical gap in Ann's argument. Even if we grant that everyone should be impartially concerned with everyone else's welfare, she immediately concludes that we should maximize total welfare. But why jump to maximizing anything? Perhaps maximization makes sense when we are talking about a single individual looking out over his or her options. But when we are talking about a society there is no single entity involved. There is no central consciousness. There is no single life to be enhanced by trade-offs. Instead, there are many different lives, and benefits for some are being traded off for the benefit of others.

- Utilitarianism has difficulty finding a way to justify strong individual rights. In my opinion, it cannot do so. That applies to the rights favored by the left (like sexual freedom) as well as the rights favored by the right (like property).

I think that you have to come up with something better, Ann. If I may say so, I think that your main problem is that you do not have a good theory of individual rights. Without that, you have no way to limit what can be done in the name of utility or welfare. That can lead to some pretty scary stuff.

*Liberal
Group:
John Speaking*

🔲🅿 COMMENT ON UTILITARIANISM

I'd like to add a few points.

Utilitarianism assumes that we can somehow measure the quantity of welfare, however we define it, in any given state of affairs and then compare various alternatives. For example, the philosopher Jeremy Bentham thought that he could develop a calculus or arithmetic of pleasure and pain. Can we really do that? I'm not so sure.

Utilitarianism also assumes that we can predict the future consequences of various rules or actions, but there are always unexpected consequences, and they are often very significant. Sometimes they are quite harmful.

In some ways, utilitarianism is counterintuitive. For example, it doesn't distinguish between what we must do and what is over and above the call of duty. For another thing, it requires us to be strictly impartial between ourselves and any other person affected by our actions. That's a pretty high bar. I think that kind of impartiality may make sense for government policy, but not for personal morality.

Liberal Group: Ann Speaking

🅜🅟 UTILITARIANISM

Hold on, guys. It has become common for philosophers to dismiss utilitarianism as a theory with fatal flaws. It's not that simple. Sure, you can do that if you construct a straw man version of utilitarianism. But it is a lot more difficult to deal with the more complex versions developed by recent philosophers.

For one thing, there are different kinds of utilitarianism. Philosophers often distinguish between what they call "rule-utilitarianism" and "act-utilitarianism." Rule-utilitarians are concerned with the consequences of adopting a set of moral or legal rules rather than the consequences of individual acts. Individual actions are judged by whether they comply with the rules. I'm a rule-utilitarian.

Dee claims that utilitarianism cannot allow for strong individual rights. I think she's mistaken. In my view, rule-utilitarians can find a place for individual rights. To allow for such rights is basically to say that a set of moral or legal rules including such rights would maximize welfare (Brandt 1992, chapter 11). Those rights would probably be what Ayesha called prima facie rights.

My point is that you shouldn't be so quick to dispose of utilitarianism. It may be necessary to develop it in a more complex way than the 19th-century utilitarians did, but this horse is far from dead.

Liberal Group: John Speaking

🅜🅟 CONTRACTARIANISM

I agree that recent writers offer more thoughtful and complex versions of utilitarianism than 19th-century philosophers did. I also agree with Ann that they show us that we shouldn't just write off utilitarianism as an ethical theory that is obviously false.

Still, I'm hesitant to embrace utilitarianism. I think Dee made some good criticisms and I have already mentioned some others. I want to take a different approach to providing foundations for modern liberalism.

Ann has already talked about John Rawls and his theory of justice. Rawls believed that he could use a hypothetical contract to select criteria for deciding whether the "basic structure" of society was just. He argued that parties in a hypothetical original position, behind a veil of ignorance, would select certain basic principles of justice. The basic structure of society could be evaluated and determined to be just or unjust by using those principles.

Now, I don't entirely agree with Rawls's basic principles, especially the principle that requires us to maximize benefits for the least well-off members of society. That principle never struck me as plausible. But I still believe that a hypothetical contract may help to provide foundations for modern liberalism.

Foundations: Hypothetical Contract

It seems to me that people making a social contract might very well agree to establish a set of liberties (just as Rawls thought) and that they would probably agree to establish a set of basic welfare rights. They would agree to those rights, in my opinion, with or without a Rawlsian veil of ignorance because they know that life is notoriously unpredictable. They might very well be born poor or suffer a serious reversal of fortune at some time in their lives. In other words, it would be in the interest of everyone to provide guarantees against poverty and misfortune.

Therefore, it seems to me that a contractarian approach can be used effectively to justify at least some of the important components of modern liberalism. I am thinking especially of the demand for basic welfare rights.

Liberal Group: Vera Speaking

🄾🄿 COMMENT ON FOUNDATIONS

I can't agree with the foundational arguments put forward by either Ann or John. So far as Ann's utilitarianism is concerned, it seems to me that once you commit to maximizing any result, you open up the possibility that some people's welfare will be traded off for the welfare of others.

But I also lack faith in John's contractarian approach. The contractarian philosophers have always assumed that everyone is ruggedly independent, roughly equal in capacity, and in the full possession of 'his' faculties. What about people who are dependent on others? What about people who are physically disabled or chronically ill? What about people who are very limited intellectually? I'm not at all sure that the social contract tradition can bring those people in as full members of society with a full set of rights. Nussbaum has discussed this problem at length and I remain skeptical.

Liberal Group: Vera Speaking

🄼🄿 EQUILIBRIUM

As I see it, the basic problem is that we are always trying to get our moral principles from a source that is outside ourselves — from conceptual analysis, game theory, theology, metaphysics, natural law, science, or somewhere else. We want to look everywhere except within ourselves. We don't want to admit that we *create* morality, and we are responsible for what we create and its consequences. We want some sort of proof to undergird our moral system so that it doesn't depend on our attitudes and our choices. In my opinion, there is no such proof. I'm skeptical about traditional attempts to provide foundations for moral and political philosophy.

But there is still something useful that we can do. We can try to systematize the morality we create. I think that Rawls's concept of reflective equilibrium is helpful here. Rawls advised us to work back and forth between possible moral generalizations and specific moral judgments until we reach an equilibrium — a logically consistent set of propositions. I think that each of us can and should do that. In that way we may be able to arrive at a set of generalizations that we can rely on when we get to the questions about which we are uncertain. Overall coherence makes the whole system credible.

Each of us can do this individually. I am quite certain of that; and, ideally, some of us can do it together, as a group.

If nothing else, working to bring our own moral views into a state of reflective equilibrium can serve as the basis for a personal social philosophy. In my case, it serves as the basis for a form of social liberalism.

*Liberal
Group:
Vera Speaking*

🄾🄿 COMMENT ON BRUCE ACKERMAN

I want to make you aware of a writer who is not as well known as Rawls or Nussbaum. His name is Bruce Ackerman. I find his work interesting because his attempt to provide foundations for modern liberalism is not based on natural law, a social contract, or utilitarianism. I'm bringing in his ideas because I have problems with the more traditional approaches. I think we need new ideas.

Ackerman (1943-present) is a professor of law and political science. In his book Social Justice in the Liberal State *(1980), he proposed a new foundation for liberalism that consists of a kind of dialogue. In that dialogue, any power relationship can be questioned, and no power relationship can be considered justified unless it can be defended without violating certain rules.*

Bruce Ackerman: Rules for Dialogue

- *Any distribution of power or material resources can be questioned. In other words, anyone has the right to ask why a given person holds this or that power or resource.*

- *When questioned, the holder of a power or resource cannot refuse to reply. Some reason or rationale for his or her holding must be offered.*

- *The reasons offered on different occasions in defense of a particular holding must be consistent with each other. They must also be comprehensive in that they show that one way of organizing power (the one being defended) is preferable to all the competing alternatives.*

- *The reasons offered in defense of a holding must meet a standard of neutrality. Neutrality requires that the holder cannot assert that his conception of the good is better than that asserted by any other citizen. It also requires that the holder cannot assert that he is intrinsically superior to any other citizen.*

- *If the holder of a power or resource cannot supply an answer that meets these criteria, then he or she must be silent. Ackerman calls this condition "constrained silence." If the holder is reduced to constrained silence, then his or her holding is illegitimate.*

Ackerman believes that those power relationships that meet his criteria form a family of cases that are properly referred to as liberal states. He believes that the modern welfare state meets his criteria.

Vera's Challenge

I want to challenge all of you to seriously think about Ackerman's method. Then, I propose that we meet again and attempt to carry on a dialogue according to his rules. He believes that that dialogue would lead us to a "liberal-democratic welfare state" (Ackerman 1980, 30). Let's find out if he's right.

Professor Sidgwick Speaking

🔲🄿 WRAPPING UP

I want to cut this off now and ask the liberal group to make a final statement. I have also asked Elijah to give us an overall evaluation of modern social liberalism.

Liberal Group: Ann Speaking

🅜🅟 FINAL STATEMENT

As a final statement, John, Vera, and I want to sum up our views as social liberals. The three of us have different views on the fundamental basis for our philosophy. I find that basis in utilitarianism. John leans toward a contractarian view. Vera relies on the possibility of a reflective equilibrium. Despite those differences, however, we agree on the ideals we seek.

The Ideals of Modern Liberalism

- Society exists for the benefit of all its members. No group should be left out or exploited for the benefit of others.

- Everyone should have the resources necessary to develop his or her capacities and pursue their concept of a good life. Furthermore, the chance of success in life should not vary greatly simply because of the different situations into which people are born. This applies especially to differences of class, race, and gender.

- We reaffirm many of the basic rights and freedoms of classical liberalism. That includes freedom of conscience, religion, expression, movement, association, and political participation. But we also stress that the basic needs of everyone should be met. We support a system of welfare rights in order to meet those needs and to guarantee that everyone has the resources required to develop his or her capacities.

- Our differences with classical liberals and modern conservatives also have to do with limiting freedom of contract and regulating property and markets. We recognize the enormous creativity and productivity of a private economy, but we believe that to achieve the goals we have set out, government regulation and some redistribution of income is necessary.

- We believe in taking steps to rectify the injustices of the past. We recognize that our country has a long history of discrimination against African-Americans, Native Americans, women, and others. Government played a role in fostering that discrimination and it should play a role in rectifying its lingering effects.

- We believe that many of the problems we face transcend state boundaries and go beyond what private individuals or private organizations can deal with effectively. A strong federal government is necessary for their solution.

- We are not utopians. We do not believe that government can solve every problem, but we do believe that active government can reduce many of our problems and make life better for us all.

That's our ideal. We believe that it embodies and fosters what most Americans hope for in life.

Libertarian Group: Elijah Speaking

🅜🅟 AN EVALUATION

It is hard for a libertarian to evaluate social liberalism dispassionately. On the one hand, the fundamental differences are huge. On the other hand, as a left-libertarian, I actually agree with some of what social liberals advocate. In any case, here are my thoughts.

Elijah's Evaluation of Modern Liberalism

- Social liberalism has put forward an ideal that includes the development of every individual's capacities in order to pursue a good life as he or she understands it. That ideal shows great faith in the potential of the average person and I think it is a step forward for humankind that it is given the focus of attention. I share that ideal even though, as a libertarian, I may not share the social liberal idea of how to reach it.

- In the United States, social liberals have led the way in the struggle to eliminate racial discrimination and discrimination against women. They deserve credit for that, even from those who may disagree with many other elements of their political philosophy.

- Social liberals retain many of the values of classical liberalism, including freedom of association, movement, expression, and political participation. I think those are values that we all share. They are of permanent value.

- Dee will disagree, but as a left-libertarian I can accept a larger role for government than right-libertarians allow. I believe that everyone has a right to benefit from our natural resources. That might allow a guaranteed income for all or some other welfare rights that social liberals support.

- On the other hand, I think that social liberalism has struggled for a century to define itself and its philosophical foundations. It has attempted to define a middle way between socialism and classical liberalism, but it has not been very clear about the nature of that middle way, and the problem of providing philosophical foundations has been equally difficult.

I agree with Vera that providing foundations isn't only a problem for social liberals. It's a problem for all of us. Human beings have more and more technical power to transform the world, but there is little agreement on ethical and political principles. We need those principles badly to decide what to do with that power.

- I think many social liberals tend to slip into a crude utilitarianism that at times walks roughshod over individual rights. As long as they think they are working toward a desirable goal, they tend to dismiss concerns about some rights, especially property rights. The result is more and more government regulation of nearly every aspect of life, much of which is intrusive and paternalistic. Dee pointed this out and I agree with her. Professor Sidgwick distinguished the right from the good and I think that this is where they may come into conflict. There are many good things that government has no right to require us to do. I also agree with Fred that regulations often have unintended, undesirable consequences.

- My main concern is that I do not think that social liberals have any way in principle to limit the powers of government. They obviously reject the constitutional limitations that were accepted in the 19th century. The problem, as Fred and Ayesha pointed out, is that they have been unable to say what limits they do accept. Therefore, my unanswered question for liberals is this: What is the principle that puts a limit on government action even when it aims at doing good?

Well, there you have it. I admire some aspects of social liberalism, but I am concerned about others. I hope I have persuaded Ann, Vera, and John to think seriously about what I have said.

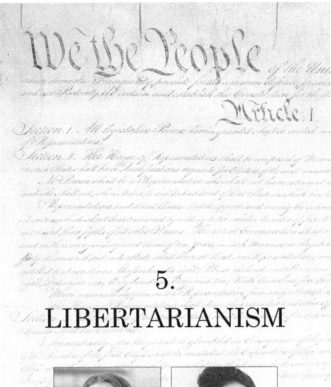

5.

LIBERTARIANISM

Presented by Dee and Elijah

Libertarian Group: Dee Speaking
◧◧ LIBERTARIANISM

Elijah and I agree on a lot of the concepts and principles that are fundamental to libertarianism. The difference is that I am a right-libertarian and he is a left-libertarian. We'll get to that later.

For now, we want to lay out some basic concepts and principles. Here's a list of the most important concepts:

Libertarianism: Basic Concepts

- **Self-ownership**
- **Individual natural rights (including property rights)**
- **Minimal government**

Libertarian Group: Elijah Speaking
◧◧ LIBERTARIANISM

We can also state some principles that make use of these concepts.

Libertarianism: Principles and Beliefs

- The principle of self-ownership states that each of us owns himself or herself. According to Peter Vallentyne, that means that each of us, at least initially, has the same rights regarding himself or herself that an owner has regarding an inanimate object. Any transfer of those rights requires the individual's consent. Any violation of those rights is unjust.

- Individual natural rights follow from self-ownership. They do not derive from government. (Hence the term 'natural.') As a matter of principle, libertarians assert that each of us has the right to determine where we go, with whom we associate, what we believe, how we worship, what we do sexually, what we take into our bodies, what risks we take, and more. Individual rights also include property rights (although left- and right-libertarians disagree on some important issues connected with property).

- Minimal government means that government should confine itself to enforcing our rights. To do so, it must protect us from aggression and enforce our voluntary agreements. Since our natural rights are not created by government, government has no right to change or eliminate them. As a matter of principle, we assert that government should protect our rights and do little or no more.

*Liberal
Group:
Vera Speaking*

🄾🄿 COMMENT ON LIBERTARIANISM

I just want to say right off that I reject several basic components of libertarianism, especially right-libertarianism. First of all, I do not think that libertarianism works for children or for people who are dependent or handicapped or chronically ill. Second, I don't see how right-libertarians can justify the strong property rights they advocate. I'll say more about this later. I just wanted you to know that I am going to take issue with some of your views.

Libertarian Group: Dee Speaking

🔳🔳 LIBERTARIANISM

Elijah and I want to stress that libertarianism is a philosophy of liberty or freedom. Of course, we believe that freedom leads to prosperity and well-being, but that is not our focus. Left liberals sometimes depict libertarians as people who care about nothing but property rights. That's false. What libertarians care about is freedom. That includes property rights, but it also includes a lot more. Consider the following:

Libertarian Freedoms

- Freedom to believe whatever you want. That includes strange religions and weird political philosophies.

- Freedom to practice your beliefs as long as you don't violate the rights of other people.

- Freedom to associate with whomever you wish. That includes other stamp collectors, people who believe the earth is flat, communists, and even Nazis.

- Freedom to live as you please. That includes sexual freedom, the freedom to take drugs, to go to nude beaches, and to listen to music that everybody else hates. You can experiment with your life. You can join a commune or live as a hermit in the desert.

- Freedom to take risks with your life and your body. You can smoke cigarettes, climb mountains, and engage in extreme sports.

- Freedom from paternalism. We reject the nanny state that attempts to protect you from yourself.

All these freedoms are freedoms from interference from other individuals or from government. The idea is to set up a framework within which people can create the lives they want to lead. They decide what is good for them.

Libertarian Group: Elijah Speaking

🅼🅿 LEFT-LIBERTARIANISM

Here's where I need to say something about the distinction between right-libertarians and left-libertarians.

The basic difference has to do with property rights to natural resources. Right-libertarians include people such as Robert Nozick, Jan Narveson, and Roger Pilon. They typically believe that people can acquire full ownership of natural resources with little or no compensation for those who do not acquire such ownership. Nozick accepts a version of what is called the Lockean proviso, but he requires minimal compensation for non-owners. The proviso goes back to John Locke's second treatise on government. Locke insisted that once individuals had mixed their labor with a natural resource like land, others lost their right to use that resource "at least where there is enough, and as good left in common for others." That last phrase is referred to as the Lockean proviso (Locke 1960, Chapter V, section 27).

Left-libertarians include people such as Peter Vallentyne, whom I have already mentioned. They believe that people can acquire full ownership in natural resources; but when they do so, they owe something to other people who do not acquire ownership.

This distinction turns out to be important when we talk about welfare rights. Dee sees welfare rights (rights to goods and services) as totally unfounded. I'm not so sure. In fact, I think that some welfare rights can be justified as a form of payment made by those who own natural resources to those who do not. I'll say more about that later.

5E EXCERPT FROM HERBERT SPENCER

Social Statics

Contemporary American libertarianism has its roots in 19th-century ideas about natural rights, individualism, economic freedom, and small government. The British philosopher Herbert Spencer (1820-1903) was a strong defender of individual freedom and a passionate opponent of government attempts to solve social problems such as poverty. In his first book, Social Statics *(1851), he developed a principle of liberty from which he derived a series of individual rights. He writes as follows:*

THUS are we brought by several routes to the same conclusion. Whether we reason our way from those fixed conditions under which only the Divine Idea— greatest happiness, can be realized—whether we draw our inferences from man's constitution, considering him as a congeries of faculties—or whether we listen to the monitions of a certain mental agency, which seems to have the function of guiding us in this matter, we are alike taught as the law of right social relationships, that— *Every man has freedom to do all that he wills, provided he infringes not the equal freedom of any other man.* Though further qualifications of the liberty of action thus asserted may be necessary, yet we have seen... that in the just regulation of a community no further qualifications of it can be recognised. Such further qualifications must ever remain for private and individual application. We must therefore adopt this law of equal freedom in its entirety, as the law on which a correct system of equity is to be based (Spencer 1851, 103).

Liberal Group: Ann Speaking

🅜🅟 LIBERTARIANISM

Here's my question for both Dee and Elijah: I know that you believe in very strong individual rights, but I do not understand the rationale or foundation for those rights.

I believe that some form of the principle of utility is the best foundation for both morals and for evaluating social institutions, policies, and actions. That principle tells us to maximize the total welfare of the people concerned. It seems to me that the individual rights you advocate, property rights especially, are incompatible with that goal.

Professor Sidgwick asked the liberal group to provide some foundations for its political philosophy. I'm asking you to do the same. What is the justification for the individual rights you advocate?

Libertarian Group: Elijah Speaking

🅼🅿 ON FOUNDATIONS

It's fair to ask for a justification of strong individual rights and for libertarianism in general, but I have to admit that libertarians don't all agree on what that justification is.

Some libertarians, including the economist Murray Rothbard, have tried to base libertarianism on natural law. Others, like law professor Richard Epstein, have tried to establish libertarianism on a consequentialist (largely utilitarian) basis. Roger Pilon of the Cato Institute has developed a reason-based system of libertarian rights based on the work of philosopher Alan Gewirth. Several libertarians have used a hypothetical contract to provide foundations for libertarian rights.

Dee and I are skeptical about natural law. Furthermore, we do not believe that utilitarianism can provide a solid basis for human rights. Dee accepts Gewirth's approach and I believe that the contractarian approach may turn out to be very fruitful.

Libertarian Group: Dee Speaking

🅜🅟 ON FOUNDATIONS

The most intuitive argument I know of for individual rights is the argument from what we have called self-ownership, but I'm going to offer a more formal argument. I want to refer you to the work of Alan Gewirth (1912-2004), formerly at the University of Chicago, and his student Roger Pilon. Gewirth constructed a reason-based system of individual rights and Pilon developed a libertarian interpretation of Gewirth's ideas. Gewirth argued that an individual agent must, to avoid logical inconsistency, hold that he or she and all others have fundamental rights to freedom and well-being. Without going into detail, I want to give you a very short summary of Gewirth's argument:

- "First, every agent holds that the purposes for which he acts are good" by his or her own criteria.

- "Second, every actual or prospective agent logically must therefore hold or accept that freedom and well-being are necessary goods for him because they are the necessary conditions of his acting for any of his purposes; hence, he holds that he *must* have them."

- "Third, he logically must therefore hold or accept that he has rights to freedom and well-being...."

- If he denies that he has these rights, "he would have to accept that other persons may remove or interfere with his freedom and well-being...."

- But he cannot accept this because it "would contradict his belief that he *must* have them."

- Finally, he must logically conclude that "all prospective purposive agents" have the same rights to freedom and well-being (Gewirth 1982, 20).

This argument bases individual rights on reason, not sentiment. That's why Gewirth might be called an ethical rationalist. The foundations are solid, and as developed by Pilon they are limited in their implications. They do not allow us to create rights to everything we need or want. They also give us a basis for limited government instead of the regulatory welfare state.

*Liberal
Group:
John Speaking*

🄳🄿 COMMENT ON GEWIRTH

I agree with Gewirth that freedom and well-being are necessary for agents to act for their own purposes. And I agree that if an agent were to claim that she had certain rights to freedom and well-being, then she would have to ascribe the same rights to others. The only way to avoid ascribing those rights to others would be to show a morally relevant difference between herself and other people, and I don't think that is possible.

The problem is that I do not agree that an agent must claim rights to freedom and well-being for herself. I see no contradiction between saying that I need freedom and well-being in order to be an agent and also saying that I do not have rights to freedom and well-being. I might even believe that others have a right to deny me the freedom and well-being I need.

Liberal Group: Vera Speaking

🅜🅟 ON GEWIRTH

Dee, I think you are making a mistake by trying to prove that your ethical principles are independent of people's attitudes and preferences. I admire Gewirth's clarity, his consistency, and his thoroughness; but in my opinion he's trying to do something that's impossible. He wants to show that we are guilty of a formal contradiction or inconsistency if we deny that people have certain rights. Very few professional moral philosophers accept his argument.

Philosopher Kai Nielsen, for example, agrees that Gewirth may have shown that all agents "want and need freedom and well-being and will typically take steps, where necessary, to protect their access to these goods." But he points out that "it doesn't follow that he must believe, if he is rational (Gewirth's sense), that he has a right to his freedom and well-being." A rational agent "could quite consistently believe that the protection of his own freedom and well-being were for him necessary goods ... and still, like Bentham, regard talk of rights as nonsense on stilts" (Nielsen 1989, 252).

Liberal Group: Vera Speaking

🅞🅟 COMMENT ON GEWIRTH

As Nielsen points out, there is no reason why a gangster cannot believe that he needs freedom and well-being to carry out his plans without asserting that he has a right to freedom and well-being (Nielsen 1989, 254).

As I said before, I do not believe that we can get our morality from theology or conceptual analysis

*Liberal
Group:
Vera Speaking*

or science. All of those approaches have been tried and failed. It's up to us to create our morality. It's our choice and our responsibility.

But let me be clear on one point. Just because there is no airtight proof that people have certain moral rights, that doesn't mean that establishing a system of rights and ascribing specific rights to people is completely arbitrary. Not at all. There can still be good reasons to protect certain human traits and capacities.

*Liberal
Group:
John Speaking*

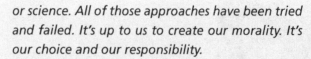 COMMENT ON GEWIRTH

I want to point out that Gewirth also argued that when the basic freedom and well-being of individuals is threatened, others who are able to do so have a strict moral obligation to provide aid. In the case of famine, for example, individuals and nations that can do so have a moral obligation to provide aid and those who are suffering have a right to that assistance. As a result, Gewirth's argument may not support the libertarian position Dee accepts. Roger Pilon argued that Gewirth had drifted from his earlier position in a dangerous direction that involved rights to "recipience." He believed that Gewirth was developing his ideas in a way that justified a "full-blown supportive state." My point is that even if we accept Gewirth's argument, it is far from clear that it implies only the libertarian rights that Dee accepts (Gewirth 1982, 201-202, 207 and Pilon 1979a, 1178).

Libertarian Group: Dee Speaking

🅼🅿 ON GEWIRTH

Wait. Wait. Wait.

I don't think you guys understand what Gewirth is claiming or how his argument works.

He isn't claiming that a gangster must believe that he has a right to the freedom he needs to rob a bank. Nor is he claiming that the gangster has a right to that freedom. That's a misunderstanding.

What Gewirth is claiming is that if we deny that others have a right to interfere with our status as "purposive agents," then we must claim that we have a right to the goods or conditions necessary for us to continue to be such agents. At the most general level, those conditions are freedom and well-being. Each of us must have those conditions if we are to be an agent at all. Furthermore, if we claim that we have those rights, we must ascribe those rights to all other agents.

I admit that Gewirth's argument is subtle and it is easy to misinterpret. Philosopher Alan White has created a more straightforward version of Gewirth's argument (White, 2020). Check it out. You might be surprised.

*Libertarian
Group:
Dee Speaking*

🄾🄿 COMMENT ON SELF-OWNERSHIP

I said that the most intuitive argument for individual rights is based on the principle of self-ownership. The principle states that each of us owns herself. It is supported by some of our strongest moral judgments, including, for example, that rape or torturing an innocent person is wrong. It implies a whole series of individual rights. As we unpack it, we can derive a right to go where we wish, take risks with our own body, engage in sexual acts of our own choosing, and more.

Libertarian Group: Elijah Speaking

🄼🄿 FOUNDATIONS

I agree with Vera and John. I respect Alan Gewirth, but I disagree with his argument. I don't think that an agent is guilty of a formal contradiction if she denies rights to freedom and well-being to herself and all other persons.

I would rather use a different sort of argument. In recent years, several philosophers in the contractarian tradition have used a hypothetical contract as a basis for individual rights. The idea here is to derive rights from prudence. Of course, the contract is hypothetical; and some people object that a hypothetical contract is not binding. I think that the hypothetical contract shows us what rational, self-interested parties would agree to. The power of the argument comes from that fact. If you would rationally pursue your own interests, the contract indicates what you should do.

I know of two writers who have argued for libertarianism on a contractarian basis: Jan Narveson and Loren Lomasky. They begin with self-interest and then, on that basis, argue for moral rules. I don't agree entirely with either Narveson or Lomasky. As a left-libertarian I take a different view of property, but I want you to be aware of what they are saying. Here's Narveson's explanation of how a contract fits into the argument for libertarianism.

A morality is a set of "rules that all are supposed to obey." In his view, to "show that a proposed morality is reasonable, then, we need to show that everyone – those being the people who are asked to comply with them – has a reason to comply." Prudence is one kind of reason. Contractarianism proposes that "the right set of principles" is the set that everyone will benefit the most from if everyone complies. Everyone "can see that he or she will do better if everyone, including himself or herself complies with those principles than if there are none or some other set." That is the set of rules to which rational people would agree (Narveson 2003, 106). Narveson believes that those rules are a form of libertarianism.

Now let me bring in Lomasky. I strongly recommend his 1987 book *Persons, Rights, and the Moral Community*. I'm going to try to summarize his view of rights, but his argument is more complicated than what I can lay out here. To begin with, he thinks of people as what he calls "project pursuers." Projects can vary greatly. Your project might be raising children, becoming an athlete, or writing a book. In any case, projects have the function of giving direction, purpose, and coherence to our lives.

Because projects are very important to us, we value the means necessary to carry them out, and we value our ability to pursue them. This implies that each project pursuer must value having "moral space" to carry out his or her projects. Our rights define that moral space. If we value our projects, we must value living in a world where we have such rights.

Since we each want rights for ourselves, we have a reason to follow a strategy that would bring about a world in which we have such rights. Using techniques from modern game theory, Lomasky concludes that a cooperative strategy is best for each of us and can be put into practice because we are not by nature entirely egoistic. It is possible to gradually develop a stable system of basic rights for all project pursuers. That system can develop without explicit bargaining or an explicit contract, but it can eventually be ratified by an explicit agreement. In other words, eventually a contract guaranteeing equal rights to all might emerge, although Lomasky admits that there is no guarantee that it will. (There is always the possibility that a community may divide into classes, and some classes may dominate others.) Nevertheless, he believes that there is a moral case for equal rights based on the fact that each individual is a project pursuer and there is no reason that one group should have more extensive rights than others.

Lomasky goes on to argue that the most stable system of equal rights is one that requires the least compromise or deference from all those involved. Systems that require more deference will encourage more individuals to withdraw from or overthrow the system. In short, in Lomasky's view, a combination of prudence, morality, and the requirements of stability lead to the establishment of a system of equal rights that are strong but quite limited.

Liberal
Group:
Vera Speaking

🄾🄿 COMMENT ON CONTRACTARIANISM

I really don't see the point to all this contract theory. First of all, I will bet you anything that when each philosopher considers the initial position in which the contract is made and decides what contract people in that position would make, it always turns out to be a contract that supports his political philosophy. Do you think it just happens that liberal John Rawls finds a contract that leads to more benefits for the poor? Or that libertarian Jan Narveson finds a contract that supports libertarian principles? Everybody finds what they want in contract theory. Here's what libertarian philosopher David Kelley had to say about a hypothetical contract:

> In Kelley's view, "An actual contract derives its binding force from consent.... The 'social contract' was never signed or spoken by anyone." Another problem is that each philosopher finds in the contract "what he thinks people would agree to if they were wise, rational, fair — that is, if they agreed with him about social policy." The bottom line is that "Hypothetical consent is not actual consent, and only the latter can bind" (Kelley 1998, 134).

Liberal Group: John Speaking

🅜🅟 ON LOMASKY

Lomasky doesn't try to prove that people have rights in the same way that Gewirth and Pilon do. Instead, he tries to show that rational people would (or might?) gradually construct a system of basic rights because it is in everyone's interest to do so. I think his argument is very plausible. My problem arises when he tries to show that the properly justified system of rights consists almost entirely of non-interference rights. He places it securely within the classical liberal tradition. In his words, it is a system that would require that we give minimal deference to others. His argument is that a minimal deference system would be the most stable. He says:

"[A] *stable regime of equal rights for all requires that the amount of required deference be close to the level of deference ideal for the least deferential members of the community*" (Lomasky 1987, 82 brackets added, italics in original).

Is that true? I think it's possible that the regime Lomasky advocates might be *less* stable than some alternatives because it requires so little deference. For example, he seems to be against minimum wage laws, but I wonder whether the absence of minimum wage laws might be just the sort of thing that makes a society unstable (Lomasky 1987, 126). His argument for stability seems to be based mainly on game theory, but I'm not sure how that translates to the real political world. I would like to see an argument for stability based on history and culture rather than an abstract game construct.

Liberal Group: John Speaking

🔲🔲 COMMENT ON LOMASKY

I want to say one more thing about Lomasky. Although the rights he advocates are almost entirely non-interference rights, he does allow for very limited welfare rights.

He argues that a regime of basic rights is based on the interests of people as project pursuers. Therefore, "If a person is otherwise unable to secure that which is necessary for his ability to live as a project pursuer, then he has a rightful claim to provision by others who have a surplus beyond what they require to live as project pursuers" (Lomasky 1987, 126).

Professor Sidgwick Speaking

🅜🅟 PROPERTY RIGHTS

It seems to me that some of the most controversial positions libertarians take have to do with property rights, welfare rights, and the distribution of wealth and income. Many libertarians advocate very strong individual property rights and criticize strong welfare rights.

I'd like to hear what you think about those issues.

Let's start with Dee. I know she takes a hard line on these things.

Libertarian Group: Dee Speaking

🅜🅟 ROBERT NOZICK

I'm glad to talk about property rights and the distribution of wealth and income. Let me introduce someone who is probably the best-known libertarian thinker of the last 50 years: Robert Nozick (1938-2002). Nozick was born in Brooklyn and attended Columbia, Princeton, and Oxford universities. As a young student, he leaned toward left-wing political ideas. Later, however, he developed a strong right-libertarian position. He published *Anarchy, State, and Utopia* in 1974. In it he argued against the theory of justice advocated by John Rawls and offered his own alternative. Nozick taught at Harvard University for many years.

Robert Nozick: Basic Ideas

- Both utilitarianism and the theory of justice advocated by John Rawls are fatally flawed.

- In place of utilitarianism and Rawls's theory, Nozick's theory of justice includes what he called "side constraints" (equivalent to strong individual rights). Side constraints are based on the principle of self-ownership and include strong property rights. Side constraints limit what it is morally permissible to do to individuals.

- Any theory of distribution that requires us to maintain a specific pattern of distribution (for example, one that seriously limits inequality of income) will require constant intervention and is incompatible with justified side constraints.

- In place of such pattern-oriented theories, Nozick proposed what he called an "entitlement" theory. Instead of seeking to maintain a pattern of distribution, the entitlement theory is historically based. A just distribution is one that results from a history of just acquisitions and just transfers. It is thus impossible to say that any particular distribution is just in itself. We need to know how it came about.

- The entitlement theory of distribution requires three sets of principles:
    - Principles of just (original) acquisition
    - Principles of just transfer
    - Principles of just rectification

- Utopia consists of a set of communities in which people freely participate and pursue their own understanding of a good life while protected by side constraints.

🔲🔲 EXCERPTS FROM ROBERT NOZICK
Anarchy, State, and Utopia

John Rawls formulated what he called the difference principle. That principle requires that society be organized so that any increase in inequality maximizes benefits for the least advantaged group. Nozick offered the following criticism of the difference principle and the Rawlsian veil of ignorance.

If things fell from heaven like manna, and no one had any special entitlement to any portion of it, and no manna would fall unless all agreed to a particular distribution, and somehow the quantity varied depending on the distribution, then it is plausible to claim that persons placed so that they couldn't make threats, or hold out for specially large shares, would agree to the difference principle rule of distribution. But is *this* the appropriate model for thinking about how the things people produce are to be distributed? Why think the same results should obtain for situations where there *are* differential entitlements as for situations where there are not?

A procedure that founds principles of distributive justice on what rational persons who know nothing about themselves or their histories would agree to *guarantees that end-state principles of justice will be taken as fundamental*....But no historical principle, it seems, could be agreed to in the first instance by the participants in Rawls' original position. For people meeting together behind a veil of ignorance to decide who gets what, knowing nothing about any special entitlements people may have, will treat anything to be distributed as manna from heaven (Nozick 1974, 198-199).

Libertarian Group: Dee Speaking

🄼🄿 DISTRIBUTIVE JUSTICE

Let's consider Nozick's entitlement theory of just distribution. That theory includes principles of original acquisition, principles of transfer, and principles of rectification.

The idea here is that the justice of the distribution of property at any particular time depends on the justice of original acquisition and the justice of later transfers. If the original acquisition was just, and the subsequent transfers were just, then the current distribution is just. It doesn't matter whether the current distribution satisfies some other moral principle such as the principle of utility. It doesn't matter whether the current distribution fits a pattern that we think is good or ideal. I think Professor Sidgwick's distinction between the good and the right applies here. It may be good in some ways to have a certain distribution of wealth or income, but that doesn't mean that it is right to require it.

Consider original acquisition. How does anyone first acquire strong property rights to anything? To answer that question, I want to take a very traditional approach by starting from what is often called the state of nature. When we imagine people in the state of nature, we are imagining them without government as part of a thought experiment. What would be the relationship between people and natural resources in that situation? Take land for example. What would be the relationship between people and the land they find around them in the state of nature? It seems to me that it would be something like this:

- People would see land around them, and none of it is owned by anyone.
- Everyone is free to make use of a piece of land. In other words, the land is available to everyone for use.
- Since no one owns any of the land, it is available to be acquired.

Now, from this starting point, what can happen? What is morally permissible? It seems to me that people would be perfectly justified in doing the following:

By taking various actions such as clearing and planting, individuals (or maybe families or even small societies of hunters and gatherers) could occupy land, work it, and raise a crop for their benefit. If people do not have the right to do this, (for example, if they needed everyone's permission to do it) then they would be morally bound to do nothing and starve. That would be morally absurd. So, we can agree that people had a right to use the available land.

Furthermore, by occupying and working the land people would acquire property rights to it and its product. After all, wouldn't we all agree that other people would be wrong to simply come in and take the land or the harvest for themselves? Again, it would be morally absurd to say that the rights of the occupiers are not violated if, after they have worked to raise a crop, others could come and take whatever they want. Remember: It is *their* labor and *their* ideas that make the difference between uncultivated land that serves no one and a farm that can feed a hundred people.

Essentially, that is how justified original acquisition could take place.

Libertarian
Group:
Dee Speaking

OP COMMENT ON DISTRIBUTIVE JUSTICE

Liberals often talk about the problem of distributive justice or the problem of inequality. But to be honest, I'm not sure just how this so-called problem arises. I want to refer you to a discussion of this question in Nozick's book (Nozick 1974, 185-186). He suggests that we think of it this way:

Libertarian Group: Dee Speaking

Let's imagine that there are ten Robinson Crusoes on ten different islands. They are not far from each other, but they don't know about each other. Each Crusoe does various things to survive – maybe planting corn or picking apples or hunting small game. Would anyone dispute the claim that each of them has the right to use and dispose of whatever he produces? I don't think so. So, in the case of completely separate Crusoes, no problem of distributive justice arises. Right?

Now suppose the Crusoes find out about each other and they start to trade some of their goods. The guy with the apples would like to have some corn, and so forth. All these trades are completely voluntary. What would we say about the new situation? Is there now a problem of distributive justice? I don't see why. It seems to me that Nozick's entitlement theory works just fine in this situation.

Now let's go one step further and assume that the Crusoes begin to cooperate on the production of new things – items that it would be hard for them to produce independently. Again, they voluntarily negotiate various arrangements to work together. Maybe one Crusoe offers a wage (or some corn) to another Crusoe to work on a project. They produce something new and sell it to the other Crusoes. Why would this increased cooperation change anything fundamental? If you can tell me why it would, I will concede that the entitlement theory is inadequate.

Liberal Group: John Speaking

🅜🅟 PROPERTY RIGHTS

I partly agree with you, Dee. I agree that there must be a way for people in the state of nature to acquire some sort of property rights, and that would include some kind of rights to land and other natural resources. But from there on it gets more complicated than you have indicated.

Take land for example. I agree that people in the state of nature have the right to work or use land. They need it to collect or grow food, and I agree that it would be morally absurd to say that they must stand by and starve because they have no right to use it. So far, so good.

I would also agree with you that acquiring or appropriating natural resources such as land in the state of nature cannot require everyone's consent or agreement. That would not be possible. Again, people would end up starving while they waited to get everyone's consent.

But I don't see how your argument gets us to really strong property rights in land (or other natural resources). A right to use something is not the right to extensive control over it and to permanently exclude others from use or control. Let's call that an *exclusive* right. I think that is what you are driving at and I don't think you have argued for it yet. You begin with the assumption that natural resources are originally unowned. I agree, but nothing about how anyone could acquire exclusive ownership rights over anything follows from that assumption.

Here's another problem with what you are saying. If no one owns anything to begin with, and if clearing and planting land confers a really strong ownership right (an exclusive right) then it follows that a few people in the state of nature could justifiably take control of all the best land and other people would have only what is left. That would be justified if your view is correct, but it seems morally unacceptable to me. More important, I think it would be morally unacceptable to the vast majority of people.

The exclusive acquisition you are advocating completely ignores and overrides the use rights that everyone had to begin with without providing any compensation whatsoever. How can that be justified?

I think Locke was right when he said that people in the state of nature had the right to use land as long as they could work it and there was "enough, and as good left in common for others" (Locke 1960, Chapter V, section 27). In other words, there must be no loss to others when the first occupiers take possession of the land and other resources. If there is a loss, some other arrangement must be made, or the others must be compensated. In my view, there can be limited property rights in the state of nature, but nothing close to the exclusive rights of classical liberalism or modern right-libertarianism.

Libertarian Group: Dee Speaking

🅜🅟 PROPERTY RIGHTS

I support strong individual property rights and in general I agree with Nozick's entitlement theory. There is one point on which I disagree with him — and that concerns the Lockean proviso. On that point, I agree with Roger Pilon of the Cato Institute. I don't think there is any obligation to abide by the proviso.

For Pilon, "Property arises...through some (very complex) act of claiming, either explicit or, as in the case at hand, implicit – through occurrent holding in the absence of any prior claim." In other words, property arises when someone does certain things to something that is unowned. Although he does not attempt to explain precisely how a person's actions generate property rights, he does offer a response to those who deny it. If acquisition were impossible, there would be "no private places to go to escape interference.... [I]t is our property that <u>enables</u> us to be free."

This is where the Lockean proviso may enter the argument. Nozick uses a relatively weak version of the proviso. Elijah accepts a stronger version. But I agree with Pilon. I don't think the proviso is relevant at all. It involves a misunderstanding.

Locke believed that God had given the Earth to humankind in common. Pilon assumes that initially no one owned the Earth. Therefore, when some people take ownership, they do not violate the rights of others. Others did not have a right to the opportunity to take and use resources. We must "bite the bullet" and face what may be "discomforting conclusions" (Pilon 1979b, 161-162, 164 brackets added).

*Liberal
Group:
Vera Speaking*

🄾🄿 COMMENT ON PROPERTY RIGHTS

OK, look. Even if it were possible to justify exclusive, individual libertarian property rights in the way Dee describes — basically through labor and first occupancy — what difference would it make? Nothing like what she describes ever happened.

Nozick's entitlement theory depends on an unbroken chain of legitimate transactions that begins with a legitimate original acquisition. That did not happen. Human history is filled with violence and theft. In fact, Nozick agrees that extensive rectification may be necessary because of what actually did happen (Nozick 1974, 231). There is no way to justify today's distribution of property based on Nozick's theory.

*Liberal
Group:
Vera Speaking*

A good libertarian might admit all that and perhaps even admit that we should carry out some sort of redistribution as a form of rectification for what actually happened. After that, she might argue, we should establish a system of strong libertarian property rights. But why should we do that?

It seems to me that we would only be required to establish a system of strong right-libertarian property rights if we could show that a regime of such rights was the only justifiable system of property. We haven't done that. At best, Nozick has shown that such a system is one possible justifiable system of property. I think that leaves us free today to look at other options for defining the rules of property. Personally, I would vote for a regime that included an element of collective choice.

*Liberal
Group:
John Speaking*

🅞🅟 COMMENT ON PROPERTY RIGHTS

Many societies around the world have recognized that the group as a whole has a responsibility for the welfare of the individual. In some peasant societies, for example, the village manages land and ensures that each family has a piece of land to farm. There is a corporate responsibility for the individual and the family. In return, of course, the individual has certain responsibilities to the group. The classical liberal and modern libertarian view changes all this. It claims that the group has minimal responsibility for the individual and, at the same time, the individual owes less to the group. In its most extreme form, this view reduces group responsibility to voluntary private charity.

I believe that we have gone too far in the classical liberal or libertarian direction. Perhaps we should reconsider the possibility that the justification for private property includes certain obligations to those who lack property. Or perhaps we should consider a greater corporate responsibility for the welfare of the individual.

Libertarian Group: Elijah Speaking

🅜🅟 PETER VALLENTYNE

I want to suggest a different perspective. We're talking about property rights, and that raises issues on which Dee and I do not agree.

My view is a lot like that of Peter Vallentyne. Vallentyne teaches at the University of Missouri and is currently one of the foremost defenders of left-libertarianism. He has written dozens of articles and coedited an anthology called *Left-Libertarianism and its Critics: The Contemporary Debate.*

The big difference between right and left-libertarianism has to do with the original acquisition of property in natural resources. How is that acquisition justified and what moral implications does it have? More specifically, what obligations does original acquisition impose on owners? These are crucial questions. If right-libertarians are correct, then the obligations of ownership are minimal. If left-libertarians are correct, they are substantial.

Peter Vallentyne: Basic Ideas

- Vallentyne believes that initially natural resources "are owned in some egalitarian manner." They "may be privately appropriated only with the permission of, or with a significant payment to, the members of society."

- Ownership of natural resources must be compatible with self-ownership. It must also allow people "to *appropriate* unappropriated natural resources without the consent of others—and with no loss of self-ownership—as long as they make an appropriate payment...."

- Private property rights "typically bring the owners benefits" and therefore these rights have a competitive value. He concludes that there is "no reason why an appropriator should be immune from paying for this competitive value."

- And finally, Vallentyne argues that paying for the competitive value is not a one-time thing. It is on-going (Vallentyne 2001, 1, 10,11).

My own view is that justice requires some sort of payment for the appropriation of natural resources. Just how large that payment should be, and how it should be collected and distributed, are complex questions. Perhaps the fair market value of the unimproved natural resources is a reasonable payment. My point is that *something* is owed to those who lose the right to use and appropriate those or similar resources. That payment might be used for lots of things, maybe even a guaranteed annual income and other welfare rights.

Liberal Group: Vera Speaking

ⓜⓟ PROPERTY RIGHTS

I want to bring in a philosopher who has written extensively on rights in general and property rights in particular. Her name is Judith Jarvis Thomson (1929-2020).

Thomson rejects the Lockean idea that the world was originally given by God to humankind in common. Originally, things were unowned, and we need some way to explain and justify ownership. Ownership here is to be taken in a strong sense including a cluster of rights, privileges, and powers — the right to use, the right to consume, the right to sell, the right to rent, the right to destroy, the right to give away or bequeath, and so forth.

Thomson asks how someone could acquire such ownership. Is it because a person applies her labor to something that she deserves to own that thing? Why would that be? Why doesn't that simply leave that thing a bit different, perhaps a bit more valuable, but still unowned? Is it because awarding that person ownership is efficient in the production of some goal? That might be true in some cases, but not in all. And even if a person deserves some reward for finding and developing a valuable resource, even if it is efficient to reward people for doing that sort of thing, why should that reward be the full cluster of rights we associate with property? Why not some other reward? Perhaps a more limited cluster of rights would work as well. Perhaps a 15-year patent would be an appropriate reward. We do that with drugs.

In the end, Thomson rejects all of the arguments offered to support the claim that a person acquires extensive rights over an unowned thing because she did something to that thing. She concludes that there are no really strong natural rights to property. Instead, she believes that property is the creation of legitimate government. I think her analysis is the most thorough and realistic one that I have seen. I conclude that we have limited use rights in the state of nature, but that more extensive and more complex property rights are the product of legitimate government. This is a case in which Professor Sidgwick's concept of legitimate government helps us to answer an important question (Thomson 1990, chapter 13).

What should those rights be? We can offer good reasons for people to have this or that right. Some rights protect people from harm. Some rights encourage economic development. Some rights have other desirable consequences. We should offer those facts as reasons for government to legislate one way or another on the subject of property.

By the way, Thomson's main book is called *The Realm of Rights*. I recommend it.

Professor Sidgwick Speaking

🅜🅟 WELFARE RIGHTS

Let's leave property rights behind and move on. What about welfare rights? That's another area in which opinions differ strongly.

I'll start again by asking Dee what she thinks.

Libertarian Group: Dee Speaking

🅜🅟 WELFARE RIGHTS

I believe in strong non-interference rights including freedom of contract. I believe in strong property rights that do not require compensation to non-owners, and I agree for the most part with Nozick's entitlement theory of distributive justice.

If my view of property rights and distributive justice is correct, then welfare rights involve an injustice. I'm thinking especially about the statutory welfare rights that governments love to create. In my opinion, typical statutory rights to income, housing, rent subsidies, food stamps, legal services, medical care, and all the rest involve illegitimate transfers of income from one group of citizens to another. They go way beyond the minimal government that I advocate. I recommend that you read David Kelley's book *A Life of One's Own* to get a libertarian view of the issues. In Kelley's words, "Lacking a moral justification, the welfare state is nothing more than a mechanism for transferring wealth from those who earned it to those who did not" (Kelley 1998, 63).

You all know that I believe in a strong principle of self-ownership. If someone has a right to demand that I provide them with, say, health care, then that person is really claiming a right to my labor. They are saying, in effect, that I must work to provide them with a benefit. I reject that because it violates my self-ownership.

Liberal Group: Ann Speaking

🅜🅟 WELFARE RIGHTS

I notice that Kelley said that "lacking a moral justification," welfare rights are just a mechanism for transferring wealth to people who haven't earned it.

I believe that there is a moral justification for welfare rights. A while ago, both John and I offered our ideas on the moral foundations of social liberalism. I suggested that utilitarianism could provide a justification for welfare rights because those rights would maximize human welfare. John suggested that a hypothetical social contract could offer a justification because people making a contract would find it in their interest to include such rights. Either of those approaches can supply the justification you require.

Liberal Group: John Speaking

🅞🅟 COMMENT ON LAWRENCE HAWORTH

I agree that the distinction between non-interference and welfare rights is very important for political philosophy. That's why I want to introduce you to a philosopher we haven't mentioned yet: Lawrence Haworth.

One approach to developing a theory of rights is to identify an ultimate value and then construct a set of rights in order to protect or foster that value. For example, Robert Nozick takes liberty as the ultimate value. Philosopher James Griffin takes personhood as the ultimate value. A 19th-century utilitarian like Jeremy Bentham took happiness or pleasure as the ultimate value.

Haworth suggests that our most fundamental value is what he calls an autonomous life. He argues, against libertarianism, that it is not liberty per se that is desirable, but "liberty autonomously exercised" (Haworth 1986, 139). He makes a similar argument against utilitarianism. Happiness is not desirable in itself, but only as part of an autonomous life.

The bedrock value underlying both libertarianism and utilitarianism is autonomy, which Haworth understands as a life characterized by critical reflection on, and choice of, values and goals. He goes on to claim that people have a right to the conditions that facilitate autonomous life. In short, he has tried to develop a theory of welfare rights based on the claim that the value of autonomy is presupposed by both libertarians and utilitarians (Haworth 1986, 209-216).

Liberal Group: Ann Speaking

🄼🄿 LIBERTARIANISM

I think we have spent enough time discussing property and welfare rights. I want to say something more general about libertarianism. These are broad criticisms.

Ann's Criticisms of Libertarianism

- It's not at all clear to me how libertarians can justify the principle of full self-ownership. It has a certain intuitive appeal here in the United States where we often talk about the importance of the individual and his or her rights. But I suspect that if we were to talk to people from cultures that stress social harmony rather than individuality, they would react differently. That means we need a justification for the libertarian view. We can't just say it's obvious, but what is that justification? Why not opt for a weaker form of self-ownership? That would allow moderately strong individual rights but also leave room for the community to require more from the individual. Doesn't that have a certain intuitive appeal as well?

- It seems to me that the minimal government required by right-libertarianism is too limited. Nozick's side-constraints are so strong that government can do almost nothing. Isn't that counter-intuitive? Do we really believe that the government must stand by and do nothing to assist the poor if private charity fails to help them?

- I also think that the right-libertarian view of property as a strong natural right that governments should not interfere with is mistaken. I can't tell you what goes on in the state of nature, but in all modern societies, property is defined by governments. I think that Judith Thomson is very persuasive on that point. In my opinion, it's best to view property rights as what Ayesha called prima facie rights created by legitimate government. That leads us back to a question that Professor Sidgwick raised about legitimacy: What is the basis of legitimate government?

- Libertarianism regards human labor as a commodity. The price of labor is to be determined by a free, competitive market, and the freedom of contract is strongly affirmed. Do we really believe that? What does that mean for people with a poor education or serious handicaps?

- Libertarianism seems to assume that everyone is an able bodied, mentally competent adult. But that's not true. Many people are handicapped, ill, or dependent on others in various ways. Where do they fit into a libertarian society?

I respect the intellectual work that has gone into developing modern libertarianism, but I think it goes too far in its emphasis on the fully competent individual and his or her rights. I think we need a philosophy that places more emphasis on the common good and guarantees more for everyone.

Catholic Group:
Ayesha
Speaking

🄾🄿 COMMENT ON LIBERTARIANISM

Let me say something from a Catholic point of view. Libertarianism as Dee presents it leaves no room for God's purposes. From the Catholic point of view, this world is God's creation and His purposes are paramount. We have an obligation to organize society in a way that helps achieve those purposes. It's not just our goals that matter. More concretely, Catholic philosophers often stress that there is a common good and that everyone deserves a share of that common good. That rules out the libertarian idea that human labor is a commodity. Individual rights, including property rights and the right to make contracts, must be compatible with the common good. Letting the price of labor float on the market is not compatible. Many Catholic thinkers believe that properly distributing the bounty of God's creation, for example, requires a living wage for the worker.

Professor Sidgwick Speaking

🅜🅟 FACTS OR PHILOSOPHY?

Before we finish up with libertarianism, I want to point out that some of the issues that divide libertarians, conservatives, and liberals aren't philosophical at all. They are factual issues, but they can be quite divisive and politically polarizing.

For example, libertarians and liberals are deeply divided on some issues concerning causes and effects. Why are some people poor? Do government anti-poverty programs work? If not, why not? Philosopher Will Kymlicka has raised some of these issues.

In Kymlicka's words, "The major arguments between the 'left' and the 'right' today are ... about several essentially empirical questions" like the following (Kymlicka 2002, 158):

- Are people poor because of their own bad choices or because of "misfortune and unequal opportunities"?

- When we create welfare programs, are we "helping the victims of unequal circumstances" or "subsidizing expensive tastes and irresponsible choices"?

- Does the welfare state help the poor "overcome their disadvantage" or create "a class of welfare dependents caught in a poverty trap"?

- Can government "remedy involuntary disadvantages" or "are the sources of social ills like poverty...so complex that state attempts to solve them will generally fail" as some conservatives believe?

We could add to Kymlicka's list. Would other anti-poverty programs work better than the ones we have? How much upward mobility is there, and why? What role does racial discrimination play in the disproportionate number of African Americans among the poor? What role does poor education play? These are all factual questions that social science should be able to answer.

I would like Dee to set aside the purely moral and philosophical issues and say something about these factual issues. Then I would like to hear a response from the liberal group.

*Liberal
Group:
John Speaking*

🄾🄿 COMMENT ON FACTUAL ISSUES

I agree with Kymlicka. We are never going to agree on some moral questions or whether government ought to do certain things. For example, we are never going to agree on whether abortion is morally wrong or whether assisted suicide should be legal. But there is at least some chance that we can agree on the extent to which social security benefits have reduced poverty among the elderly or the extent to which the programs of the Great Society reduced poverty in general. If we can agree on those kinds of issues, we may be able to agree on policy.

Libertarian Group: Dee Speaking

🅜🅟 FACTUAL ISSUES

OK. Let's set aside our philosophical differences for a minute and talk about the factual issues that Professor Sidgwick is referring to. Some of what I'm going to say comes from David Kelley.

- We have had lots of government programs to fight poverty. For example, we have had AFDC (now TANF), general assistance, and food stamps (now SNAP). I think that the best studies show that these programs do very little. The percent of people who are poor goes up and down slightly, but the federal war on poverty has been lost. Despite the fact that they are well-intended, government anti-poverty programs don't work very well. The only thing they do well is to create good jobs for the middle-class people who staff them.

- The main cause of chronic poverty is the bad choices that some people make. They drop out of school. They join a gang and get in trouble with the law. They have a child before they finish high school and before they can support it. They have children without getting married. They do not learn to read well. They fail to acquire marketable skills. They take drugs. They also accept the notion that someone else, usually the government, should provide for them and their children. That results in a state of dependency based on years of receiving government aid of one kind or another.

- In some ways, government policy actually creates poverty. This is especially true in the case of minimum wage laws. At present, welfare state liberals are demanding a $15 per hour minimum wage. A wage requirement that high would be a disaster for many people. Why would any business pay $15 an hour to a semi-literate person with minimal skills and a sketchy job history? The fact is, it won't.

- I would like to add that there are other solutions to the problem of poverty that welfare state liberals tend to ignore. Private charity is less expensive and more effective than government programs. And besides that, it is voluntary. If we want to have a society that cares for the deserving poor and preserves freedom, we should look to private organizations for solutions.

Liberal
Group:
Vera Speaking

🄾🄿 COMMENT ON FACTUAL ISSUES

I can hardly believe what you are saying, Dee. This is a classic case of blaming the victim. You are talking about the people in our society who have the least. They attend the worst schools. They have the most limited resources. They struggle with crime and violence all around them in neighborhoods that no one in this room would want to live in, but all you can do is blame them for being poor.

Everyone responds to the conditions in which they live. Change the conditions and they will change what they do. Provide good schools and make jobs available. That's the solution.

Liberal Group: Ann Speaking

⌊m⌋⌊p⌋ FACTUAL ISSUES

Kymlicka is right. We do disagree on a series of empirical or factual questions. In a general way, Dee is making what is called a culture of poverty argument. The idea is that the overall way of life of the poor makes them poor or keeps them poor. In my opinion, it's not that simple.

- I am not going to deny that some of the poor are poor because they have made bad choices like dropping out of school and taking drugs. But you are characterizing the whole group that way, and that's a mistake.

- You are also ignoring the special problems that the very poor and chronically unemployed have in the job market. If you do not own a car, it is almost impossible to get to many jobs. If you do not have a telephone, it is almost impossible for employers to get in touch with you to set up a job interview. If you are homeless, there may be no address that you can put down on a job application. If you cannot afford childcare, you may not be able to show up at work day after day the way employers expect. These are problems that middle-class people don't have and never think about, but they are very real for the poor and the chronically unemployed.

- Besides that, you are completely ignoring the reality of racial discrimination. Most of the poor are white, but a disproportionate number are black. We can show from lots of studies that there is considerable discrimination that operates against blacks in the job market. For example, studies have shown repeatedly that white and black applicants can send in identical resumes (except for names that make the race of the applicant obvious) and the white applicants get many more favorable responses.

- Many of the poorest Americans — people who are homeless — have serious mental, emotional, and health-related problems. It is totally unrealistic to think that they will become self-supporting. They need treatment and financial support. There's no way around that.

*Liberal
Group:
Vera Speaking*

🅞🅟 **COMMENT ON FACTUAL ISSUES**

I think Dee is asking the wrong question. The question is not "Did poor people make bad choices?" The question is "Is there a way in which we can intervene to change their economic condition?" Dee is saying that the government cannot identify an effective way to intervene. I think it can. We know how to create incentives that will get the private sector to hire more of the chronically unemployed. We know how to create public service jobs that will hire even more. We have done these things at times, and we could do them again. A large number of people will take those jobs if they are made available.

*Catholic
Group:
Ayesha Speaking*

🅞🅟 **COMMENT ON FACTUAL ISSUES**

Dee mentioned private charity. I admire private charity as much as anyone. We couldn't survive as a humane society without it. I'm sure that my church and Diego's church are very active helping the poor. But I think that it is a mistake to think that private charity alone can address the larger problems of the poor effectively. Consider the cost of medical care. A week in a hospital can cost tens of thousands of dollars. There is no way that private charity could cover those costs for 20 or 30 million poor people. The only institution with the resources to do the job is government.

Liberal Group: John Speaking

🅜🅟 FACTUAL ISSUES

It seems to me that there are two approaches to explaining the persistence of poverty. One stresses the choices that poor people make. The other stresses the conditions in which they live.

We sometimes assume that this is an either/or situation, but I am not at all sure that those two approaches are logically incompatible. At least some of the claims are compatible. For example, it may be true that there are cases in which poor persons continue to be poor because of bad choices like dropping out of school, but it may also be true that many more people will make that choice under certain conditions. If that is true, then a complete explanation of persistent poverty requires understanding both the choices made and the conditions that encourage those choices. Most important: A change in either choices or conditions can reduce the incidence of poverty.

Liberal Group: Vera Speaking

🅞🅟 COMMENT ON FACTUAL ISSUES

I don't want to be cynical, but I wouldn't bet the farm on liberals and conservatives reaching agreement on these factual issues.

For over a century there have been people who have hoped and believed that economics or sociology would come to our rescue and tell us how to solve our social problems.

> *Unfortunately, the way it actually works out is that each political perspective has its own sociologists and economists who support its views. The right has its Milton Friedmans and Charles Murrays. The left has its Paul Krugmans and William Julius Wilsons. Don't expect agreement anytime soon.*

Professor Sidgwick Speaking

🅜🅟 WRAPPING UP

I want to step in and ask Dee and Elijah to make a closing statement on libertarianism. This is their chance to appeal to our hearts.

Then, after Dee and Elijah are finished, I have asked John to try to give us a final evaluation of libertarianism. I know that's a bit unfair. He's not a libertarian and he can't speak for all of you, but I want him to try to get a little above the fray and look at the larger picture. We'll see how he does with that.

Libertarian Group: Dee Speaking

ⓜⓟ FINAL STATEMENT

Elijah and I feel as if we were in court and about to make our closing statement to the jury. OK, here it is.

Libertarianism is about freedom. It rests upon the age-old dream of freedom from the arbitrary rule of kings and lords. It takes up the quintessential American virtue, the love of liberty, and builds upon it, making it the center of its philosophy. In doing so, it combines elements of the left and elements of the right. Along with the left it asserts that individuals must be free to choose their lifestyle. That means the freedom to experiment, including sexual freedom, the freedom to take drugs, to speak outrageously, to create new kinds of art, and to scorn tradition. Along with the right it asserts that strong property rights are an essential part of freedom, markets should be free, the right of contract should be recognized, and government should be minimal.

Robert Nozick put it well when he wrote about libertarianism as a "framework for utopias" — not because it prescribes in detail how everyone should live, but precisely because it does not attempt to do so. Instead, it offers a framework, a set of rules, that prevents others from forcing the individual to conform to their way of thinking. It allows each of us the freedom, the space, in which to live out his or her conception of the good life (Nozick 1974, 312).

In Nozick's words, libertarianism offers "a wide and diverse range of communities which people can enter if they are admitted, leave if they wish to, [and] shape according to their wishes." In these various communities, "experimentation can be tried" and "alternative visions of the good can be individually or jointly pursued" (Nozick 1974, 307 brackets added).

*Libertarian
Group:
Elijah Speaking*

**O P COMMENT ON
LEFT-LIBERTARIANISM**

I agree with Dee on the centrality of self-ownership and freedom; but as I have said before, I also agree with social liberals up to a point. I believe that when individuals or groups take exclusive ownership of unowned natural resources, there must be some sort of payment made to those who lose the opportunity to use or own similar resources. That payment could take the form of welfare rights that Dee rejects. For example, it might be the basis of a guaranteed annual income.

This isn't a crazy idea. Look at Norway. It has a sovereign wealth fund based on oil revenues that provides benefits to citizens. Our own state of Alaska has a fund based on oil revenues that pays a dividend to Alaskans. What I'm suggesting can be done in the real world.

Liberal Group: John Speaking

🅜🅟 AN EVALUATION

Professor Sidgwick has asked me to provide an overall evaluation of libertarianism. I'll give you my thoughts, but remember that I don't speak for anyone else. I have included some questions that I would like to have answered.

John's Evaluation of Libertarianism

- Libertarianism stresses non-interference rights. There is no question that those rights have been an enormous step forward morally for humanity. If fully implemented, they would prevent a great deal of harm. Social liberals may see them as old hat, but that wasn't always the case. If we lost them, we would soon rediscover their value.

- The philosopher Ronald Dworkin has suggested that the best political philosophy must guarantee equal concern and respect for all citizens. That implies that we must not trade off the good of some for the good of others. John Rawls and Robert Nozick both recognized that tradeoffs like that are a problem for traditional utilitarianism. In libertarianism those tradeoffs are prevented by rights or side-constraints. I believe that the recognition that certain kinds of tradeoffs cannot be allowed is something of permanent value. Libertarianism puts it front and center.

- Libertarianism has stressed the harm done by states and the subsequent need to limit state power. Again, this is of permanent value. When we think about the great crimes of history — the transatlantic slave trade, the two World Wars, the Holocaust of the 1940s, the genocide in Rwanda, the killing of the Armenians in the Ottoman Empire, and so on — we see that most of them were either carried out by states or required state support.

- One possible basis for individual rights is the principle of self-ownership. I think that here again libertarianism is emphasizing something of permanent value.

- On the other hand, it seems to me that we can question some of the assumptions and conclusions of libertarianism, especially right-libertarianism. Does the principle of full self-ownership go too far? Are right-libertarian property rights too strong? Are the limits on government advocated by most libertarians too great? Do they make it impossible for us to solve problems like pollution and global warming? Does equal concern and respect require that we give the government a greater role in helping those who do poorly in a market-oriented society? I think it is fair to press libertarians for better answers to those questions.

- Vera and I questioned the right-libertarian view of property, especially the nature of original acquisition. How is it possible for one person or one group to acquire exclusive property rights to natural resources? Philosopher Judith Thomson, who is not a libertarian, has argued that strong, complex property rights are the creation of legitimate government. I think that what she says is very plausible.

- I think Vera is right to ask whether libertarianism works fairly for people who are not in the full possession of adult faculties. What about children? What about the disabled? The chronically ill? As we move away from the fully capable adult pictured in libertarian theory, we have to deal with those cases. I think it is fair to say that libertarians have not done enough in that area.

- My questions for libertarians are already pretty obvious. What is the basis for such a strong principle of self-ownership? What is the basis for the strong right-libertarian rights of property? How does libertarianism apply to children and those who are handicapped or otherwise dependent on others?

Those are my thoughts. You can see that I think highly of libertarianism even though I would not describe myself as a libertarian. I think it offers real gains that we must not lose sight of. Any acceptable political philosophy must incorporate those gains in some fashion.

*Conservative
Group:
Fred Speaking*

O P COMMENT ON LIBERTARIANISM

As a conservative, I think it may be useful to view libertarianism from a Burkean perspective. Libertarians tend to develop an ahistorical argument for a set of individual rights and then deduce the implications of those rights for society. In other words, most forms of libertarianism impose an abstract plan or model with little regard for the history of any particular society. Recall how Burke ridiculed the abstract rights of man, but firmly supported the historically developed rights of Englishmen. He might well say something similar about modern libertarianism. Does it ignore too many of the traditions of each individual society? If so, that may make many of its recommendations unworkable.

6.
CATHOLIC SOCIAL THOUGHT

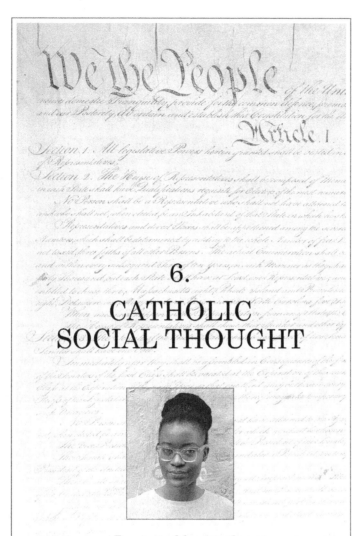

Presented by Ayesha

Catholic Group: Ayesha Speaking

🅼🅿 CATHOLIC SOCIAL THOUGHT

Catholic social thought has a long history. Like conservatism and liberalism, it shows great variety. It would be naive to expect anything else from an organization that is more than a thousand years old and has more than a billion members. As a result, I can't give you a summary of all that has been written in the Catholic tradition concerning social life and politics. I can say that since the late nineteenth century, the Church has made a concerted effort to come to grips with the modern world, including industrialization, personal liberty, and democratic government. In a series of papal encyclicals, certain key ideas have developed on economics, poverty, the working classes, democracy, human rights, and government. I think I can give you a sense of those ideas.

First of all, I want to lay out some basic concepts and principles of Catholic social thought. Here's a list of some of the important concepts.

Catholic Social Thought: Basic Concepts

- **God**
- **Natural moral law**
- **Human dignity and human rights**
- **An organic society with a common good**
- **A preferential option for the poor**
- **A third way between capitalism and socialism**
- **Subsidiarity**

Each of those concepts is fundamental. They can be embodied in principles that give us the essence of Catholic social philosophy.

Catholic Social Thought: Principles and Beliefs

- God is not only the creator of all things but created all things for a purpose. Therefore, as a matter of principle, we must work toward that purpose. In particular, God created the resources of this earth for the benefit of all his creatures, especially humankind.

- There is a natural moral law. Human reason can determine that law from a study of the nature of human beings, their history, and the conditions under which they live. That moral law is also supported by divine revelation.

- Human dignity is based on the fact that human beings were created in the image of God. It is the basis of human rights. Those rights are part of the natural moral law.

- There is a common good for human beings. It includes the good of the whole society, but it also includes the good of each and every individual. This implies that everyone should share in the bounty of God's gifts to humankind and no one's good can be ignored or traded off for the good of others. The existence of a common good is incompatible with the idea that different social classes have fundamentally antagonistic interests. In modern times, the common good consists largely in protecting the rights of all.

- An economic system must be judged within an ethical framework. That framework tells us, for example, that everyone should share in the benefits of economic progress, that labor is not a commodity, and that we should choose policies that protect and assist the poorest among us.

- There is a middle way between extreme individualism and extreme collectivism in the proper organization of society. That middle way values private property as a natural right but also stresses that property should be widely distributed and must be used to promote the common good.

- Because the resources of the earth are intended for the benefit of all human beings, we must act as stewards of those resources on behalf of future generations.

- The chief function of the state is to promote the common good and protect individual rights.

- The principle of subsidiarity tells us that decisions should be made, and problems dealt with, at the lowest effective level. Decision-making should not be centralized to an unnecessary degree.

Catholic Group:
Ayesha
Speaking

🅞🅟 COMMENT ON
AMERICAN CATHOLICISM

I should also say that Catholic thought in the United States has always had a distinctive twist to it. Catholics in the US found themselves in a Protestant country with a democratic tradition. There was always a tension between some traditional Catholic ideas and the dominant political and social ideas here in the US. Americans believe in republican government, free speech, and the separation of church and state. American Catholics have had to come to grips with those ideas. Nevertheless, there have been some standout Catholic thinkers in the US, including people like John Ryan, Dorothy Day, and John Courtney Murray. These people have worked to bring together the Catholic and the American traditions.

Catholic Group: Ayesha Speaking

🔲🔲 POPE LEO XIII

Most historians agree that modern Catholic social thought began in earnest with the encyclicals of Pope Leo XIII (1810-1903). Leo was born near Rome. He attended a Jesuit school in Rome and was ordained a priest (although not a Jesuit) in 1837. He was elected pope in 1878.

In the mid-19th century the Catholic Church struggled to come to grips with a rapidly changing world. Not only were the Papal States lost by the Church in the process of Italian unification, but broad trends such as industrialization, urbanization, the spread of democratic political systems, the creation of political parties, the rise of labor unions, and the spread of socialist ideas were all part of a changing social order. At times, the Church seemed to reject the newer ideas and institutions, but Leo took a different approach. He sought instead to develop a distinctly Catholic social doctrine as an alternative to both market-driven capitalism and socialism.

In 1891 Leo published his most famous encyclical, *Rerum Novarum*, which contains the essence of his social doctrine. Here are some of his key ideas:

Pope Leo XIII: Basic Ideas

- God has created the earth for the "use and enjoyment of the whole human race." Although the rights of private property are affirmed by natural law, the wealthy have strong moral obligations to the poor and needy (par. 8).

- Great inequality exists between owners and workers. The condition of the working classes is "little better than that of slavery itself." This is in part due to the lack of guilds to protect workers and in part to the unchecked greed and competition among employers (par. 3).

- Socialists attack property rights, preach class war, seek to establish a community of goods, and hope to overthrow existing political authorities. Socialism thus threatens society and does not solve the problems of working people.

- Although those who possess great property have rights of ownership, they may not use their property in just any way they choose. They must share their wealth with those in need. They must use their wealth "as the steward of God's providence, for the benefit of others" (par. 22).

- Wages must be such that they are sufficient to support a "frugal and well-behaved wage-earner." The law should encourage as many people as possible to become owners. Guilds of working men or workers and employers should also be encouraged (par. 45).

- Civil society exists for the "common good" and is concerned with "the interests of all." The state must serve the common good and regard the interests of all as equal (par. 51. See Gilson 1954 for one of many editions.).

I think the thrust of Leo's views was in the right direction. Church and state must defend ordinary people and labor is not a commodity. I believe that, and my church believes it too.

58 EXCERPTS FROM POPE LEO XIII
Rerum Novarum

Leo XIII issued Rerum Novarum *(Rights and Duties of Capital and Labor) in 1891. It is generally regarded as the beginning of modern Catholic social thought. The following paragraphs will help to summarize Leo's social philosophy. The paragraphs of encyclicals are numbered for reference.*

3. In any case we clearly see, and on this there is general agreement, that some opportune remedy must be found quickly for the misery and wretchedness pressing so unjustly on the majority of the working class: for the ancient working-men's guilds were abolished in the last century, and no other protective organization took their place.

19. The great mistake made in regard to the matter now under consideration is to take up with the notion that class is naturally hostile to class, and that the wealthy and the working men are intended by nature to live in mutual conflict. So irrational and so false is this view that the direct contrary is the truth.... Each needs the other: capital cannot do without labor, nor labor without capital.

43. We now approach a subject of great importance, and one in respect of which, if extremes are to be avoided, right notions are absolutely necessary. Wages, as we are told, are regulated by free consent, and therefore the employer, when he pays what was agreed upon, has done his part and seemingly is not called upon to do anything beyond.

44. To this kind of argument a fair-minded man will not easily or entirely assent; it is not complete, for there are important considerations which it leaves out of account altogether.

45. Let the working man and the employer make free agreements, and in particular let them agree freely as to the wages; nevertheless, there underlies a dictate of natural justice more imperious and ancient than any bargain between man and man, namely, that wages ought not to be insufficient to support a frugal and well-behaved wage-earner. If through necessity or fear of a worse evil the workman accept harder conditions because an employer or contractor will afford him no better, he is made the victim of force and injustice.

48. In the last place, employers and workmen may of themselves effect much, in the matter We are treating, by means of such associations and organizations as afford opportune aid to those who are in distress, and which draw the two classes more closely together.

49. The most important of all are workingmen's unions, for these virtually include all the rest. History attests what excellent results were brought about by the artificers' guilds of olden times. They were the means of affording... many advantages to the workmen.... Such unions should be suited to the requirements of this our age....

Catholic Group: Ayesha Speaking

🅼🅿 FATHER JOHN RYAN

Leo XIII may seem like a faraway character, but there were Catholic thinkers here in the United States who adapted his ideas to our country. Father John Augustine Ryan (1869-1945) was the most influential. Ryan was born in Vermillion, Minnesota. He attended a series of Catholic schools, became a priest in 1898, and received his doctorate in sacred theology from the Catholic University of America (CUA) in 1906. He taught first at the St. Paul Seminary and later at the Catholic University until his retirement in 1939. A biographical note provided by the university describes him as "the foremost social justice advocate and theoretician in the Catholic Church during the first half in [*sic*] the 20th century" (CUA, Biographical Note).

Ryan studied both moral theology and economics. His work was a synthesis of both. In his view, an economic system, such as that of the United States, exists to serve moral purposes and must be guided by moral principles. Ryan's doctoral dissertation was published as *A Living Wage* in 1906. *Distributive Justice* followed in 1916. He drafted the "Bishops' Program of Social Reconstruction" in 1919.

Ryan was profoundly influenced by the social teachings of the Church, especially that of Pope Leo XIII and Pope Pius XI. His interpretation of *Rerum Novarum* allowed him to develop a form of Catholic progressivism similar in many ways to the non-Catholic progressivism of the early 20th century. *A Living Wage* was dedicated to the progressive economist Richard Ely. Ely, for his part, wrote an introduction to Ryan's book. According to historian Jay Dolan, "The genius of Ryan was his ability to merge Catholic social thought with the American current of reform. The basis for this merger was the natural law tradition." Ryan "gave to American Catholics the foundations of a social gospel" (Dolan 1992, 343). In the 1930s Ryan was a strong supporter of Franklin Roosevelt's New Deal.

Ryan also denounced the views of the popular radio priest Charles Coughlin, writing in 1936 that Coughlin's "economic theories and proposals have no positive support in the encyclicals of Leo and Pius or in any other authoritative Catholic source" (Ryan 1936).

Here are some of Ryan's basic ideas and a few of his practical proposals.

John Ryan: Basic Ideas and Practical Proposals

- All human beings have equal intrinsic worth and equal claims to "sustenance from the common bounty of the earth" (Ryan 1935, 149).

- An economic system must be judged within a moral framework.

- Private property is justified as stewardship but limited in its use by moral principles.

- Extreme economic individualism, centralized state socialism, and the totalitarian fascist state are all morally unacceptable.

- A just distribution of income requires a living wage for the worker.

- Workers should have the right to form unions.

- There should be a system of unemployment insurance for workers. (In the 1940s, Ryan also advocated a system of public health insurance.)

- Workers and employers should form associations to manage some aspects of production.

Catholic Group:
Ayesha
Speaking

🅞🅟 COMMENT ON
RYAN'S THEORY OF RIGHTS

Father Ryan was an unusual mix of philosopher, economist, and political activist. He developed a theory of rights that undergirded his views on reforming our economy. Here's a short summary of his views:

- *A right can be defined as "an inviolable moral claim to some personal good."*

- *Individuals have rights because of their rational nature.*

- *These rights are natural and not positive rights. In other words, they are not conferred by the state. Their "ultimate source is to be found in the Reason and Will of God."*

- *Natural rights are the "moral means or opportunities by which the individual attains the end appointed to him by nature."*

- *That end is "right and reasonable life." Right and reasonable life consists in "the development of man's personality through the harmonious and properly ordered exercise of his faculties." Furthermore, "Natural rights are necessary means of right and reasonable living. They are essential to the welfare of a human being, a person."*

> • *The most important of these rights are the "rights to life, to liberty, to property, to a livelihood, to marriage, to religious worship, to intellectual and moral education."*
>
> For Ryan, the individual is sacred. He or she is an "end in himself." The individual has "intrinsic dignity" (Ryan, 1996, 161-165).

🆂🅴 EXCERPTS FROM FATHER JOHN RYAN
A Better Economic Order

John Ryan (1869–1945) attempted to apply Catholic principles, especially those in the encyclicals of Leo XIII and Pius XI, to moral-economic questions. He wrote extensively on economic justice, a just wage, the rights of property, and the role of government. The following excerpts are taken from A Better Economic Order, *published in 1935.*

In order to be just, an economic system must rest upon and be permeated by certain definite ethical principles. Lacking these, the system can exemplify only partial, pragmatic, and irregular justice....

The first of these principles is that the earth and its potentialities belong to all members of the human race without distinction. This is a corollary of the doctrine of equal natural rights. Before God and by reason of their nature, human beings possess intrinsic worth and are essentially equal....

Since all persons are morally equal and endowed with equal moral rights, they all have equal claims to sustenance from the common bounty of the earth. The Creator has not given any group of men exceptional rights over the natural bounty....

The second fundamental principle is that men are morally obliged to use the goods and opportunities of the earth in accordance with the laws of justice and charity. While the particular implications of the principle are too numerous to be described here, a few of the most important and fundamental should be stated.

The first of these implications or conclusions is that the institution of private property is morally right because it is necessary for human welfare. The second is that the holders of private property, the owners of particular portions of the earth or its derived goods or advantages, are morally obliged to exercise this power in such a way that the non-owners will have access to these things on reasonable terms; for example, through contracts which enable them to obtain employment at just rates of remuneration....

The third implication was thus stated by Aristotle: "It is evident then that it is better to have property private, but make the use of it common...."

According to the order of nature instituted by Divine Providence, the goods of the earth are designed to supply the needs of men. The division of goods and their appropriation through human law do not thwart this purpose. Therefore, the goods which a man has in superfluity are due by the natural law to the sustenance of the poor.

This is the traditional Christian conception of ownership as stewardship. The private proprietor is not the absolute owner of the things that he calls his. He is merely the trustee, responsible to God for such use of his possessions as will not frustrate the divinely destined end of all created goods, namely, the sustenance of all the people (Ryan 1935, 148-151).

Catholic Group:
Ayesha
Speaking

🅞🅟 COMMENT ON DISTRIBUTISM

There were a number of 20th-century Catholic writers who were called "distributists" and their social philosophy was known as distributism. The group included Hilaire Belloc and Harold Robbins. They emphasized the importance of a wide distribution of property both for justice and independence. Robbins (1888-1954) published The Sun of Justice: An Essay on the Social Teaching of the Catholic Church *in 1938. Here are some of his ideas:*

Harold Robbins: Distributism

- *Man has been created in the image of God and therefore must be afforded "a certain ample measure of dignity and sufficiency in the world in which he has been placed" (Robbins 2011, Kindle location 246).*

- *People have natural rights to marriage and to property. Property is the "buttress" of the family and freedom. It gives the person and the family the independence needed to flourish. This realization leads immediately to the need for widely distributed property (Robbins 2011, Kindle locations 413, 602).*

- *Under the current system of large-scale mechanized industrialism, we have lost widely distributed property. Employees are little more than slaves to machines.*

- *The ideal solution to this problem is a return to small family-owned farms, craft production, and craft guilds.*

*Catholic Group:
Ayesha
Speaking*

I don't think that we can solve our economic problems by a return to the land or to small-scale craft production. That would lower the standard of living more than the American people would accept. But I think there is a lot to be said for reducing the size of the largest business enterprises and encouraging small business and home ownership. Property can give people independence and a sense of who they are.

Conservative Group: Fred Speaking

🅼🅿 FATHER EDWARD KELLER

I respect Father Ryan. I believe that his intentions were good and that he genuinely cared about ordinary working people. Still, I think he misinterpreted the papal message and gave it too much of a progressive slant. As a counterweight to Ryan, let me introduce another Catholic economist, Father Edward Keller (1903-1989). Keller was a member of the Congregation of the Holy Cross. He taught at the University of Notre Dame and published his best-known work, *Christianity and American Capitalism*, in 1953. His ideas give us an example of a more conservative interpretation of Catholic social thought.

Keller paid serious attention to the social encyclicals of the popes, but he also defended what he considered the basic assumptions and institutions of American capitalism, including private property, free competition, free enterprise, and freedom of contract. His main concern was to criticize trends, ideas, and institutions that he believed would lead to a centrally planned economy in the United States. He was also concerned to dispute what he saw as a leftist or collectivist interpretation of the papal encyclicals.

Keller did not defend "unrestricted capitalism," and understood that Leo XIII and Pius XI had condemned it. He sought to defend a middle way between a planned economy and one that is entirely unregulated. He believed that the US had developed a set of laws and institutions that provided for the proper degree of regulation. Those laws and institutions guaranteed that American capitalism served the common good.

Keller warned against the dangers of "big government" and was especially concerned with the shifting of power from states to the federal level. He saw this transition as a violation of the Catholic principle of subsidiarity. It also depersonalized life by wrapping the individual in ever more federal regulation. He believed that because of competition and anti-trust laws, "big business" was less of a danger than "big labor." As a solution, he supported right-to-work laws that made union membership voluntary and the application of anti-trust laws to some labor organizations. In his view, big business and big labor must both be limited in order to serve the common good.

I don't agree with Keller on everything. That's not the point. I'm bringing him into our discussion because I don't want all of you to think that Catholic social thought is just another form of modern liberalism. I want you to know that alongside Ryan and the liberal tradition, there has also been a more conservative Catholic tradition. I'll say more about it later.

Conservative Group: Fred Speaking

🄾🄿 COMMENT ON EDWARD KELLER

In a more positive vein, Keller advocated moral reform and the "social reconstruction of capitalistic institutions by the establishment of a system of voluntary, self-regulatory bodies in each industry and profession" (Keller 1953, 74). These bodies would include representatives of both employers and employees. They would be formed at various levels (local, company, industrial, and national).

*Conservative
Group:
Fred Speaking*

The functions of these cooperative associations would be limited, however. They would not be concerned with "the fixing of wages, profits and prices; the determination of what products would be produced and what their quality and quantity would be; [or] the determination of the allocation of capital facilities, etc." (Keller 1953, 89 brackets added). They would instead be limited to matters such as "methods of hiring and firing; the improvement of production; the fixing of safety regulations; the determination of job classifications and of incentive systems, seniority rights, retirement plans, [and] the joint administration of welfare programs..." (Keller 1953, 90 brackets added).

Catholic Group: Ayesha Speaking

🅼🅿 POPE JOHN XXIII

Pope Leo XIII, Father Ryan, and Father Keller all focused on economic issues. I want to jump now to someone who placed a major emphasis on human rights: Pope John XXIII (1881-1963). He came from a family of Italian farmers, was ordained a priest in 1904, and elected pope in 1958. Although his time as pope was short, he is regarded as one of the great reformers of the modern

Catholic Church. John called the Second Vatican Council, which changed the liturgy and doctrine of the Church in ways that are still controversial.

He issued eight encyclicals, including *Mater et Magistra* in 1961 and *Pacem in Terris* in 1963. The latter stressed the importance of human rights, both non-interference rights and social or welfare rights.

John's views, and the changes that emerged from Vatican II, were enthusiastically greeted by liberal Catholics and many non-Catholics. *Pacem in Terris* was published in full in *The New York Times* and was well received by many people around the world. Catholic conservatives, on the other hand, feared that Vatican II had gone far beyond changing the church liturgy and had in fact changed basic Catholic doctrines. Some political and economic conservatives in the United States criticized John's encyclicals as bad docrine and bad economics. I love John, but I have to say in all honesty that Fred, my fellow Catholic, interprets his encyclicals in a more conservative way than I do.

Here is a taste of what John said in *Pacem in Terris*.

Pope John XXIII: *Pacem in Terris*

- The pope begins the encyclical by describing man's relationship to God. "God also created man in His own 'image and likeness,' endowed him with intelligence and freedom, and made him lord of creation..." (par. 3).

- He then reiterates the traditional Catholic natural law view of morality. "[T]he Creator of the world has imprinted in man's heart an order which his conscience reveals to him and enjoins him to obey...." This order is written "in the nature of man" (par. 5 and 6 brackets added).

- In John's interpretation of natural law there is a marked emphasis on human rights. All persons have certain rights because they have "intelligence and free will. By virtue of this, he [each person] has rights and duties of his own, flowing directly and simultaneously from his very nature. These rights are therefore universal, inviolable and inalienable" (par. 9 brackets added).

- He went on to identify a list of specific rights, including the right to life, bodily integrity, food, shelter, clothing, rest, medical care, social services, and security in cases of sickness, unemployment, and old age (par. 11).

- He also reaffirmed the right to private property, saying that it "derives from the nature of man." At the same time, he stressed the traditional Catholic view that "there is a social duty inherent in the right of private property" (par. 21-22).

Catholic Group: Ayesha Speaking

🅜🅟 NATURAL LAW

I would like to say a little more about the natural law tradition. I'm no expert, but I think I can clarify some of the basic ideas. Before I do, let me make a couple of comments. First, the natural law tradition has changed and developed over time. Many different writers have made contributions. So what I am giving you here is only one view with which others might disagree. Second, in my view, natural law moral philosophy is not based on any premises that are specifically Catholic. There have been many non-Catholic writers in the natural law tradition.

Natural Moral Law

- The natural moral law is different from both the positive law enacted by the state and the revealed law found in holy scripture. It refers to a moral law that is independent of both those sources. (However, revealed moral law confirms and extends the natural law.)

- The natural law is based on human nature and what can be shown to be good for human beings.

- We can discover the contents of natural moral law through the use of our reason. Discovery does not require a divine revelation. Sometimes the law is said to be written in our hearts.

- The most general principle, as enunciated by the 13th-century theologian Thomas Aquinas, is the obligation to do good and avoid evil. Other moral rules can be derived directly or indirectly from that principle.

- Although the content of natural law is universal, particular circumstances must be considered when it is applied.

- A law passed by a government is invalid if it conflicts with the natural law. Martin Luther King, Jr. in his "Letter from Birmingham Jail" referred to Aquinas with approval and defined an unjust law as a "law that is not rooted in eternal law and natural law" (King 1963).

I want to stress that natural law ethics is based on an idea of the human good or what is good for human beings. That idea is crucial. For Father Ryan, for example, that good included the "harmonious and properly ordered exercise of his faculties" (Ryan 1996, 163).

Also, I want to add that Catholic social thought is not based entirely on the natural law tradition. It is also based on scripture, Church tradition, and modern psychology and social science. I'm stressing natural law at this point because I think you may be less familiar with that element of the overall Catholic view.

Liberal Group: Vera Speaking

🔲🔲 NATURAL LAW

Ayesha, I certainly agree with Martin Luther King when he criticized segregation laws as unjust. But I have problems with the whole natural law tradition. I'm skeptical. Here's what bothers me:

Vera's Criticisms of Natural Moral Law

- If we assume that there is a God and that we know God's purposes, then perhaps we can derive some general rules about how we ought to live. But do we know those things? Most Americans believe in God, but there seems to be a lot of disagreement about what God wants for us. Can such uncertain premises serve as a basis for our morality or our political philosophy? I doubt that they will help with the controversial issues, especially those concerning women, gender, and sexuality.

- If we attempt to develop a non-theistic version of natural law, we will be forced to derive moral principles from human nature and circumstances. But that brings us face to face with the problem raised by the philosopher David Hume — how do we derive 'ought' from 'is'? In other words, how do we get from facts to moral obligations?

- We may be able to study history and discover some general rules of prudence that will guide us in our lives, but those are not moral rules. How do we get from prudence to morality? Morality tells us not simply what is prudent, but what we are obliged to do or not to do (even when it is not in our interest). That's a big leap. I don't see how we can do it.

- Some writers have said that the natural law is written in men's hearts, but what is written in the heart varies a lot from culture to culture. Oliver Wendell Holmes, Jr. once wrote that "The jurists who believe in natural law seem to me to be in that naive state of mind that accepts what has been familiar and accepted by them and their neighbors as something that must be accepted by all men everywhere" (Holmes 1918, 41). Maybe Holmes was right.

I think you may be assuming a set of universally agreed-upon moral notions that does not exist. I question whether that is a solid basis for our political ideas.

*Liberal
Group:
Vera Speaking*

🄾🄿 COMMENT ON NATURAL LAW

I want to add a concrete example of the dangers of natural law thinking. When the popes make natural law arguments, they often assume that they know God's purposes and that they understand human nature. From that they derive moral principles and apply them to specific issues. I personally don't see how that can be done. In my opinion, it is more likely that someone will read his or her personal attitudes into what they call natural law.

I think that in his 1968 encyclical Humanae Vitae, *Pope Paul VI did exactly that. He believed that he knew why God made our bodies the way they are and how we should use them to have children. Here's what the pope wrote:*

"Responsible parenthood also and above all implies a more profound relationship to the objective moral order established by God, of which a right conscience is the faithful interpreter. The responsible exercise of parenthood implies, therefore, that husband and wife recognize fully their own duties towards God, towards themselves, towards the family and towards society, in a correct hierarchy of values.

In the task of transmitting life, therefore, they are not free to proceed completely at will, as if they could determine in a wholly autonomous way the honest path to follow; but they must conform their activity to the creative intention of God, expressed in the very nature of marriage and of its acts, and manifested by the constant teaching of the Church" (Humanae Vitae, par. 10).

*Liberal
Group:
Vera Speaking*

"In fact, as experience bears witness, not every conjugal act is followed by a new life. God has wisely disposed natural laws and rhythms of fecundity which, of themselves, cause a separation in the succession of births. Nonetheless the Church, calling men back to the observance of the norms of the natural law, as interpreted by her constant doctrine, teaches that each and every marriage act (quilibet matrimonii usus) must remain open to the transmission of life" (Humanae Vitae, par. 11).

Basically, the pope said that it is morally wrong (against the natural law) for women to use modern artificial birth control. You can see by looking at this passage that the whole concept of a natural moral law is vague enough that it can be used to support whatever policies one wants to support.

Now let me make a different point. In my opinion, the doctrine in Humanae Vitae *is a prime example of how the Catholic Church has failed to keep up with changing attitudes toward sex, gender, and especially women.*

There are some very fine elements in Catholic social thought, but if the Church doesn't make the change, it is going to lose credibility with more and more people.

I think that what the Catholic Church needs is another John XXIII who can bring the Church into line with current conditions and current thinking about sexuality and women. Can Pope Francis do that? I'll be watching.

🄢🄔 EXCERPT FROM H. L. A. HART
The Concept of Law

The British legal philosopher H. L. A. Hart argued that there was a "core of indisputable truth" in the doctrines of natural law. That core, however, was far less powerful as a moral mandate than Catholic philosophers have claimed. Hart writes as follows:

We have, indeed, insisted that in all moral codes there will be found some form of prohibition of the use of violence, to persons or things, and requirements of truthfulness, fair, dealing, and respect for promises. These things, granted only certain very obvious truisms about human nature and the character of the physical world, can be seen in fact to be essential if human beings are to live continuously together in close proximity; and it therefore would be extraordinary if rules providing for them were not everywhere endowed with the moral importance and status which we have described. It seems clear that the sacrifice of personal interest which such rules *demand* is the price which must be paid in a world such as ours for living with others, and the protection they *afford* is the minimum which, for beings such as ourselves, makes living with others worth while. These simple facts constitute, as we argue in the next chapter, a core of indisputable truth in the doctrines of Natural Law (Hart 1961, 176).

Catholic Group: Ayesha Speaking

🅜🅟 MORE APPLICATIONS

I want to say a little more about how Catholic principles can be applied in the United States. Keep in mind that Catholic principles stress the dignity of the human person, the pursuit of the common good, the condemnation of a completely market-driven labor market, and a preferential option for the poor. The ideas I'm offering here come partly from *Economic Justice for All*, a pastoral letter from the National Conference of Catholic Bishops published in 1986.

Concrete Applications

- Employment should be regarded as a right. Government should adopt policies that promote full employment. This may include creating public service employment jobs or granting subsidies for employing specific groups of people in the private sector. It may also include expanding opportunities for job training.

- Each working person has a right to a living wage earned under safe conditions. Labor is not a commodity with a price to be determined by supply and demand.

- As the wealth of society increases due to the application of better technology, everyone should benefit.

- The basic needs of each individual, including employment, housing, food, and medical care, must be provided for. When private means fail to do so, the state should intervene and guarantee that those needs are met.

- Justice requires a preferential option or consideration for the poor when considering all social policies.

- Public assistance programs should be designed to help people to become self-sufficient through employment.

I think that should give you some idea of how Catholic principles can be applied. They clash with Dee's libertarian views and also with Fred's conservative views. Notice that Catholic principles imply more than non-interference rights. They imply welfare rights as well.

Liberal Group: Vera Speaking

Ⓜ️Ⓟ LIBERATION THEOLOGY

Despite my skepticism about natural law, I want to be clear that there are certain kinds of Catholic social thought that I admire. There seem to be many different varieties, and I am not so sure that they can all be reconciled with each other. It may even be a mistake to refer to "Catholic social thought" as if it were a single unified set of ideas. For me, the most impressive variety is the liberation theology developed in Latin America. I am thinking especially of the work of Father Gustavo Gutiérrez, including his 1971 book *A Theology of Liberation*. Here's my summary of some of his main points. I will quote his own words where I can in order to give you a sense of the passion with which he writes.

Gustavo Gutiérrez : Basic Ideas

- The most important development of our time is the "struggle to construct a just and fraternal society" (Gutiérrez 1973, x).

- The "theological meaning of liberation is, in truth, a question *about the very meaning of Christianity and about the mission of the Church*" (Gutiérrez 1973, xi).

- Theology must be informed not only by abstract reason and philosophy, but by the modern social sciences. This requires an understanding of the dependence of some nations on others and the domination of some classes and nations over others.

- Charity must be recognized as the center of Christian life and become the foundation of the *"praxis"* of the Christian. Theology must be a "criticism of society" linked to "historical praxis" or action (Gutiérrez 1973, 6-7, 11).

- Critical theology must be a "protest against trampled human dignity." It must be engaged in the "struggle against the plunder of the vast majority of people." It will be engaged where "nations, social classes, people struggle to free themselves from domination and oppression by other nations, classes, and people" (Gutiérrez 1973, 15, 13).

This is a Christianity that is committed to improving the lives of the poor and the oppressed. To the extent that the Catholic Church embraces this kind of thinking, I support it 100 percent. But in my opinion, this kind of thinking does not represent the dominant view within the Catholic Church. I wish it did.

5E EXCERPTS FROM GUSTAVO GUTIÉRREZ
"Notes for a Theology of Liberation"

Gustavo Gutiérrez (1928 - present) is a Peruvian Dominican priest who has taught at several universities, including the University of Notre Dame. He writes as follows:

Underdevelopment, as a global social fact, can be seen as the historical subproduct of the development of other countries. The dynamics of capitalistic economics lead simultaneously to the creation of greater wealth for fewer, and of greater poverty for more. Our national oligarchies, teamed up in complicity with these centers of power, perpetuate, for their own benefit and through various subterfuges, a situation of domination within each country. And the inequality between developed and underdeveloped countries is worse if we turn to the cultural point of view. The poor, dominated countries keep getting farther and farther behind. If things go on this way, we will soon be able to speak of two human groups, two kinds of men (Gutiérrez 1970, 249).

The point to remember is this: the scope and importance of the process of liberation are such that to ask its meaning is to ask the meaning of Christianity itself, and the mission of the Church in the world. These are the root questions explicitly or implicitly behind the involvement of Christians in the fight against injustice. Only this approach will allow us to see with new eyes what liberation means in the light of faith (Gutiérrez 1970, 254).

Libertarian Group: Dee Speaking

🅼🅿 A REPLY TO AYESHA

Ayesha, I don't want to be disrespectful of your religion, but you have brought it into the center of a political discussion, so I'm going to criticize your position. I have always thought of the Catholic Church as a pretty conservative institution, but nothing you say sounds very conservative to me.

Dee's Criticisms of Ayesha's Views

• What you are saying sounds like welfare state liberalism with a gloss of religious language. The American bishops seem to be claiming that the biblical view of man and society implies modern liberalism. I am not at all sure that is true. I know lots of Christians, including Catholics, who would disagree. I think Fred is going to say something about that. There is very little solid argument in the bishops' letter. It is a well-written appeal to noble sentiments, but not much more.

- I think your interpretation of Catholic social thought gives too great a role to the state. The bishops say that they are against statist or collectivist institutions and solutions, but that's exactly what they are advocating. It is the state that will have to create jobs, care for the poor, and tax the better-off to do it.

- The bishops talk about achieving justice, but they seem to be thinking almost entirely in terms of results, not historical process. What if outcomes are fair and just because of the historical process that produces them instead of any pattern they display? I think the bishops should read Robert Nozick.

*Conservative
Group:
Fred Speaking*

O P COMMENT ON AYESHA'S VIEWS

The bishops are afraid of blaming the victim; and, as a result, they are unwilling to even suggest that anyone is poor because of bad choices that he or she has made. That may be politically correct in the liberal community, but it is not realistic. At least some people are poor or unemployed because of their own behavior.

The bishops want to ascribe our economic problems to the vices and bad attitudes of the rich and powerful. It is greed that causes our problems. But that is not a serious economic analysis of the situation. A semi-literate adult is not unemployed because the people who run Exxon are greedy. That person is unemployed because he or she can't read. What that person needs is education.

Conservative Group: Fred Speaking

🄜🄿 A REPLY TO AYESHA

I have to jump in here. I'm Catholic too, but I disagree with the way that Ayesha has presented Catholic social thought. Her version is seriously biased toward a leftist interpretation.

Let me make a few points. I am going to rely mostly on the work of the Lay Commission on Catholic Social Teaching and the U.S. Economy. The Commission issued a report on the final draft of the bishops' pastoral letter *Economic Justice for All* that Ayesha mentioned. Their report was respectful but critical.

Fred's Criticisms of Ayesha's Views

- The bishops seem to endorse a *"preferential option for the state."* They look to the state for solutions "more often and more quickly than is likely to help." The Lay Commission believes that the proper role of the state is to make sure that economic activity is "open, free, legally accessible to all, easy to enter, broadly supported in law." That will allow the poor to prosper through their own creativity and enterprise. The bishops seem not to understand this and look to the state for more direct welfare programs that are likely to be less effective (Lay Commission 1986, Section 2, item 2).

- The bishops do not properly understand the view of human rights found in Pope John's encyclical *Pacem in Terris*. They treat it as though it advocates a set of unqualified welfare rights including the right to a job, the right to a family wage, the right to medical care, and so on (National

Conference of Catholic Bishops 1986, par. 80). The Lay Commission disagrees. In its view, Pope John believed that it is individuals who are primarily responsible for providing those things for themselves. The state or the community is only obliged to step in when the individual is unable to provide for himself or herself through no fault of their own (Lay Commission 1986, Section 2, item 4).

- The bishops seem to think that inequalities in the United States are extreme and that opportunities are very limited. I question that. I think that our system has fostered a great deal of upward mobility. Many people have come here and done well. Immigrants from India are a recent example. In other words, the system provides opportunity as it is. It works.

- The bishops don't really understand poverty. They fail to see that much of the poverty in the United States is caused by changes in family structure. "No other cause of poverty ranks as high as family breakdown" (Lay Commission 1986, Section 2, item 8(d)). Single mothers are likely to be poor. Their problem isn't due to corporate greed. It's due to their family situation. Another group is poor because of its low level of education. Again, this has nothing to do with anyone's greed.

- The bishops do not seem to understand the importance of a free economy for reducing poverty. They are committed to government programs, but the real solution is strong families plus freedom and creativity on the part of individuals.

I want to refer you to Michael Novak's work and to the report of the Lay Commission. Novak wrote lots of articles that are available on the Internet. If nothing else, his work reminds us again that there is more than one interpretation of Catholic social thought. Along with the liberals, there are respectable conservatives who claim the name Catholic.

Catholic Group: Ayesha Speaking

🅜🅟 A REPLY TO FRED

I think that Novak and the Lay Commission are missing the essence of the modern Catholic tradition. Instead, they are trying to assimilate Catholic social thought into the mainstream of American conservatism. Now, some of that can be done. The Church has made its peace with democratic government and the standard classical liberal freedoms like freedom of religion, freedom of speech, and the separation of church and state. But the merger of the two traditions, Catholic and conservative, is not complete.

The Church simply will not allow that human labor is a commodity or that the goods of this world are justly distributed by a free market. The operations of the labor market must be judged within a moral framework. Finally, the Church does not accept the notion that human rights are limited to the non-interference rights that American conservatives support.

Ayesha's Reply to Fred

- In the Catholic view, each human being has dignity or value because he or she was created in the image of God. In a more secular version of this claim, each person has dignity because he or she has intelligence and free will.

- To maintain that dignity, people require certain conditions. Those conditions can be thought of as rights.

- The common good can be defined as the sum total of conditions required to preserve human dignity.

- The implication is that non-interference rights are not sufficient. To maintain human dignity, people also need the opportunity to work and learn plus rights to food, to shelter, and to medical care.

- The role of government is to promote the common good, and that necessarily means protecting human rights as the conditions required to achieve that good.

When Novak criticizes the bishops' pastoral letter, he relies partly on his interpretation of Pope John's *Pacem in Terris*. He claims that the welfare rights that Pope John supports only apply to those cases in which a person is deprived "through no fault of his own." But although John does use that phrase, the rights he advocates are not limited to that case. His view is much more general. He tells us that "every man has the right to life, to bodily integrity, and to the means which are necessary and suitable for the proper development of life" (par. 11). He includes all the rights that I have mentioned and more.

Even if we did interpret Pope John as Novak does, there would still be a great many people with a right to assistance. At the very least, I think that children, the elderly, and those who are physically or mentally too ill to work would qualify. We should also add those who are making a serious effort to find work and cannot do so plus those discriminated against because of race or sex. Certainly, in all these cases, the popes are claiming that those individuals have a right to assistance provided by their fellow citizens.

Libertarian Group: Dee Speaking

O P COMMENT ON AYESHA'S VIEW

Fred and I agree that Ayesha is going way too far here. She is not making the right distinctions.

Of course, it would be a wonderful world if everyone had a good job, a solid education, an old-age pension, and the latest medical care. We all agree to that, but that's not the issue. We are talking about rights, not what is good or ideal. Professor Sidgwick helped clarify that distinction.

Ayesha has to make a distinction between what people would have in an ideal world and what people have a right to.

As she presents it, Catholic social thought seems to derive a whole set of welfare rights from basic human needs. The need for a job generates a right to a job. The need for medical care generates a right to medical care. The need for housing generates a right to housing, and so on. Libertarians have criticized that view again and again. First of all, there is no limit to the rights that can be generated that way. That by itself suggests that there is something wrong with the argument. More importantly, how can one person's need give them a right to the product of another person's labor? The argument assumes that everyone has a claim on the talents, energy, work, and income of others. That's totally incompatible with self-ownership, which I believe is the most obvious basis for individual rights.

Liberal Group: Vera Speaking

🅜🅟 DIFFERENT VIEWS

Hold on. Can't you guys see what's happening here? Everyone is looking at Catholic social thought and finding what they want to find. Ayesha finds 20th-century liberalism. Fred finds 20th-century conservatism. As for me, I focus on Latin American liberation theology.

I have already said that philosophers who are contractarians seem to find what they want in a hypothetical social contract. The Catholic Church is a big place with lots of popes, bishops, and intellectuals. You can find what you want there too. It's like reading the Bible. The Catholic bishops read the Bible and find welfare rights. Michael Novak reads the Bible and finds free enterprise.

All this is very, very human. We all do it. I do it myself. I'm only suggesting that we should be aware of it when we do. In the case of Catholicism, it may be impossible to determine the one true interpretation of Catholic social thought.

Catholic Group: Ayesha Speaking

🅜🅟 DAVID HOLLENBACH, S.J.

Pope John emphasized human rights in his encyclical *Pacem in Terris*. I want to tell you about one recent Catholic philosopher who has made the concept of human rights central to his work. The man I have in mind is Father David Hollenbach, a Jesuit priest who has written extensively about human rights.

Hollenbach (1942-present) was born in Philadelphia, Pennsylvania and attended St. Joseph's University and Yale University. He has taught at Boston College, Georgetown, and other schools. He published *Claims in Conflict: Retrieving and Renewing the Catholic Human Rights Tradition* in 1979 and *The Common Good and Christian Ethics* in 2002. He also helped draft the bishops' letter on economic justice that I have already mentioned.

David Hollenbach, S. J.: Basic Ideas

- The liberal and socialist traditions stress two different types of human rights: political and civil rights on the one hand and social and economic rights on the other. We need a moral framework that can justify both types of rights.

- The Roman Catholic tradition offers the necessary framework. It founds both types of rights on the concept of human dignity or worth. Rights are the conditions necessary for human dignity to be protected and fostered. The most complete list of these rights can be found in Pope John XXIII's encyclical *Pacem in Terris*.

- The Catholic theory of rights encompasses the whole human being in his or her bodily, economic, social, religious, political, and associative aspects.

- Writing after the Second Vatican Council, Hollenbach described the Catholic view of human rights as moving away from a natural law view that emphasized universal reason and toward a view that recognizes religious and cultural pluralism. In this newer approach, there is a stress on human beings as made in the image of God, on dialogue, and on the centrality of love and human solidarity (Hollenbach 1979, 131-133).

- The most pressing need at that time was for an emphasis on "social rights" such as the right to food, clothing, shelter, medical care, political participation, and more.

- The following three "priority principles" should be adopted:
    - "The needs of the poor take priority over the wants of the rich."
    - "The freedom of the dominated takes priority over the liberty of the powerful."
    - "The participation of marginalized groups takes priority over the preservation of an order which excludes them" (Hollenbach 1979, 203-204).

Liberal Group: Vera Speaking

🅜🅟 **POPE FRANCIS**

I want to say something here in praise of one of the most recent developments in Catholic social thought.

Looking back over the last 125 years, we could say that Pope Leo XIII addressed the problems of labor in the 1890s, Pope Pius XI addressed the problems of reconstructing economic institutions in the 1930s, and Pope John XXIII elaborated the Catholic view of human rights in the 1960s. Today, Pope Francis is venturing into new territory. In his 2015 encyclical *Ladauto Si' (On Care for Our Common Home)* he has addressed the most serious ecological and environmental issues of our time. He has made it clear that these problems are not only scientific and economic but also moral.

I'm not a Catholic, and I have problems with some Catholic views. You all know that. But I want to support Ayesha on this. I think her church has taken a strong position — it may prove to be a leadership position — on the current ecological threats to human life and well-being. I want the Catholic Church to go further, but I also want to praise it for what it has done so far.

🄂🄴 EXCERPTS FROM POPE FRANCIS
Laudato Si'

Pope Francis published his encyclical Laudato Si' *in 2015. In it he addressed current environmental and ecological issues. He writes as follows:*

The climate is a common good, belonging to all and meant for all (par. 23).

Whether believers or not, we are agreed today that the earth is essentially a shared inheritance, whose fruits are meant to benefit everyone. For believers, this becomes a question of fidelity to the Creator, since God created the world for everyone. Hence every ecological approach needs to incorporate a social perspective which takes into account the fundamental rights of the poor and the underprivileged. The principle of the subordination of private property to the universal destination of goods, and thus the right of everyone to their use, is a golden rule of social conduct and 'the first principle of the whole ethical and social order' (par. 93).

Climate change is a global problem with grave implications: environmental, social, economic, political and for the distribution of goods. It represents one of the principal challenges facing humanity in our day. Its worst impact will probably be felt by developing countries in coming decades. Many of the poor live in areas particularly affected by phenomena related to warming, and their means of subsistence are largely dependent on natural reserves and ecosystemic services such as agriculture, fishing and forestry. They have no other financial activities or resources which can enable them to adapt to climate change or to face natural disasters, and their access to social services and protection is very limited (par. 25).

The problem is that we still lack the culture needed to confront this crisis. We lack leadership capable of striking out on new paths and meeting the needs of the present with concern for all and without prejudice towards coming generations. The establishment of a legal framework which can set clear boundaries and ensure the protection of ecosystems has become indispensable; otherwise, the new power structures based on the techno-economic paradigm may overwhelm not only our politics but also freedom and justice (par. 53).

Enforceable international agreements are urgently needed, since local authorities are not always capable of effective intervention (par. 173).

*Liberal
Group:
Vera Speaking*

🅞🅟 **COMMENT ON BIRTH CONTROL**

The pope's encyclical has brought the Catholic Church into an alliance with people working to stop the pollution and warming of our planet. Still, I have to say that I do not think he has done enough to address the problems of sex and gender. For example, he does not address birth control, and there is no way that we can deal effectively with the problems he raises if we do not confront that issue. The rapid increase in population has contributed enormously to pollution, poverty, and stress on the environment. The only way to slow that down is to use modern birth control. The bottom line is that women must have control over their reproductive capacity.

Conservative Group: Fred Speaking

🅼🅿 A CONSERVATIVE VIEW

I am not saying that there is no climate change, and I agree that we need to talk about possible scenarios and solutions. But I will also tell you my chief concern right up front: I am worried that liberals and radicals here in the United States will use the need to solve environmental problems as an excuse to create a whole new layer of government control over our economy, and they are grabbing on to Pope Francis to build support for their agenda.

I look to the pope, and to my church, for spiritual guidance, not economic policy. Having said that, let me make a few comments on *Laudato Si'*.

A Conservative View of *Laudato Si'*

- First of all, I agree with Pope Francis that we need self-restraint, humility, and a return to values that embrace more than material things. I also agree that we should not view nature as simply a thing to be dominated and exploited to satisfy our every desire.

- Nevertheless, I think that the pope is venturing into areas where he has no expertise and no authority. He should limit himself to spiritual and moral guidance, leaving controversial scientific and economic issues to others.

- We need balanced economic growth to reduce poverty and achieve the integrated development that Pope Francis desires. That will involve difficult tradeoffs that his encyclical does not address.

- At times in this encyclical the pope appears to equate markets and capitalism with selfishness, greed, and exploitation; but that is a biased view. The reality is that nothing has done more to reduce poverty than free-market capitalism.

- At one point, Francis quotes Pope Benedict XVI and tells us that we need a "true world political authority" that will be able to "manage the global economy." I am here to tell you, as an American conservative, that that is scary talk. I think that it is a very dangerous road to go down, and I do not think that the Catholic Church should be promoting the idea (Francis 2015, par. 175). What happened to the principle of subsidiarity?

Catholic Group: Ayesha Speaking

🅜🅟 A MORE RADICAL VIEW

Fred, I hate to tell you this, but there are Catholic thinkers today who go way beyond what Pope Francis said in *Laudato Si'*. One of those thinkers is philosopher Theodore Nunez. His book, *Sustainable Abundance for All: Catholic Social Thought and Action in a Risky, Runaway World* (2018), is an attempt to radically reimagine the world in which we live.

Nunez believes that we are faced with two serious problems that he and others call the "Great Acceleration" and the rise of a "world risk society." The Great Acceleration is what Pope Francis called "rapidification." It consists of the "relentless process of social speed-up driven by technological innovation for the sake of profit." The world risk society is one in which "technological and environmental mega-hazards call into question taken-for-granted conceptions of progress" (Nunez 2018, Kindle locations 208, 171, 209).

Ted Nunez : Problems and Solutions

"The social question addressed by Pope Leo XIII in *Rerum Novarum* (1891) has morphed into a more complex eco-social question...." The question has now become "What constitutes the good life, and how can persons and communities sustain hope for and move responsibly and creatively toward human and planetary flourishing in a risky, runaway world?" (Nunez 2018, Kindle locations 255-256).

Nunez identifies three approaches to the problems of acceleration and risk. First, the neoliberal approach that emphasizes expanded markets and limited governmental intervention. Second, the ecological modernizing approach that emphasizes high environmental standards and clean technologies. And finally, the green communitarian approach that emphasizes "egalitarian visions of 'just sustainability' based on a decentralized, pluralist approach to governance and a local/bio-regional model of cooperative economy" (Nunez 2018, Kindle location 747).

In his view, sustainable abundance is possible, but we can achieve it "only by renouncing the dangerous dogma of economic growth and constructing dynamic, steady-state economies within bounded communities" (Nunez 2018, Kindle location 277).

Nunez is thinking not only of the scientific, technical, and economic problems involved in the Great Acceleration and current mega-risks, he is also urging us to redefine our understanding of the good life — changing our focus from wealth and consumption to what really matters. He advocates two major institutional changes. These are focused on the problems that may result from accelerated automation and the loss of more and more well-paying jobs:

- Establishing a basic income guarantee (BIG). A BIG would guarantee every citizen of a certain age a minimum annual income. Everyone eligible for the BIG would receive that income with no strings attached.
- Establishing a 30-hour work week.

Nunez believes that the combination of accelerated automation, a guaranteed income, and a 30-hour work week could lead us to a "post-jobs" society — a society in which people refuse to make "holding a full-time job the central focus of individual identity and social life" (Nunez 2018, Kindle locations 3594, 3977). The hope is that this new society would open up possibilities for human flourishing that have never before existed.

🄢🄔 EXCERPTS FROM TED NUNEZ
Sustainable Abundance for All

Ted Nunez teaches ethics and Catholic social thought at Villanova University. His work embraces traditional Catholic thought but extends it to deal with current social and ecological problems. He writes as follows:

To date, modern Catholic social teaching since Pope Leo XIII has dealt with the imbalance of power between capital and labor by emphasizing the duty of employers to pay workers a living wage as a way of satisfying the basic needs of worker households, recognizing labor's contribution to wealth creation, and offering frugal workers the opportunity to save and invest in wealth-generating resources (e.g., a parcel of land, a house, stock holdings). In the context of an industrial society characterized by Fordist production, the church also upheld the right of workers to organize unions and collectively bargain for a just share of socially-produced wealth. However, from the early 1970s onward, the context for evaluating questions of economic justice and power has been changing: owners and managers of capital have responded to rising costs and declining profits with a neoliberal strategy that flexibilizes and atomizes the labor process, erodes welfare-state protections, reduces or eliminates company benefits, automates and/or outsources jobs aggressively, and thus shifts the *risks* associated with unemployment, poverty, and debt onto workers. As noted earlier, both the (self-identifying) middle class and working poor have registered these changes in high levels of stress and economic insecurity. In recent decades, the "precariat"... [workers relegated to temporary or part-time roles] has grown, while safety-net programs designed for a twentieth-century economy have not been modernized. Given this new reality, the time has come for the church to rethink its emphasis on a living wage and union formation as the primary policy tools for empowering workers. Today, the wider distribution of wealth and economic opportunity called for in Catholic social teaching can be achieved more effectively through additional policies, namely a basic income and thirty-hour work week (Nunez 2018, Kindle location 3927 brackets added).

Liberal Group: Vera Speaking

🅞🅟 COMMENT ON NUNEZ

I agree with a lot of what Nunez says. I agree that we are facing huge risks including massive unemployment due to automation. I also think that we need major institutional change to stop global warming as soon as possible. That's why I support the Green New Deal proposed by Congresswoman Alexandria Ocasio-Cortez. Hopefully, it will create lots of new jobs in clean-energy industries.

Conservative Group: Fred Speaking

🅞🅟 COMMENT ON NUNEZ

As a Catholic and an American conservative, I disagree with Ayesha and Nunez. I also disagree with Vera's Green New Deal.

- *The program Nunez describes is Utopian. Much of it is rhetorical, and the more concrete parts are very unlikely to be enacted into law.*

- *To carry out Nunez's program the government would have to massively regulate the whole economy.*

- *Nunez doesn't even mention American principles of limited government and constitutionality.*

- *As far as the Green New Deal goes, the costs would be astronomical, and the unintended consequences could be disastrous.*

Catholic Group: Ayesha Speaking

🅜🅟 FINAL STATEMENT

Instead of a final statement of my own, I want to show you a simplified version of a diagram that Father Hollenbach has used to illustrate the Catholic view of human rights. The diagram places human dignity at the center and surrounds it with the various kinds of human rights that support it (Hollenbach 1979, 98).

Rights to communication, free expression, education, and to be informed truthfully	*Rights to life, bodily integrity, food, medical care, and security in sickness and old age*	*Rights to self-determination and legal protection of political participation and due process*
Rights to religious belief, expression of belief, and religious freedom	*Human Dignity*	*Rights to free movement, nationality, residence, and migration*
Rights to choose a state in life, to found a family, and to have the conditions needed for family life.	*Rights to work, proper working conditions, a just wage, union organization, and private property*	*Rights to social intercourse, assembly, association, and to form societies*

Human dignity itself is founded on the creation of human beings in the image of God. I believe that if we unpack that concept, we will have a political and social philosophy that we can all be proud of.

*Liberal
Group:
John Speaking*

🅞🅟 COMMENT ON RIGHTS

Although Ayesha is coming at the subject of human rights from a Catholic perspective, I think that what she is saying has a lot in common with what some secular philosophers have said. Her diagram raises basic questions for all of us.

Lots of philosophers have attempted to ground human rights in some feature or capacity of human beings. That feature occupies the position that human dignity has for Catholics. It might be happiness, personhood, liberty, autonomy, intrinsic value, or something else. Ayesha's diagram might help all of us to organize our thinking about rights. I'd like to see all of us take it home to think about.

John's 'Homework' Assignment

- *How would each of us fill in Ayesha's diagram based on our own view of human rights? Can each of us fit our view into a diagram like this? If not, why not?*

- *What would you put in the box at the center of the diagram? Why is that feature so important? Why is it worthy of the protection afforded by human rights and, perhaps, legal rights?*

- *How would you fill in the remaining boxes? How would your entries differ from Ayesha's and why?*

Liberal Group: Vera Speaking

🅼🅿 AN EVALUATION

Professor Sidgwick has asked me to provide an overall evaluation of Catholic social thought. I'm not a Catholic, but I'll try.

Vera's Evaluation of Catholic Social Thought

- The Catholic view stresses the notion that all social life, including economic life, exists within a moral framework. The Catholic framework tells us, for example, that it is morally wrong to regard human labor as a commodity with a price determined by a free market. We all need to think about what the proper framework should be like. From a libertarian point of view, a system of free exchange, devoid of force and fraud, is sufficient. For many others, protection from force and fraud is not enough. So the Catholic view leads us to the recurring questions: What sort of moral framework is best for social and economic life? How is that framework to be developed and enforced? Those are perennial questions that all of us need to answer.

- Like libertarianism, the Catholic view avoids some of the problems of utilitarianism because it does not allow the well-being of one person to be traded off for the well-being of others. It doesn't try to maximize an aggregate. Since each person is made in the image of God, each person is sacred. Each person has infinite value.

- John has already pointed out that the Catholic view, like some secular views, identifies a single human feature or capacity (human dignity) and builds its theory of rights around that feature as a core value. I think that is a model we can all follow. For Catholics, people have dignity because they are made in the image of God. Secular thinkers will have to justify their core value in a way that does not depend on theology. For example, John told us a little about Lawrence Haworth, who has argued that we should place autonomy at the center of our thinking about rights. I hope we all work through John's homework assignment and try to fill in Ayesha's chart with our own ideas.

- I am glad that the popes have wholeheartedly adopted the language of human rights and in recent years have consistently promoted the protection of rights. Pope John XXIII was a great example. I can accept Pope John's list of basic rights, but I know that many others feel that it is dangerously long. As a result, I think that liberal Catholics need to provide clearer foundations for the welfare rights they advocate.

- I said before that I was very much in favor of some of the ideas that make up Catholic liberation theology, but I think the Church has pulled back from those ideas. In my opinion, Catholic leaders need to reassert the Church's commitment to the poor throughout the world.

- In my view, Catholic thought has not kept pace with changes in our ideas about sex, gender, and women in particular. For me, that is extremely important because it makes it more difficult to address the problems that women face all over the world. Pope Francis has taken some steps in the right direction. For example, he seems to approve of civil unions for gay couples. On the other hand, he has said that the Church cannot bless same-sex marriages. He seems to be walking a very fine line between liberals and conservatives inside the Church. I hope he takes more steps in a liberal direction, including perhaps a married priesthood, women as priests, and the use of modern birth control. In my opinion, if the Church doesn't change, it will become less and less relevant to contemporary problems.

- I get the impression that the natural law perspective is not as important in Catholic thought today as it once was. Does the Church still claim that human reason alone (without a scriptural or theological basis) can discern a natural moral law? If so, I don't see much support for that claim in what Ayesha has said. But for the Church to be most effective, it needs to find a way to speak to those who are not theists.

- In the end I have two questions: What is the basis for the Catholic view of natural moral law, and what can the Church do to adapt to modern views on gender and sexuality?

Well, that's it. I've done the best I can to give a fair hearing to Catholic social thought.

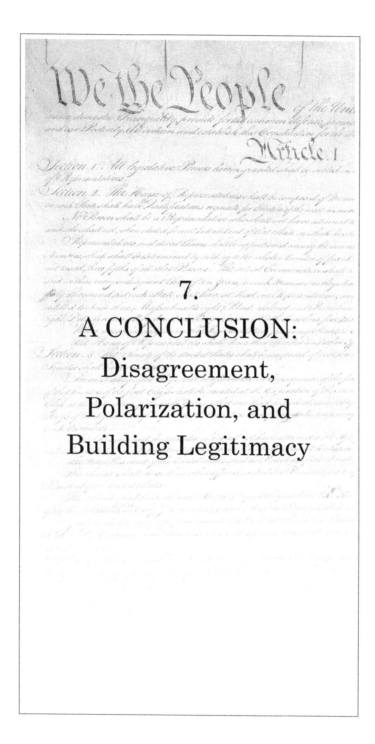

7.

A CONCLUSION:
Disagreement, Polarization, and Building Legitimacy

Professor Sidgwick Speaking

🄜🄟 DISAGREEMENT

It's time to bring this discussion to a conclusion. Our purpose today was to get a clearer view of the basic political ideas that form the frameworks around American political activity. You all attempted to lay out the key concepts and principles in each of your philosophies. You talked about lots of ideas, including non-interference rights, welfare rights, the role of religious ideas in politics, the ethical foundations for your views, the nature of property rights, the idea of legitimate government, and more. In this part of our discussion, I want us to focus on that last idea, the idea of legitimate government, because I think we, as a country, may be approaching a crisis in that area.

But first, let's look back on the discussion we had today. You disagreed on many issues, and I would love to be able to give you the final answers to your questions. I would like to be able to give you the Truth with a capital 'T,' but I can't.

The complexity of American society, with its many different groups of people with different occupations, different functions, different religious traditions, different levels of wealth, different ethnic and racial backgrounds, and different economic interests will always generate different opinions, ideals, and values. Rawls would say that wherever there is freedom, there will always be fundamental differences in ideas — different "comprehensive doctrines" and different understandings of a life that is good for human beings. That is not an argument for or against any particular political philosophy. It's just a fact, and we have to live with it.

I have asked Ayesha to give us a short summary of your views, just to review some of the different political ideas that are widespread in our country.

*Liberal
Group:
Ann Speaking*

🅞🅟 COMMENT ON DISAGREEMENT

In addition to the differences in income, wealth, occupation, race, religion, and ethnicity, there are what Rawls called the "burdens of judgment" that must be dealt with by even the most reasonable people. Those burdens include conflicting evidence, vague concepts, differences in total life experience, and conflicting values attached to different alternatives (Rawls 2001, 35). For all these reasons, he believed that there will always be competing views of the world that are the natural result of the use of human reason.

Catholic Group: Ayesha Speaking

🅜🅟 SHORT SUMMARIES

I'll try. We heard four presentations on different political philosophies. They included American conservatism (two varieties), modern liberalism, libertarianism (both left and right), and Catholic social thought. I think everybody did a great job. Here are my way-too-short summaries of what you said.

A Short Summary of Views

- Fred and Diego presented different versions of American conservatism. Fred stressed the importance of constitutionally limited government, federalism, individual rights (including property rights), free markets, traditional values, and well-established institutions. Diego, as an evangelical Christian, put emphasis on the importance of strong families and resistance to moral decline.

- John, Ann, and Vera presented modern social liberalism. They differed on some points, but they agreed that government policy ought to be designed to create a society in which every person has the basic resources required to develop his or her capacities and has a fair chance to live a good life as they understand it. They advocate a strong state that regulates economic markets, guarantees some resources to all, remedies historical injustice, and attempts to deal with current social and environmental problems.

- Dee and Elijah presented two different forms of libertarianism. They agreed on the importance of self-ownership, strong individual rights, and minimal government. They disagreed on questions concerning the original acquisition of property in natural resources. That might seem like an academic dispute, but it has important implications. For Dee, government should be minimal and welfare rights should be extremely limited if they exist at all. Elijah believes that owners of natural resources owe compensation to non-owners. Compensation could take many forms, including welfare rights.

- I presented Catholic social thought. I tried to stress the idea that human beings have value or dignity because they were created in the image of God. That dignity is the foundation of human rights, both non-interference rights and welfare rights. I think it is fair to say that I presented a liberal interpretation of Catholic thought. Fred, who is also a Catholic, disagreed, and presented a more conservative interpretation of Catholic thinking. One of these days I'm going to convince Fred that he's wrong.

*Catholic
Group:
Ayesha Speaking*

🄾🄿 COMMENT ON SUMMARIES

We also heard four evaluations of the four frameworks, and there were several questions raised in those evaluations.

I evaluated American conservatism and I asked whether the constitutionally limited government that conservatives advocate can deal with the large-scale problems like pollution, pandemics, and global warming that we confront today. I also wanted to know more about how conservatives can provide a basis for the natural rights they support.

Elijah evaluated modern social liberalism and he asked what principle liberals could offer that places limits on the scope and power of our federal government.

John evaluated libertarianism and he wanted to know more about the basis for the libertarian principle of self-ownership and the very strong property rights advocated by right-libertarians.

Vera evaluated Catholic social thought and she asked to know more about the basis for the Catholic view of natural moral law. She also asked what the Catholic Church can do to adapt to modern views on gender and sexuality.

I know we can't answer those questions today, but they give us something to think about for the future.

Professor Sidgwick Speaking

🅜🅟 DISAGREEMENT

Thank you, Ayesha. I have already suggested why I think that the broad philosophical differences that came out in today's discussion are likely to persist. The most obvious divide among you is between the social liberals who believe in a very active federal government that will aggressively attack problems and the conservatives and libertarians who want a more limited federal government. Another divide is between those of you who want our politics to be conducted in purely secular terms and those who want to bring in religious concepts and arguments.

Unfortunately, those are not the only disagreements we have to confront in our politics. There are others that we did not even mention today. Consider the following questions:

- What type of cultural change is desirable? For example, how are we to define gender? What is the proper role of women in society? How much immigration and what categories of immigrants should be welcomed into our nation? To what extent should we provide asylum for people from other countries?

- What laws and policies should we have concerning intensely emotional moral issues such as abortion and gay marriage?

- What restitution, if any, should be made for past injustices? For example, what should be done today because of slavery, Jim Crow, Indian removal, and the long history of unfair discrimination against women?

- Finally, there are questions that arise out of the tension between those who have benefitted from the economic and technical development of the last 40 years and those who have not. This often comes down to those who have reaped the benefits of globalization and higher education and those who haven't. This conflict has led to many disagreements, especially over foreign trade policy.

There is disagreement over all these questions, and it threatens to increase our political polarization and reduce our common ground of shared political values and principles. If Rawls is correct, we need that common ground as a basis for legitimate government.

In my opinion, Rawls is right; and the problem is getting worse. We may be approaching a crisis — one that is very well symbolized by the need to bring a large number of troops to Washington, D.C. to maintain peace on the day of Joe Biden's presidential inauguration. It is for that reason that I want us to focus now on the loss of common ground and the resulting threat to legitimacy.

For this discussion, I want us to assume that something similar to Rawls's principle of legitimacy is the best principle for a diverse modern democracy to embrace. If that is true, and if we are slowly losing the common ground that binds us together, what can we do to stop the loss and rebuild legitimacy? That is our main question.

It may help to recall some of Michael Perry's ideas, so I have asked John to remind us of Perry's thoughts on political dialogue. I want you to ask yourselves whether Perry's ideas can help us expand our common ground of political values and principles.

*Conservative
Group:
Diego Speaking*

🔲🔲 COMMENT ON DISAGREEMENT

I agree that Americans have all sorts of disagreements. There is the big versus small government issue and all the others that Professor Sidgwick mentioned, but there is also some important common ground. We shouldn't forget that.

All of us believe in democratic government, free speech, equality before the law, freedom of belief and movement, and some other political values. At a deeper level, all of us agree that the individual human being has intrinsic value and should be accorded certain rights. The problem is that our common ground is probably insufficient to give us a detailed understanding of those rights, and it will not resolve some of our most controversial political issues such as those concerning welfare rights, gay marriage, or the right to an abortion.

*Professor
Sidgwick
Speaking*

🔲🔲 COMMENT ON LEGITIMACY

I want to remind you of a couple of things. First of all, the nature of legitimacy. The crucial point is that a legitimate government is justified in using coercion to enforce its laws and policies. Citizens, on the other hand, normally have a moral obligation to abide by the laws and policies of a legitimate government.

Second, there are many different principles of legitimacy that have been accepted historically. In a monarchy, for example, a dynasty may be considered legitimate because of an alleged ancient compact with the people. A king may be considered legitimate because he is the son of the previous king. In a theocracy, a ruler may be considered legitimate because he is believed to have a special relationship with God.

Rawls proposed what he called the liberal principle of legitimacy. He said that "political power is legitimate when it is exercised in accordance with a constitution ... the essentials of which all citizens, as reasonable and rational, can endorse in the light of their common human reason." He added that "In matters of constitutional essentials, as well as on questions of basic justice, we try to appeal only to principles and values each citizen can endorse" (Rawls 2001, 41).

If we hope to apply this principle in the United States, we must find common values and principles that "each citizen can endorse." Otherwise we lose the conditions required for legitimate government and, in time, faith in the legitimacy of that government.

Liberal Group: John Speaking

🅜🅟 ECUMENICAL DIALOGUE

I'm glad to bring Perry in again. He writes about "ecumenical dialogue," "ecumenical tolerance," and "ecumenical politics." I think his ideas may help us extend our common ground, but I'm not sure by how much.

Michael Perry's Concept of Ecumenical Dialogue

In Perry's view, Americans already agree on certain constitutional essentials. They also agree on certain "general moral premises" that are often derived from their religious traditions. This agreement can help form the basis of a political community, but Americans also disagree on the "particular interpretations" of those premises (Perry 1991, 96). Perry believes that we can bring these different interpretations into a new ecumenical politics characterized by ecumenical dialogue and ecumenical tolerance. The requirements of such a dialogue include being well informed, respectful, empathic, honest, and sincere. In addition, it is crucial for the people involved to accept what he calls "fallibilism" and "pluralism." To accept fallibilism is to be willing to be self-critical. To accept pluralism is to believe that a society with many different moral points of view may lead to "deepening moral insight" (Perry 1991, 100). In practice, some of the views expressed in ecumenical dialogue will use religious symbols and language. Perry believes that these religious elements are entirely appropriate if they are used in a way that is publicly intelligible, non-sectarian, and non-authoritarian. In his 2020 presidential campaign, Joe Biden, who is a Catholic, suggested that we should be "guided by the words of Pope John Paul II, words drawn from the scripture, 'Be not afraid.'" I think that may be an example of the sort of religious language that Perry would approve.

The overall thrust of Perry's approach is to open up political dialogue to many points of view, both religious and secular, that offer different visions of the good for human beings.

Liberal Group: Ann Speaking

m P **PERRY'S DIALOGUE**

I think the kind of dialogue Perry is advocating would make our political debates better informed, more tolerant, more civil, and more respectful. Like John said, it would also open them up to some religious ideas and to different ideas about what is good for human beings.

All of that is good, but how much would it expand our shared political values and principles? I'm not sure.

Civility and the rest are welcome improvements, but they are not the same as agreement.

Catholic Group: Ayesha Speaking

m P **PERRY'S DIALOGUE**

I think that in one way Perry's ecumenical dialogue might help. Learning more about each other and being willing to admit when we are mistaken can eliminate some misunderstandings that we have about each other.

For example, in an honest dialogue, people who are concerned about the number of illegal immigrants in this country might come to understand that Democrats do not really advocate open borders. On the other hand, those who are more liberal on immigration might come to understand that many conservatives really do sympathize with Latinos who were brought here illegally as small children. In other words, there are times when good information can expand common ground by showing people that some of the differences they are concerned about do not really exist.

Conservative Group: Diego Speaking

🅜🅟 PERRY'S DIALOGUE

I think that ecumenical dialogue can help. As a Christian, I certainly like the idea of opening up political dialogue to more religious ideas, but I think its potential for expanding our common ground is limited. It can work to an extent if everyone wants it to work, but some of our differences run pretty deep.

I'm really sorry to say that, but I have to agree with Ann. Civility and respect may lower the temperature of our debates, but they do not usually eliminate basic disagreements.

That reminds me of what I said about Rawls a while ago. Rawls wanted an overlapping consensus on political values and principles that was more than a "modus vivendi" based on self-interest (Rawls 1996, 147). I think that kind of consensus is the ideal, and it is possible in some cases; but in other cases an agreement on goals and procedures based on similar interests may be all that we can reach. I don't think we should devalue that agreement. It may be helpful in building legitimacy.

*Libertarian
Group:
Elijah Speaking*

🄾🄿 COMMENT ON DIALOGUE

I think it is pretty obvious that as of today we do not have this sort of dialogue and this sort of politics, but maybe we can work toward it. Maybe we have begun working toward it here in our own group.

I know it would be foolish to think that Americans will end up agreeing on all the important issues. But perhaps another of Perry's insights can be of value to us. In Perry's view, the goal of dialogue is not always agreement. Sometimes, the goal is community, and community may be possible in spite of disagreement.

Professor Sidgwick Speaking

🄼🄿 DELIBERATIVE DEMOCRACY

You all want dialogue to expand our common ground, but you think it may be rather limited in what it can do. I can see that. Let me bring in two more authors who may be able to help.

Amy Gutmann and Dennis Thompson, in their book *Democracy and Disagreement*, ask this question: How should a democracy deal with fundamental moral disagreements? Their answer consists in what they call "deliberative democracy" and "deliberative disagreement."

I have asked Elijah to give us a short summary of their view of deliberative democracy. As with Perry, I'm asking you to consider their proposals and whether they can help us to expand our common ground of political values and principles.

Libertarian Group: Elijah Speaking

🅜🅟 DELIBERATIVE DEMOCRACY

I'll try. The main idea is that deliberative democracy would be structured to "promote extensive moral argument about the merits of public policies in public forums, with the aim of reaching provisional moral agreement and maintaining mutual respect among citizens" (Gutmann and Thompson 1996, 12). Here are the main ideas:

Gutmann and Thompson: Deliberative Democracy

- Moral disagreement is inevitable. Deliberation must recognize, discuss, and manage moral disputes.
- There are three principles that should guide the process of deliberation:
  - Reciprocity
  - Publicity
  - Accountability
- There are three more principles that should govern the content of the results of deliberation:
  - Basic liberty
  - Basic opportunity
  - Fair opportunity

The process principles tell us how to deliberate. The content principles place limits on the final outcome of deliberation. The outcome, for example, cannot violate the basic liberties of citizens.

The principle of reciprocity is the most important of the process principles. It "asks us to appeal to reasons that are shared or could come to be shared by our fellow citizens." It also requires that our "empirical claims in political argument be consistent with reliable methods of inquiry…" (Gutmann and Thompson 1996, 14-15).

I think that if we were to practice what Gutmann and Thompson are advocating, it might be possible to reduce political and moral polarization or at least the anger that fuels it. I say that because I think part of that anger exists because millions of people feel that no one listens to them or pays any attention to what they care about.

Of course, Gutmann and Thompson know that some moral disagreements are so fundamental that they cannot be resolved using shared values and principles. I think that abortion, euthanasia, gay sex, and some welfare rights may be examples. In cases like that, they argue that citizens should practice "moral accommodation" based on "mutual respect" (Gutmann and Thompson 1996, 79-85). I have asked Dee to tell us more about that.

Libertarian Group: Dee Speaking

🅜🅟 MORAL ACCOMMODATION

I don't know to what extent dialogue can increase our common ground, but I agree that it is worth trying. I think that it sometimes works, and that's what counts. Perhaps legitimacy is a matter of degree and we can gradually build more of it.

As Elijah said, Gutmann and Thompson know that some conflicts involve fundamental values and moral issues. It's very unlikely that we can find enough common ground to settle those disputes and agree on laws and policies concerning those issues. In those cases, they propose what they call moral accommodation. That includes the following:

Elements of Moral Accommodation

- Acknowledge the moral nature of the positions taken by others and do not question their character and motives.
- Be open to the possibility of changing one's mind.
- Be consistent in speech and action.
- Accept the "broader implications of the principles presupposed by one's moral positions."
- Seek an "economy of moral disagreement" by using moral arguments that minimize the rejection of the opposing position.
- Seek an "economy of factual disagreement" by attempting to focus on agreed-upon facts (Gutmann and Thompson 1996, 81, 85).

If we could do all of those things, it would help build common ground. I believe that, but can we do them? That's the question. The polarization that Professor Sidgwick described carries intense emotions with it. There is anger and bitterness on all sides. Can we overcome that? I don't know, but we can try.

Catholic Group: Ayesha Speaking

☐☐ COMMENT ON DELIBERATIVE DEMOCRACY

I think we all want to end on an optimistic note. I know I do. So I want to quote a little more of what Gutmann and Thompson say about deliberative democracy.

They believe that if deliberative democracy were practiced, "the decisions that citizens and their representatives make would be more morally

> *legitimate, public-spirited, mutually respectful, and self-correcting."*
> *They know that deliberative democracy isn't perfect. They know that*
> *it offers "only provisionally justified decisions," but the point is that*
> *those decisions are "justifiable to all citizens who are bound by them."*
> *I think we all agree that that is something we lack today. Gutmann and*
> *Thompson hope that by "making democracy more deliberative, citizens*
> *stand a better chance of resolving some of their moral disagreements,*
> *and living with those that will inevitably persist, on terms that all can*
> *accept" (Gutmann and Thompson 1996, 51).*
>
> *I think it's worth working toward a democracy like that.*

Professor Sidgwick Speaking

🔳🔳 SUBSTANCE AND PROCEDURE

I want to point out something about what Gutmann and Thompson are saying. They distinguish between values and principles governing content and those governing process. That is roughly the same distinction that Vera introduced earlier today when she distinguished substantive values and principles from procedural values and principles.

Examples of substantive values include equality before the law and freedom of speech, religion, association, and movement. A substantive principle might indicate, for example, that the well-being of all persons is of equal value or that all persons have the same civil rights.

Procedural values include parliamentary rules, periodic elections, and public debates. A procedural principle might tell us that representatives are to be elected every two years, that voters must be over a certain age, that certain decisions require a supermajority, or that the size of electoral districts must follow certain rules.

Vera pointed out that our common ground consists of *both* substantive and procedural values and principles. I think that may turn out to be crucially important in resolving or at least mitigating our legitimacy crisis.

Liberal Group: John Speaking

🅼🅿 DIALOGUE

I don't know whether Americans will ever practice the kind of dialogue that Perry or Gutmann and Thompson advocate. Perry's criteria for non-sectarian and non-authoritarian arguments are probably too strict for most of us to adhere to. Gutmann and Thompson may be too idealistic. But I think we *can* commit to a search for common ground that will help us to reduce the level of conflict and find solutions to concrete problems. Indirectly that may help to restore the legitimacy Professor Sidgwick has talked about.

I heard about something recently that made me optimistic. It was an experiment called *America in One Room*. The experiment was sponsored by several organizations, including the Center for Deliberative Democracy at Stanford University. It involved over 500 Americans with different political perspectives talking about contentious issues including immigration, health care, the economy, the environment, and foreign policy. Everyone involved was given solid information reviewed by experts on all sides. Without getting into details, I can say that in many ways people actually came together. The more extreme positions lost support and many people moved toward the political center. The important thing is that they found more extensive common ground.

*Libertarian
Group:
Elijah Speaking*

🅞🅟 COMMENT ON DIALOGUE

I agree with Ayesha that there are cases in which respectful dialogue can show us that we were wrong about what other people believe and there is no fundamental disagreement. On the other hand, I also agree with Diego that when a fundamental disagreement does exist it is unlikely to be resolved by dialogue.

My guess is that dialogue helps the most when disagreements are based on factual issues. The America in One Room experiment that John referred to proves that. If people have good information, they can resolve some of those issues and come together at the level of practical policy.

Bringing people together on policy can be important. It can help to restore confidence in the procedures we use to make decisions. I think it can help if we are willing to commit to it.

Professor Sidgwick Speaking

🅜🅟 LEGITIMACY

I started off by saying that I believe we may be facing a crisis of legitimacy because we do not have enough shared political values and principles. As disagreement turns to polarization, a crisis becomes more likely. The problem was exacerbated by the Trump presidency, but it will not be solved by simply electing a new president. It is likely to persist for decades, but it is not necessarily immune to every treatment. If we think about the problem correctly, we may be able to find at least a partial solution.

You all agree that we already have considerable common ground in our political values and principles. In addition, you all agree that dialogue of the sort that Perry and Gutmann and Thompson advocate may help to expand our agreement, but it probably will not, by itself, solve the problem. It will not provide enough common ground on substantive issues to answer all of our fundamental questions about human rights, welfare rights, abortion, gay marriage, and other issues. Disagreement will continue on these and other issues.

This is where Vera's distinction may be helpful. She suggested that in addition to certain substantive political values and principles, we may be able to agree on certain procedures (such as abiding by majority rule or supermajorities or popular elections). The *combination* of the two might provide the common ground that makes legitimate government possible. Once we accept the government as legitimate, we can agree to abide by laws and policies if we believe that the proper procedures have been followed. To put it a little crudely, agreement on procedure can make up for the fact that we do not always agree on substance.

That makes the recent loss of faith in procedures and institutions especially important. We are losing confidence in the very procedures and institutions we need in order to preserve common ground and legitimacy. For example, the entire electoral system has been called into question in the last few years. Millions of voters believe that the 2020 presidential election was rigged or stolen. Many believe that election results have been distorted by gerrymandering. Millions of others believe that there have been attempts at massive voter suppression or that the electoral college is an obstacle to democracy. Whatever the truth in these claims, and I think some of them are quite correct, they show us that if we are to rebuild legitimacy, we need to restore confidence in our democratic procedures and institutions.

Professor Sidgwick Speaking

🅜🅟 SUGGESTIONS

To wind up, let me make a few suggestions. One place to begin is with leadership at all levels. We need respected leaders from both major political parties to explain the problem of legitimacy, tell everyone what is at stake, and underscore its importance. That leadership is crucial. Then, of course, we also need reforms to procedures and institutions. Voting, for example, should be done in a way that convinces virtually everyone that fraud is very unlikely. National standards could prevent voter suppression. Perhaps the electoral college should be reformed. Gerrymandering can be reduced by having independent commissions draw the boundaries of electoral districts. Emergency presidential powers could be more widely understood and subject to more effective Congressional review. Dialogue of the sort that Perry and Gutmann and Thompson recommend along with more discussion like the Stanford experiment could be strongly encouraged and practiced by schools, churches, unions, and both major political parties. Important economic interests that both political parties have ignored for decades should be addressed. For example, we could greatly improve the quality of education and job training for people in declining industries.

I believe that with credible leadership, dialogue, and institutional reforms it may be possible to rebuild the common ground we need to provide both the necessary conditions for legitimate government and a renewed faith in that government.

I hope that we have begun the process of rebuilding legitimacy with our dialogue today. Thank you for coming and for sharing your ideas.

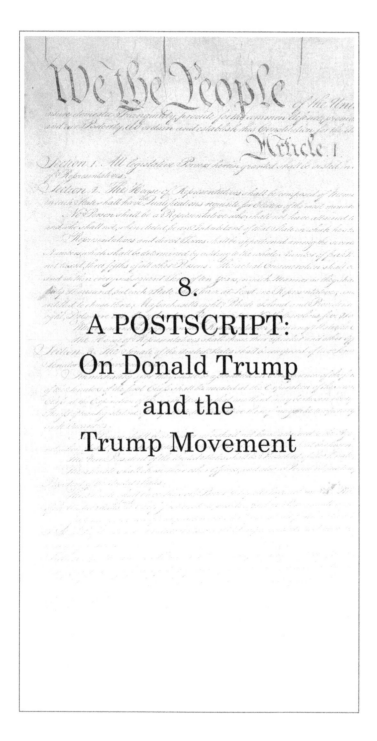

8.

A POSTSCRIPT:
On Donald Trump
and the
Trump Movement

Professor Sidgwick Speaking

🅜🅟 DONALD TRUMP

I'm glad you could come back for another discussion. In our previous dialogue, we talked about political ideas, but we didn't talk about the most dramatic turn of political events since the election of Ronald Reagan in 1980: the emergence of Donald Trump as a politician. Trump had been known for decades as a real estate developer and, more recently, as a TV personality; but he had never held elected office. In 2012 he sought the Republican Party nomination for president and was ridiculed by most political commentators. In 2016 he returned, and this time he garnered the support of a solid core of people in the Republican primaries. He defeated 16 other Republicans and emerged as the party's candidate for the presidency. Several leaders in his own party opposed his nomination. A number of prominent conservative intellectuals criticized him and eventually left the party. *National Review*, the conservative magazine founded by William F. Buckley in the 1950s, devoted a cover story to criticizing Trump. Experts who study polls predicted that former Secretary of State Hillary Clinton would win easily, but they were wrong. On November 8, 2016 Donald Trump lost the popular vote but won a majority in the electoral college.

Four years later Trump lost the 2020 election to former Vice President Joseph Biden. Despite that fact, he has a devoted following; and we are left with important questions to consider:

Questions about Donald Trump and the Trump Movement

- Trump's critics have repeatedly said that he is "unfit" to be president. His supporters think he is perfect for the job. What do you think?

- How should we describe Trump? He has been called a conservative, a populist, a demagogue, a xenophobe, a fascist, a Nazi, a patriot, a nationalist, a white nationalist, an economic nationalist, a racist, a sexist, a member of the alt-right, and more. What do you think is the best way to describe him?

- Who are Trump's core supporters and what are their concerns? I'm thinking here of the people who supported him early on in the 2016 presidential campaign.

- What are the lessons and the likely consequences of the Trump movement and the Trump presidency?

There has been a lot written about these questions. What I would like each of you to do is to look at Trump from your own perspective. Apply the principles you presented in our dialogue on political ideas and tell us what you think of the Trump phenomenon.

By the way, I have asked someone new to join us for this discussion. His name is Mike and he's a student in the political science department. I brought him in because I know that he is pro-Trump, and I thought it would be helpful to have someone here to give us a solidly pro-Trump point of view.

The Unknown Future

President Trump lost the 2020 election, but it is still important for us to understand the Trump phenomenon, its background, its consequences, and its lessons. This is true in part because Trump increased the political polarization that already existed in our country. It is also true because the conditions that made Trump popular will persist and he may continue to exert considerable political influence. Our future as a functioning democracy and a world leader may depend upon what we learn from the Trump presidency.

Liberal Group: John Speaking

🄼🄿 TRUMP'S FITNESS

In my opinion, there are many Republicans and Democrats who are fit to be president. Mitt Romney, Jeb Bush, Hillary Clinton, and Joe Biden have the character, knowledge, and temperament to hold the office. There is something different about Donald Trump. His personality, his character, his store of knowledge, and his attitudes are all outside the normal range for presidents. Let me try to break that down a little.

Personality, Character, and Temperament

- Trump is arrogant, self-absorbed, impulsive, belligerent, vindictive, bombastic, and mean-spirited. Is that really the kind of person we want making major decisions? Can such a person lead our country?

- He lacks a basic respect for established norms, institutions, and international relationships. He thinks nothing of criticizing and ridiculing the FBI, the CIA, the leaders of our armed forces, or long-standing allies.

Truth and Knowledge

- Trump's attitude toward the truth is that of a promoter or salesman. He does not care how much he exaggerates or fabricates as long as he makes a sale. He's the guy outside the tent at a carnival who tells you that for $5.00 you can see a woman with three heads. In fact, there is no woman with three heads, but to him that doesn't matter.

- Trump's ignorance is astounding. He knows almost nothing about history, economics, foreign policy, or domestic policy.

- The greater problem, however, is that Trump does not know that he is ignorant. During the 2016 campaign, for example, he claimed that he knew more about ISIS than our generals. When the COVID-19 pandemic hit, he seemed to believe that his personal insights on how to treat the virus were as useful as those of epidemiologists. With that attitude, he cannot educate himself as other presidents have done.

I know that Mike may disagree with what I have said, but I'm just telling it to you the way I see it. It seems to me that a person like the one I have described is obviously unfit for the presidency.

*Liberal
Group:
Vera Speaking*

🄾🄿 COMMENT ON TRUTH

I agree that Trump says all sorts of things that are not true. He told us that Mexico would pay for a wall on our southern border. He said that if he were elected Americans would have better health care at a fraction of the cost. He insisted that millions of people voted illegally in the 2016 election and that there was massive fraud in the 2020 election. The list goes on and on.

But for me the most disturbing thing is not so much what Trump says, but the fact that more and more people live in their own 'truth silos.' That goes for liberals and conservatives alike. They listen to the same sources of news day after day. The same claims are reinforced over and over. Some people have said that the whole notion of objective truth is slipping away. I don't think that's true. I believe that people still think that their claims are objectively true, but we cannot agree on how to settle our disputes. For example, we cannot agree on which sources of information to trust. Trump

*Liberal
Group:
Vera Speaking*

does not help us solve this problem. When he says that the major media generate fake news, he makes it worse.

Will our republic fail if citizens cannot agree on how to verify their different claims? Does republican government assume that there is a truth that we can work together to discover? If so, where does that leave us? I'm worried.

*Libertarian
Group:
Elijah Speaking*

🅞🅟 COMMENT ON TRUTH AND ARGUMENT

I agree with John and Vera, but I want to make a few comments on the connection between Trump and the ordinary notions of truth, evidence, and argument.

All of these notions are being lost or distorted or replaced with something else that is fundamentally different. We are almost to the point at which they do not matter at all. In other words, we are almost to the point at which rational discourse has broken down, but we need it more than ever.

Evidence, Argument, and Solutions

- *Trump substituted repetition for evidence. For example, he said over and over that Mexico would pay for a wall on our southern border. It doesn't seem to matter that there was never any reason to believe that it would happen.*

- *He substituted ridicule for argument and rational criticism. He did this repeatedly in*

*his campaigns by referring to "low energy Jeb," "little Marco,"
"Pocahontas," and "sleepy Joe" Biden.*

- *He substituted attitude and unlimited self-confidence for serious
  political and economic positions. His followers love the "f**k you"
  attitude he portrays, but he seldom offers well thought out plans
  to address problems. For example, he expressed the anger and
  fear of those people who work in declining industries like coal,
  but he had no plan to bring back their jobs or to help them find
  new jobs in new industries.*

Pro-Trump: Mike Speaking

🅜🅟 TRUMP'S FITNESS

Hi. I'm Mike, and I voted twice for Donald Trump. Wow! I feel like I'm at
an Alcoholics Anonymous meeting admitting to my addiction. But seriously,
I did vote for Trump, and I don't regret it. I came here because I want to
explain to you that you just don't understand what Trump is about and why
so many people support him.

Look, I am not going to defend everything Trump does. I'm not going to
defend all of his boorish behavior. I don't like the name calling and I wish he
didn't tweet so much. But, I will also say that what you call crude behavior
is exactly what allows him to communicate with millions of Americans who
don't have two or three college degrees to pin on the wall. A few years ago,
there was a country song with words that went something like "I like people
who buy their coffee ground." Can you understand that? There are people
out there who are sick and tired of being looked down upon by people with

stock portfolios and electric cars and kids in private schools who get taken to Paris when they 'graduate' from junior high. These are people who were working in factories while Hillary Clinton was going to Wellesley. Trump speaks to those people, and they listen to him. He speaks their language and he talks about their problems.

A lot of what you think makes him unfit to be president is seen very differently by the people who support him. For example:

Fitness or Unfitness?

- What you see as arrogance, his supporters see as self-confidence.
- What you see as belligerence, his supporters see as a fighting spirit — a willingness to strike back against nations that have taken advantage of us time and time again.
- What you see as impulsiveness, his supporters see as a willingness to cut through red tape and act quickly and decisively.
- What you see as crude talk, his supporters see as a willingness to break the rules of political correctness and speak the truth in plain English.
- What you see as an unscrupulous promoter who disregards the truth, his supporters see as a skillful negotiator preparing the atmosphere for a good deal.
- As far as knowledge goes, I think you are forgetting that people learn in very different ways. Trump doesn't sit around reading textbooks on economics and foreign policy. I'll give you that. But he learns from real life experience and by talking to lots of different people and absorbing what they say. That's what counts.

The bottom line is that in my opinion, and in the opinion of Trump's core supporters, a confident person willing to fight for American interests and to take bold action is entirely fit to be president. That's what we want.

For All Four Women: Ayesha Speaking

🅼🅿 TRUMP'S FITNESS

"Entirely fit to be president?" We're sorry, Mike, but we tend to agree with John. You won't get all four of us women together on a lot of issues, but on that we agree. We also have something to add to what John said.

All through his campaigns, and during his years in office, Trump showed that he has no concern at all about sexism, racism, and nativism. He is completely unaware of the problems many people have because of their sex, their race, or where they come from. For example, he has been completely indifferent to the problems of immigrants from Latin America.

Republican Senator John McCain once said that there was a dark side to American populism, and he walked away from it. Trump is well aware of that dark side, but he cultivates it as the basis of his political appeal. We feel that all of this makes him unfit to be our president.

Sexism, Racism, Nativism, and Cruelty

- During the 2016 campaign, a sound recording of Trump made it clear that he liked grabbing women "by the pussy" and that he thought he could get away with it because he was a celebrity. At times he has referred to women as pigs, slobs, and dogs.

- Trump initially built his political appeal on the claim that President Obama may not have been born in the United States and was therefore ineligible to be president. He has been slow to reject the support of white supremacist groups and antisemitic neo-Nazis. He picked out black athletes who knelt during the national anthem for condemnation even though their protest was quiet and dignified. In his 2020 campaign he repeatedly tried to frighten white suburbanites by suggesting that the Democrats would bring droves of poor people (meaning black people) from the cities into their neighborhoods.

- Trump's attack on undocumented immigrants has been non-stop. He has referred to people coming from Mexico as criminals, rapists, and "bad hombres." He has also made it clear that he would like to ban all Muslim immigrants to the US, build a wall between the US and Mexico, and end birthright citizenship. He claimed that a judge of Mexican descent could not treat him fairly in court. In short, he has worked constantly to construct our image of Mexicans and Muslims as people that we should fear and punish.

- The Trump administration has demonstrated a streak of cruelty toward people in a position of weakness. The worst instance of this was its policy of separating young children from their parents in the case of migrants and asylum seekers from Latin America. Trump seems incapable of any empathy for the weak and vulnerable.

We don't see how you can even consider a person like Trump as president. Elect a conservative, someone like Mitt Romney or Jeb Bush. That's fine. But make it a person who appeals to the best in America, not the worst.

*Catholic
Group:
Ayesha Speaking*

ⓞⓟ COMMENT ON FITNESS

The ultimate proof that Trump is unfit to be president became clear when the COVID-19 crisis hit. His style of leadership failed the country.

There are cases when the salesman or the carnival barker can motivate his audience and make things happen. Sometimes perception becomes reality, but that's not true in a pandemic. All of Trump's talk about how the pandemic was a hoax, the number of cases was small, it was all going to go away, and how great we were doing with testing — it was useless. It was all sales talk, and it did nothing to solve the real problem.

> *Trump was undone by the flaws in his own character. He may have believed that the major media outlets were exaggerating the COVID problem in order to hurt him politically. He may have believed that if he downplayed the problem it would go away by itself. In any case, he failed to confront the problem head-on and lead the country in the fight against the pandemic. While some Asian countries experienced only a handful of deaths, we experienced hundreds of thousands.*
>
> *The irony is that if he had taken decisive federal action to contain the virus and assist its victims, he would have been seen as a hero and it would have helped him enormously in the 2020 election.*

Pro-Trump: Mike Speaking

🅼🅿 BASIC ISSUES

I still think Trump is fit to be president, and I'll try once more to tell you why.

I will not defend Trump's sexist attitudes and his vulgarity. Many of his statements about illegal Latino migrants and Muslims are insulting. I agree with you on that.

But look, we have a president who speaks in hyperbole. Everything is either the greatest or the worst. We know that's how he talks. You shouldn't take him literally.

Furthermore, focusing on Trump's exaggerations and distortions misses the point. If you want to understand Trump, you have got to look elsewhere. Let me suggest that there are three basic issues for Trump and his hard-core supporters — the people who supported him all through the Republican primary elections in 2016 and continue to do so.

The Basic Issues

- The loss of good-paying jobs for people with a high school education or less. Those jobs were mostly in manufacturing, but they were also in some other declining industries like coal mining.

- Uncontrolled illegal immigration and massive legal immigration from cultures quite different from our own.

- Government indifference to the interests of straight, white, working people. Those people feel that the government cares about everybody but them.

If you focus on these issues you can understand the Trump movement. The insults aimed at women and African Americans are secondary. These three issues connect with many others — globalization, free trade, crime, loss of social status, the changing distribution of income, taxes, loss of cultural dominance, and lots of other things — but these three are at the core. What makes Trump fit to be president in the eyes of his supporters is that he "gets it" on these core issues. He pays attention to their concerns and their fears while the elite in both parties couldn't care less.

*Liberal
Group:
Vera Speaking*

🔲🅿️ **COMMENT ON BASIC ISSUES**

I disagree with you when you suggest that the insulting remarks Trump makes about women and African Americans are secondary. They are part of the way he stokes his audience and cultivates their support. I think race is way more important to Trump's core supporters than you let on, especially the race of immigrants.

But I won't stress that right now. On the three core issues that you mention, I agree that the loss of good jobs for people with a high school education or less is important. That should be addressed and both parties have done too little. There has also been a great deal of immigration since the legal

> changes of the 1960s. That scares a lot of people. They see the world changing around them and it makes them very uncomfortable. But Donald Trump has no idea how to deal with either of those problems. He can't bring back millions of jobs and he can't do much to reduce immigration because our economy needs more workers.
>
> The most charitable way to put it is to say that Trump is misleading a lot of people by giving them false hopes instead of real solutions.

Professor Sidgwick Speaking

🅜🅟 DESCRIBING TRUMP

Most of you feel that Donald Trump is unfit to be president. You cite his character, personality, lack of knowledge, and disregard for the truth. Mike sees things differently. Where most of you see impulsiveness, he sees boldness. Where some of you see belligerence, he sees fighting spirit, and so on.

Let's move on. Trump has been described in many ways. Here's a list of the labels commonly applied to him by his critics. Do any of them apply? What do you think?

How Should We Describe Donald Trump?

- Political conservative?
- Extreme conservative?
- Patriot?
- Populist?
- Fascist?

- Nativist?
- Economic nationalist?
- White nationalist?
- Xenophobe?
- Racist?

Conservative Group: Fred Speaking

🅼🅿 CONSERVATIVE CRITICISM

I'll go first. Trump ran twice as the Republican Party nominee, but I don't see him as a conservative of any kind. It would be more correct to say that Trump appealed to a minority within the Republican Party and managed to take over the party. Since then, he has remade it. As a Reagan conservative, I voted against Trump. Here's why:

Fred's Conservative Criticisms of Trump

- He appears to know nothing about the philosophy of limited government and a strict interpretation of the Constitution.

- During his term, he ignored the rule of law and made it clear that he would love to be an autocrat. He expanded presidential power by using emergency powers and executive orders. He even joked about being president for life. After the 2020 election, he refused to accept the results for months and urged his followers to prevent the certification of the electoral college votes.

- He has harshly criticized important American institutions such as the FBI and the CIA.

- His tax reform will add to the federal deficit.

- He does not believe in strong defensive alliances with other countries. Instead, he has insulted traditional allies and refused to criticize Vladimir Putin, the autocratic leader of America's most powerful enemy.

- He is gradually giving up American global leadership by taking a narrow, short-term view of our national interests and withdrawing from international organizations and agreements.

- He has opposed free trade and advocated protectionism as a solution to economic problems.

- He has refused to quickly and categorically condemn white supremacist groups.

- He has repeatedly criticized the press as the "enemy of the people" despite its role as an essential element in a well-functioning republic.

- He has harshly criticized many immigrants and asylum seekers and catered to nativism in general. In doing so, he has seriously damaged the image of America as a place symbolizing hope for a better life to people around the world.

There are lots of thoughtful conservatives who reject Trump. In *The Corrosion of Conservatism*, historian and foreign policy expert Max Boot summarized his conservative philosophy and added immediately that "Trump does not understand or believe in a single one of these principles" (Boot 2018, xx). I agree completely.

Conservative Group: Fred Speaking

🅞🅟 CONSERVATIVES ON TRUMP

There were many conservatives who criticized candidate Trump in the February 15, 2016 issue of National Review. Here are some samples, just to give you a flavor of the criticism.

David Boaz: "Not since George Wallace has there been a presidential candidate who made racial and religious scapegoating so central to his campaign."

Ben Domenech: "Trump assures voters that he will use authoritarian power for good," but Americans fought to "defeat a tyrannical monarch and establish a government of laws, not men."

*Conservative
Group:
Fred Speaking*

Mark Helprin: "He doesn't know the Constitution, history, law, political philosophy, nuclear strategy, diplomacy, defense, economics beyond real estate, or even, despite his low-level-mafioso comportment, how ordinary people live." Trump is a "man who simply grasps anything that floats by."

John Podhoretz: "Trump is an unbalanced force. He is the politicized American id. Should his election results match his polls, he would be, unquestionably, the worst thing to happen to the American common culture in my lifetime."

Thomas Sowell: "A shoot-from-the-hip, belligerent show-off is the last thing we need or can afford."

Bill Kristol asked whether Trump was "the very epitome of vulgarity?" in part because he is concerned only with success.

Mona Charen: "Put aside for a moment Trump's countless past departures from conservative principle on defense, racial quotas, abortion, taxes, single-payer health care, and immigration.... The man has demonstrated an emotional immaturity bordering on personality disorder, and it ought to disqualify him from being a mayor, to say nothing of a commander-in-chief."

Katie Pavlich asked "Do we truly believe in our long-held principles....Or are we willing to throw these principles away because an entertainer who has been a liberal Democrat for decades simply says some of the right things?"

Conservative Group: Diego Speaking

🄼🄿 AN EVANGELICAL DEFENSE

Trump is not a Christian conservative, but I voted for him. Here's why.

Diego's Evangelical Defense

I know that Trump has no record of Bible-oriented church involvement or any other Christian activity. His personal lifestyle is anything but Christian. He has pursued many extramarital affairs and placed money making and personal prestige above all other values. His self-absorption and lack of humility are obvious.

But that's not all there is to it. I was voting for a president, not a minister. Trump was the best hope for placing judicial conservatives on the Supreme Court and possibly overturning *Roe v. Wade*. He's done that with people like Brett Kavanaugh and Amy Coney Barrett. That was the bottom line for me and for millions of other evangelical conservatives.

Liberal Group: Vera Speaking

🅼🅿 TRUMP AND FASCISM

I agree that Trump is not a typical American conservative, but I will go further. If it walks like a duck and talks like a duck, then it's a duck. Donald Trump walks like a fascist and talks like a fascist, so he is a fascist. If we don't recognize it, we are going to lose our republic.

I am not the only person who thinks this. Lots of people, both conservatives and liberals, agree. David Frum, a conservative commentator and former speech writer for George W. Bush, has said it. Max Boot, a conservative writer and fellow at the Council on Foreign Relations, has said it. Jason Stanley, a Yale philosopher, has said it. Robert Reich, former Secretary of Labor, has said it. As late as January 2021, days before the end of the president's term of office, news commentator Joe Scarborough said it again.

Think of the obvious signs and similarities that we have seen over and over. Here are just a few:

Why We Should Call Trump a Fascist

- Trump has a solid popular base that blindly follows him and believes that he has extraordinary personal powers. He has claimed that he alone can solve our nation's problems, and they believe him.

- Trump has subtly urged his followers to use violence against opponents. At rallies in 2016, for example, he said that he would pay their legal fees if they roughed up protestors. As late as January 2021 he urged his followers to march on the Capital Building and "fight like Hell." They proceeded to vandalize the building and several people were killed. The president was subsequently impeached for "incitement of insurrection."

- It is obvious that Trump would like to rule as an autocrat. You can see it in the executive orders he has issued. He said that he wanted to ban all Muslims from entering the United States, and he would have done it if he hadn't been blocked. He unilaterally diverted funds from military projects to extend the wall between the US and Mexico. He has repeatedly expressed admiration for autocrats like Vladimir Putin in Russia or Rodrigo Duterte in the Philippines.

- Trump demonizes weak minority groups, saying that they are criminals and the source of important social problems. I'm thinking especially of the way he has demonized undocumented Latino immigrants.

- Trump has also demonized certain foreign nations, blaming our problems on them. He has done this repeatedly with China and Mexico. He insisted that they were stealing our manufacturing jobs and impoverishing American workers. He repeatedly referred to the COVID-19 virus as the China virus.

- Trump preaches a kind of hypernationalism. He talks over and over about "making America great again" and putting America first.

- Trump makes thinly veiled appeals to white people as white people. He stokes white fear and anger, and he knows it. That's what all the talk about law and order is really about.

- Trump relishes a kind of exaggerated masculinity — his many affairs, his supermodel wife, and his arrogant claims to be able to do whatever he wants with women because of his celebrity status.

*Liberal
Group:
Vera Speaking*

⊡⊡ COMMENT ON
TRUMP AND FASCISM

Let me focus on just one example of the writers who have referred to Trump as a fascist. During the 2016 campaign, Robert Reich wrote an article called "The American Fascist." He pointed out parallels between Trump and the fascists of the early 20th century. Like the earlier fascists, Trump focused on "the angers of white working people who have been losing economic ground for years." Those workers were "easy prey for demagogues seeking to build their own power by scapegoating others." They had suffered economically and also suffered from "failed expectations." Many believed that they or their children would move up economically, but it wasn't happening.

According to Reich, Trump, like earlier fascists, identifies specific groups as scapegoats. He hits hard on Mexican migrants and Muslims. Earlier fascists developed personality cults around their leaders — people like Hitler or Mussolini. Trump has done the same. "Trump's entire campaign similarly revolves around his assumed strength and confidence." Earlier fascists used violence, and Trump has hinted at violence as well. His supporters "have attacked Muslims, the homeless, and African-Americans — and Trump has all but excused their behavior."

> The old fascists "glorified national power and greatness." Trump does the same. His "entire foreign policy consists of asserting American power against other nations."
>
> In Reich's view, recognizing all these parallels with European fascists "who used economic stresses to scapegoat others, created cults of personality, intimidated opponents, incited violence, glorified their nations and disregarded international law" can help us understand "what Trump is doing and how he is succeeding" (Reich 2016).

Liberal Group: John Speaking

🅜🅟 TRUMP AND FASCISM

I will agree that there are similarities between the Trump movement and fascism. Trump has a popular following and at times rails against elites. He also blames illegal migrants for all sorts of things. Still, I think there are good reasons to avoid the word 'fascist.'

Why 'Fascist' is the Wrong Word to Use

- Most (but not all) of Trump's agenda is pretty standard Republican stuff. He pushed to get rid of Obamacare, lower individual and corporate taxes, reduce regulation, build up the military, and put judicial conservatives on the Supreme Court. None of that is fascist by anyone's definition.

- Historians do not agree on the essence of what we call fascism and therefore they do not agree on the meaning of the term. Everyone agrees that Mussolini was a fascist and that his regime was a fascist regime. Beyond that, there is endless debate. The bottom line is that the term 'fascist' has become so ambiguous and vague that it simply does not help us to communicate. As George Orwell said in his 1946 essay "Politics and the English Language," it means only that something is not desirable.

- The word 'fascist' is overused to the point of absurdity. Rush Limbaugh said that Obama's agenda was fascist. Jonah Goldberg, in his book *Liberal Fascism*, labeled the whole progressive agenda since the early 20th century as fascist. George W. Bush referred to militant Islam as Islamo-fascism. Some liberals called Bush himself a fascist or a proto-fascist. The point is that the term is used indiscriminately and therefore it is essentially useless.

- We need a solid understanding of the Trump movement, and that means identifying the social conditions that gave rise to it. Labeling Trump a fascist provides only the illusion of an understanding. It doesn't really help us at all, but it makes us feel good. It is self-deception to think that putting Trump in a box labeled fascist is going to help us solve the problems we face. It may even prevent us from developing a proper understanding by allowing us to think that we already have one.

Having said all that, if I had to choose two words to describe Donald Trump, I would call him a populist demagogue.

Libertarian Group: Elijah Speaking

🅾️🅿️ **COMMENT ON TRUMP AND FASCISM**

Let me make a suggestion: When we are tempted to describe Trump as a fascist, we should ask ourselves what characteristics have prompted us to do so. Instead of using the word 'fascist,' we should identify those characteristics. For example, if Trump is anti-immigrant or autocratic or sexist, use those terms instead of calling him a fascist. In that way, we can communicate more clearly, and that will help us to identify and solve our problems.

Conservative Group: Fred Speaking

🅜🅟 TRUMP AND FASCISM

I agree with John that calling Trump a fascist is a mistake. Don't get me wrong, I'm against Trump. He has taken over my Republican Party and masqueraded as a conservative. He's not a conservative by my standards, but that doesn't make him a fascist.

I think that we would be better off to look at the American traditions of populism, nativism, and economic nationalism in order to get a fix on Trump.

Let's think for a minute about what those three traditions involve. If we put them all together, I think we get a pretty good description of Donald Trump.

Populism, Nativism, and Economic Nationalism

- American populists typically have a solid popular base. Populism is not an elite movement.

- Populists typically express the economic grievances of ordinary people. In the late 19th century, populists expressed the grievances of farmers against railroads and banks. Animosity is often directed against elites, although it may also be directed against weak minority groups.

- Nativism is driven by animosity directed at foreigners. Nativists believe that the interests of native-born Americans are threatened by immigrants. They may claim that immigrants lower wages, that immigrants have a different religion, that immigrants commit crimes, or that immigrants are culturally un-American.

- Economic nationalists believe that our economic problems are due to our economic relationships with other countries. We need different relationships so that others cannot take advantage of us. Free trade may be viewed with suspicion. Tariffs and other restrictions are typically offered as solutions. This view is especially attractive to people working in declining industries.

Populism, nativism, and economic nationalism don't completely describe Trump. I know that. But I think they go a long way to position him within our American political traditions. The word 'fascist' doesn't help at all.

By the way, if you're looking for some good books on populism, try John Judis *The Populist Explosion* or Michael Kazin *The Populist Persuasion*.

Pro-Trump: Mike Speaking

🅼🅿 POPULISM

I agree with parts of what you are saying. Trump is in the populist tradition. Just don't try to make it sound as though everyone in that tradition is one of the bad guys.

Populist movements don't come from nowhere. They usually express legitimate grievances, like those of the farmers in the 19th-century farmers' alliances and the People's Party. Trump is in that tradition and he is expressing the grievances of ordinary working people.

One of Trump's early supporters (who later became a critic) was Anthony Scaramucci, a guy from an Italian working-class family who went to good schools, made a lot of money, and worked on the 2016 Trump campaign. Here's what he had to say in his book *Trump: The Blue-Collar President* about the people at a Trump rally in Albuquerque.

Scaramucci on Trump's Supporters

"They were angry with elites, with Washington, and with the people who'd negotiated all the deals that sent their jobs overseas." Not only that, but "They had seen their communities begin to disappear, and their ways of life change dramatically." Some "had been fired from their jobs and had no expectation of being hired again; others were saddled with massive debt...." From their point of view, "no one had been speaking for them or listening to them, including me." Scaramucci admits that maybe he was "too wrapped up in my high-octane success to notice that my neighborhood had gone from one of aspiration to one of desperation." The same was true elsewhere, "in hundreds of other places such as Scranton, Beaumont, and Albuquerque" (Scaramucci 2018, 207).

If you listen carefully to what Scaramucci is saying and understand what the people at that rally were feeling, then I think you can understand where the Trump movement came from.

Do any of you really want to call those people fascists? I don't think that will get you anywhere. What you need to do instead is figure out how to solve their problems. They are caught in the process of economic and cultural globalization. They are the ones who have paid the price of those transformations. Now what are you going to do about it?

Pro-Trump:
Mike Speaking

🅞🅟 COMMENT ON
TRUMP'S SUPPORTERS

I have been stressing the economic problems of a lot of Trump's supporters, but there is more to it than that.

A few years ago, there was a study done at Princeton University that found an increase in deaths among middle-aged white men in the United States. Those white men were the only group to show such an increase.

The study also concluded that the increase was largely due to drugs, alcohol, and suicide. It was worse for the less educated men (Case and Deaton 2015, abstract).

For decades, most of us have assumed that the white male could take care of himself. He had all the advantages. He benefitted from centuries of discrimination against women and African Americans. All of that is undeniable. But the numbers in this study tell us that something has changed. Not only are wages flat for whites without a college education, but the men are literally dying.

I think that Donald Trump is speaking to those people, and we need to pay attention. These are people who need help.

5E EXCERPTS FROM PHYLLIS SCHLAFLY, ED MARTIN, AND BRETT DECKER
The Conservative Case for Trump

Although George Will, Max Boot, and David Brooks do not consider Donald Trump to be a true American conservative, there are others who do. Phyllis Schlafly (1924-2016) was a conservative leader for 50 years. She is well known among conservatives for her 1964 book A Choice Not an Echo *and for her leadership of the Eagle Forum. Schlafly supported Barry Goldwater in 1964 and strongly opposed the Equal Rights Amendment.*

In 2016 Schlafly, Ed Martin, and Brett Decker published The Conservative Case for Trump *in which they argued that Trump was the most conservative presidential candidate since Ronald Reagan. In the excerpts below, they argue that Trump will benefit the American working class.*

Before Donald Trump, there had been no effective national political spokesman for the American worker. Now there is. Trump states unequivocally that, "Trade deals are absolutely killing our country." An increasingly large majority of Americans agree with him.... A growing number of Americans no longer feel the economic system works for them and are expressing frustration that they are being locked out of the global economy by our own corporations and our own politicians. The outpouring of support in this election for Donald Trump, and to a certain degree for Bernie Sanders in the Democratic primaries as well, is a manifestation of this frustration and the feeling that establishment politicians do not care or are not even aware of the plight of regular people across the country.

Generations of Americans have believed that if they worked hard they could improve their economic standing and give a better future to their children. By blithely trading away American jobs, especially blue collar jobs, in order to pursue free trade and its alleged benefits for the consumer, our political class has left many Americans no longer believing that the American Dream is within their grasp; instead, they find themselves shunted out of well-paying manufacturing jobs and into lower paid service jobs (Schlafly 2016, 34-35).

As financial theorist William J. Bernstein notes, "The pain and dislocation in the lives of individuals, industries, and nations caused by the globalization of the planet's economy are real." The interests of the rest of the world are not always in sync with America's interests, and when that's the case, American leaders need to put America first (Schlafly 2016, 38).

Liberal Group: Vera Speaking

🅜🅟 A REPLY TO MIKE AND DIEGO

Wait a minute, Mike. Sure, the people who make up the core of Trump's supporters have problems. Who doesn't? They have been neglected by our two main political parties, but there is more to it than that. The way that Trump has approached those problems is all wrong. When he calls Mexicans rapists, insists that the major media are the enemy of the people, and says that COVID-19 is a hoax, he's not doing anything to help his supporters.

Diego, I'm really surprised at your position. You have always said that personal character is important in political leaders. You have always looked for leaders who find their values in the Bible. And now, what are you doing? You have sold your soul to get conservative justices on the Supreme Court. Is it worth it?

Trump's core followers have problems. That's true, but there are appropriate ways to deal with those problems and other ways that are simply not acceptable in a diverse country like ours. We need to bring people together, not put them at odds with each other. We need to think about the common good. Some people are caught in declining industries and they have suffered, but the solution is not economic nationalism. The real solution to those problems is investment in new industries, new jobs, and better education.

*Libertarian
Group:
Elijah Speaking*

🔲🔲 COMMENT ON DECLINING INDUSTRIES

I know that many of Trump's core supporters are caught in so-called declining industries, but I want to point out that historically there have been many industries that have prospered and subsequently declined. Eastern Pennsylvania, where I live, was once loaded with iron furnaces and forges. They are all gone now except for a few that are tourist attractions. They were replaced by modern iron and steel works. The newer technology was enormously more productive, and that is what matters if you want to raise the standard of living for everyone. Every part of the country has gone through such transitions. It's part of what some economists have called "creative destruction" and it has made us a wealthy nation. Trying to stop it is short-sighted. You might as well shoot yourself in the foot.

Pro-Trump: Mike Speaking

🅼🅿 POPULISM

I won't defend Trump's vulgarity or the mean-spirited things he says about illegal immigrants. I don't approve of any of that stuff. But I still believe that Trump has really good instincts on much more important issues.

Trump understands that there are millions of American workers who have been hurt by factory closings and cheap foreign competition. There are some economists who agree with him and have made solid arguments in favor of his program. Here's a part of what Stephen Moore and Arthur Laffer said in their book *Trumponomics: Inside the America First Plan to Revive Our Economy.*

Moore and Laffer's "Populist Agenda"

- Put America's interests before those of other nations.
- Restore patriotism.
- Reject governmental paternalism.
- Rebuild America's inner cities.
- Protect our borders from "drug runners, terrorists, illegal immigrants, and criminals."
- Support American business.
- Reject identity politics. Stop dividing Americans by "race, sexual orientation, ethnicity, and class."
- Cut unnecessary regulations.
- Cut tax rates to improve competitiveness.
- Replace welfare with work.

- Use America's natural resources.

- Modernize America's infrastructure.

- Improve health care and education by encouraging choice and competition.

- Promote free and fair trade agreements.

- Reduce government spending.

- Establish a merit-based immigration system. A merit system would select on the basis of skills, investment capital, and education (Moore and Laffer 2018, chapter 4).

Moore and Laffer call this a populist agenda. I agree. All I ask of you is that we find a way to rationally discuss the components of the program without going off on a tangent calling Trump a fascist or a racist. The left has been so freaked out about Trump that they can't discuss anything. Some thought that he was going to start a nuclear war. Others thought that he was going to cancel the 2020 election. What we all need is to take a deep breath and start talking about the real issues.

Liberal Group: Vera Speaking

🅞🅟 COMMENT ON POPULISM

I think this so-called populist program is mostly old Republican ideas wrapped up in pro-working-class rhetoric. It basically lets big business do whatever it wants.

Moore and Laffer talk about slashing regulations and exploiting American energy resources. I'm concerned that that will amount to a wholesale retreat from environmental protection. Moore and

*Liberal
Group:
Vera Speaking*

Laffer want to mine and drill everywhere — on federal lands, in Alaska, off the coasts, all over the place. In their book, they make it clear that they love fracking for oil and gas. They don't deal with the damage done to ground water by fracking.

In my view, backing off on environmental protection is a very short-sighted policy that will degrade our environment and cost us more in the long run.

*Pro-Trump:
Mike Speaking*

🅞🅟 COMMENT ON TRUMP'S ECONOMICS

Moore and Laffer have also put forward a boiled-down three-part version of their plan to boost the American economy, increase the growth rate, and create lots of good working-class jobs. Here it is in a nutshell:

Moore and Laffer's Three-part Growth Program

- Cut taxes.

- Slash regulations.

- Produce American energy (Moore and Laffer 2018, 213).

Each of these components is important, but I want to call your attention to the last one: produce American energy. This country is bursting with sources of energy. In the last 20 years, there has been a revolution in the production of oil and gas from shale. The people who thought that we were about to run out of oil were simply wrong. The

> very opposite is happening. In a few years, the US may be the leading producer and exporter of oil and gas. That means more jobs here at home and less dependence on oil from politically unstable foreign countries. Who can be against that?
>
> Moore and Laffer believe that this three-pronged approach can increase our annual economic growth rate to somewhere between 3 and 4 percent. That's exactly what those people in Albuquerque want to hear.

Liberal Group: Vera Speaking

🅜🅟 TRUMP'S SUPPORTERS

Mike, there is more involved here than people who have been left behind economically. I sympathize with those people and I want the government to help them with better education and training. You and I probably agree on that.

The problem is that some of Trump's supporters are white supremacists, and some are intensely antisemitic. I'm not saying that all of his followers are like that, but some are. They are people who simply do not want black or brown or Jewish people in this country. They have been fighting against equality for decades and in general they have been losing. They see Trump as someone who can lead them in a restoration. For them, making American great again means making it white again. As president, it was Trump's responsibility to strongly condemn them and repudiate their support. He was slow to do that; and when he did, it was halfhearted at best.

Another group of his supporters believes in the QAnon conspiracy theories. They appear to believe that an elite group practices pedophilia and secretly controls all sorts of things. Some of those people showed up in Washington D.C. and attacked the Capital Building in January 2021. Trump should have repudiated them long before that, but he didn't.

My point is that it's a mistake to talk about Trump's followers as just a group of hard-working people who have been hurt by globalization. Some of them represent the worst elements in our society.

Conservative Group: Fred Speaking

🅜🅟 TRUMP'S ECONOMICS

Trump is not a conservative in the Goldwater-Reagan tradition. He is also vulgar, ignorant, and says all kinds of things that are not true. That said, I do agree with some of his economic ideas. The corporate tax cut contained in the Trump tax reform is the most important example. For decades, other countries have lowered their corporate tax rate, leaving the United States with one of the highest rates in the world. That has hurt American companies and the people who work for them. Moore and Laffer made a simple argument on this issue. Here is the gist of it in their own words:

Moore and Laffer on the Trump Tax Cut

- "Better wages come from better productivity. Better productivity comes from better tools. And better tools come from capital investment."

- "Thus, first, lower corporate tax rates mean more capital investment by businesses in the United States."

- "Second, capital investment is a major factor in making workers more productive."

- "Third, worker productivity is the major driver of higher salaries and benefits to American workers" (Moore and Laffer 2018, 131).

I think that Moore and Laffer are correct. I hope that the corporate tax cut will usher in an era of prosperity that includes lots of good jobs. Furthermore, if we can boost economic growth to an average of 3% per year, we will be able to lower our deficits, pay down the national debt, and help fund the huge entitlements that the federal government has created.

Liberal Group: John Speaking

🅜🅟 CONSEQUENCES AND LESSONS

Fred and I want to get beyond the controversies about whether Trump is fit to be president or whether he is a fascist or a populist. We want to move on to Professor Sidgwick's next question: What are the consequences of the Trump movement and the lessons we can derive from it? We are asking each of you to identify the single most important consequence or the single most important lesson. I'll start.

John: The Most Important Consequence of the Trump Movement

- I think the most important consequence of the Trump movement has been the withdrawal of the United States from its role as leader of the two most important global systems: the nation state system and the world market system. There are serious problems that affect the whole world, and they require leadership and cooperation in order to be effectively managed. Trump and his followers seem to believe that it is in our national interest to withdraw from multilateral agreements on trade, nuclear proliferation, pollution, disease, global warming, and other problems. I think that approach is the opposite of what we need, and I'm hoping that President Biden will change it.

- The United States is far from perfect, but without American leadership the options are not very pretty. One option is a major increase in conflict and chaos around the world as powerful states like China and Russia fight for regional control. Any number of smaller nations could be ground up in that struggle. Another option is that world leadership will be taken over by a single power. That might be China or Russia, but neither of those nations has a strong tradition of democratic government, religious freedom, freedom of movement, and freedom of expression. In a world of increasingly close connections, with people communicating, traveling, and migrating more than ever, with demands everywhere for greater political participation, and with greater diversity of religion, opinion, gender, and sexuality, we need a governing philosophy that can accommodate that diversity. The liberal tradition has shown itself capable of embracing those differences. I for one do not want to see the world dominated by a state that lacks such a tradition.

Conservative Group: Fred Speaking

🅼🅿 CONSEQUENCES AND LESSONS

I agree with John, but I have another concern that is more of a domestic issue.

Fred: The Most Important Consequence of the Trump Movement

- I think the most important consequence has been the destruction of the Republican Party as an American conservative party. Because of Trump, the Republican Party has already lost some of its leading public intellectuals — people like George Will, Max Boot, David Frum, Steve Schmidt, and Bill Kristol, to name just a few. No political party can succeed without people of that caliber to formulate its message and defend its positions.

- The party may survive as a populist party or as a mixture of conflicting factions, but it will not be the party that a generation of conservatives hoped it would be. Trump's Republican Party is also becoming a white person's party. I reject that. It is wrong morally and it will fail politically in the long run. There are simply not enough white working people without a college degree. Conservatives need to show the country that their ideas can benefit everyone.

- My conservatism advocates constitutionally limited government and limited market regulation. It is internationalist, not isolationist. It hopes to lead the world, not withdraw from it. And it is inclusive, not nativist or racist.

In the words of columnist David Brooks, the Republican leadership made a Faustian bargain with Trump. They may accomplish parts of their agenda, but it will "cost them their soul" (Brooks 2017).

Liberal Group: Vera Speaking

🅼🅿 CONSEQUENCES AND LESSONS

I have some ideas on the lessons and the consequences of the Trump movement. Here's what I think:

Vera: The Most Important Consequence of the Trump Movement

- The lesson from the Trump movement is that the dark side of the American character persists. It includes racism, nativism, and sexism. Trump has a very well-tuned gut feeling for those ideas and attitudes, and he stoked and legitimized them in order to become president.

- The most important consequence of the Trump movement may be an increase in the number of overt nativists, white nationalists, and other bigots. Those people are coming out of hiding to do their work. Right now, the target is undocumented Latin American immigrants and Muslims. Tomorrow? Who knows! You may or may not want to call it fascism, but this stuff is dangerous.

Catholic Group: Ayesha Speaking

🅼🅿 CONSEQUENCES AND LESSONS

I tend to agree with what others have said, but I'll add some ideas of my own.

Ayesha: The Most Important Consequence of the Trump Movement

- I am afraid that we are losing certain ideas that are fundamental to a well-functioning republican government. We have lost the idea of a common good, the idea of a loyal opposition, the idea that reasonable people can disagree, and the idea of mutually beneficial compromise. We may have lost the very idea of a liberal society in the older sense of a society characterized by individual freedom and the free exchange of ideas.

- Linked to the idea of a loyal opposition is the assumption that while people are often mistaken, they are seldom lying and seldom morally corrupt. We no longer make that distinction. Instead, people on all sides assume that whomever they disagree with is probably both lying and corrupt. Trump's critics take every false statement of his as a lie. His supporters say his critics are creating "fake news." A thriving liberal society must assume that there are honest differences of opinion that should be vigorously debated, not just enemies who lie to each other.

I'm concerned that a liberal republican society cannot survive with these changing ideas and attitudes.

*Liberal
Group:
Vera Speaking*

**O P COMMENT ON
CONSEQUENCES AND LESSONS**

I want to mention another lesson of a general nature. It is this: An election can give a man power, but it cannot give him wisdom. It cannot give him knowledge, prudence, a long-term view of the future, or a sense of the proper role of a leading nation in history. The character of the man matters.

Pro-Trump: Mike Speaking

M P CONSEQUENCES AND LESSONS

Diego and I both voted for Donald Trump, and we think the most important lessons and consequences are different from what you have been suggesting.

Mike: The Most Important Consequence Of the Trump Movement

- A large group of Americans, mostly white and with less than a college degree, have been left behind by the economic progress of the last 40 years. For decades the number of well-paid jobs (especially manufacturing jobs) open to people with a high school education has declined. The number of unionized jobs in the private sector has declined. The real wages of many people have risen very little or not at all while the salaries of better educated people have risen substantially. In short, the benefits of economic growth have been distributed very unevenly. During that period, the elites who run both political parties did very little for those people. The Democrats claimed to support unions, and the Republicans claimed they would lower taxes and defend traditional values. In the end, it was mostly talk. The Democrats focused on African Americans, feminists, and gays. The Republicans focused on big business, lowering taxes on the rich, and limiting regulation. Both parties favored economic globalization. The lesson is that we must not allow large groups of people to be left behind.

- The most important consequence may be that we finally do something for the people who helped build America and were then ignored and forgotten.

Conservative Group: Diego Speaking

🅜🅟 CONSEQUENCES AND LESSONS

I agree with Mike that Trump's economic policies are important. A lot of ordinary people have been ignored; but my concern is chiefly moral, not economic. As a Christian, I am concerned first of all with the moral decline of our country. If we cannot change that, we will never get back on the right track.

Diego: The Most Important Consequence Of the Trump Movement

- I think the most important consequence of the Trump movement is yet to come. Trump appointed pro-life judges to the Supreme Court. In a few years, I believe that *Roe v. Wade* will be reversed. The law on abortion will be sent back to the states where it belongs, and the people in most states will place stricter limits on legal abortions. When that happens, it will be the greatest moral reversal in modern times.

- Don't get me wrong. I believe that abortion should be allowed if a woman has been raped, if incest has occurred, or if pregnancy threatens the mother's life. I also think that most laws passed by the states will contain similar qualifications.

*Conservative
Group:
Fred Speaking*

🄾🄿 COMMENT ON PROBLEMS AND SOLUTIONS

Trump does point to some important problems, but he is not the man to solve them. In 2013, foreign policy expert Richard Haass wrote Foreign Policy Begins at Home. *He described many of our problems and proposed some solutions, but he also said that effective solutions require "real leadership." In the absence of real leadership, Haass listed three alternatives: drift, crisis, and "faux leadership in the form of populism." Donald Trump is not a conservative. He is that faux leadership, relying on ignorance, simplistic solutions, and animosity (Haass 2014, 163).*

Libertarian Group: Elijah Speaking

🄼🄿 CONSEQUENCES AND LESSONS

As libertarians, Dee and I can hardly support Trump.

Sure, we appreciate Trump's efforts to cut taxes and regulation, but there is a lot more to it than that. Broadly speaking, Trump is not at all libertarian. He admires autocrats like Putin and Duterte. He repeatedly attacks the press for criticizing him. He would love to ban Muslim immigrants, deport undocumented migrants, and reduce the number of legal immigrants. He has talked about using the death penalty against drug dealers. His tax law will produce a large deficit. His first attorney general came out solidly against the legalization of marijuana, and some of his high-level appointees are well-known foreign policy hawks. None of that is libertarian.

Elijah and Dee: The Most Important Consequence Of the Trump Movement

- The single most important problem with Donald Trump and his movement is his complete misunderstanding of how international trade works and how it benefits the United States as well as other countries. Trade is not a zero-sum game. Furthermore, trade should not be approached on a country by country basis. Trump seems to believe that if the United States negotiates bilateral agreements with a series of countries, and if each agreement (taken by itself) is good for the US, then we end up with the best trade arrangement possible. That's a mistake. He also seems to think that trade deficits are killing the American economy and that tariffs and other trade restrictions are the answer. Again, that's a mistake. Tariffs, for example, may be advantageous to a few companies and their employees; but they are essentially an added cost for everyone else. Is that the way to help American workers?

- The most important consequence of Trump's administration may be that we stop moving toward freer trade and shoot ourselves in the foot with a short-sighted economic nationalism. We hope that the Biden administration can reverse that trend. The solution to declining industries is new industries, not tariffs.

*Liberal
Group:
Vera Speaking*

🅾🅿 **COMMENT ON
CONSEQUENCES AND LESSONS**

I agree that Trump misunderstands how international trade works and how it benefits the United States. But I can't go all the way with libertarians in favor of completely free trade.

I think we can find a middle way. We can have freer trade that still has restrictions built in that protect the environment, hold up wages, and create safer working conditions in developing countries.

Liberal Group: Ann Speaking

🅜🅿 **TRUMP'S GIFTS**

I want to finish up with something a little different. I recently read David Frum's book *Trumpocracy*. Frum is a conservative who worked as a speech writer for President George W. Bush.

In *Trumpocracy*, Frum offers a list of "gifts" that Trump has given to all of us. I would like to list some of those gifts here. I'm going to paraphrase Frum's own account (Frum 2018, chapter 12).

Ann: The Gifts of Donald Trump

- We need a wider political vision. Trump has made us all realize that a large number of Americans have been ignored for decades. We have neglected "the ravages of drug addiction, the costs of immigration, the cultural and economic decline of the industrial working class."

- We need to rediscover the importance of truth. It is self-destructive to think of truth as a fiction or simply a tool of the powerful. We must reject the idea that everyone has their own truth. Remember this: If we want to say that someone is mistaken, then we must agree that there is a truth that can be known.

- Trump has reminded us that a bully is a coward, and we do not want a bully as our president.

- Trump has reminded the left that the institutions of national security are of great value to us all.

- Trump may have opened up the possibility of major reform within the Republican Party.

- Trump may have proven to both major political parties that moderation within each party needs to be cultivated.

Now let me add a gift idea of my own.

Ann: One More Gift

The rise of Donald Trump brought together an unusual group of allies. Liberals and conservatives who rejected Trump joined together to criticize him and his policies. My hope is that this will lead some of us to a greater appreciation of people we once regarded as political opponents. Most of my friends are liberals, but I hope that when they hear conservatives like David Frum, David Brooks, Max Boot, Bret Stephens, and George Will criticize Trump, they will realize that these are conservative humanists with serious convictions. I hope we will be able to work together in the future.

Professor Sidgwick Speaking

🅜🅟 CONSEQUENCES AND LESSONS

I hadn't planned on saying anything about the consequences of the Trump presidency, but I'm going to do so anyway.

I raised the problem of legitimacy in our other dialogue. John Rawls believed that the legitimacy of a democratic government depends on reasoning from common ground on issues of basic justice and basic institutions. In my opinion, part of that common ground consists of trusted procedures and institutions. Trump and some of his supporters have called those procedures and institutions into question. If our elections are fraudulent, if Congress is a "swamp," if the major media outlets are spreading lies, if our military leaders and our intelligence agencies are incompetent, why should anyone regard our government as legitimate? Why should anyone abide by its laws? By fostering those ideas, Trump has undermined our common ground and our faith in legitimate government more than any other development in recent years. That may be the most important consequence of his presidency.

Liberal Group: John Speaking

🅼🅿 FINAL THOUGHTS

Professor Sidgwick has asked me to offer some final thoughts on Donald Trump and the Trump movement. In part I will summarize what has been said, but I will add a few thoughts of my own. Even though Biden won the 2020 election, we need to understand and apply the lessons of the Trump presidency for the sake of our future as a republic.

John: Final Thoughts on Donald Trump

- Trump has identified some very real problems that a lot of people have ignored. Static incomes, lost jobs, Chinese investment and trade policies, and long foreign wars are good examples.

- At the same time, Trump has concocted or wildly exaggerated other problems. This has misled many people instead of providing effective leadership. Think of his suggestion that Barack Obama was not born in the US, his characterization of illegal immigrants as criminals, and his claims that millions of people voted illegally in the 2016 and the 2020 elections.

- When recognizing and focusing on real problems, Trump has done a service to our country. We may dislike his style, but we must acknowledge that the elites of both parties neglected those problems for many years. Now, I think, we realize that they can no longer be ignored. On the other hand, when focusing on phony problems, Trump has done us a great disservice.

- Even when Trump focused on significant problems, the solutions he proposed were of little value. Instead of facing the complexity and uncertainty of the world we live in, he offered illusions and slogans that can never be the basis of real solutions. A southern wall, for example, would do little to stop illegal migrants or the flow of drugs. A ban on Muslims would do little to stop terrorist attacks. Withdrawing from international organizations and agreements only makes it more difficult for the US to exercise leadership.

- In some ways, Trump has done us all a service by doing things that most of us criticize. By attacking established institutions, he has reminded us of their value. He has also reminded us that presidents have powers that can be abused, and, therefore, shown us how important the personal character of the president is.

Having said all of that, I believe that we must take up the challenge that Trump embodies. We must look the real problems he has identified in the face and develop solutions that are both effective and humane.

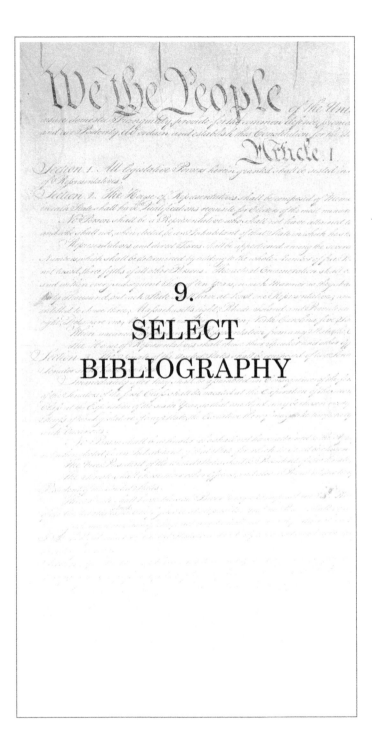

9.
SELECT
BIBLIOGRAPHY

BIBLIOGRAPHY

There is a large literature on political and social philosophy that includes many different points of view. The following works may be of value when you are working out your own position on issues. This bibliography includes the works quoted in the dialogues plus a selection of others.

Ackerman, Bruce.

Social Justice in the Liberal State. New Haven: Yale University Press, 1980.

Becker, Lawrence C.

Property Rights: Philosophic Foundations. London: Routledge & Kegan Paul, 1977.

Benn, S. I. and R. S. Peters.

The Principles of Political Thought. New York: The Free Press, 1959.

Berlin, Isaiah.

Four Essays on Liberty. London: Oxford University Press, 1969.

Boot, Max.

The Corrosion of Conservatism: Why I Left the Right. New York: Liveright Publishing Corporation, 2018.

Brandt, Richard B.

Ethical Theory. Englewood Cliffs: Prentice-Hall, Inc., 1959.

ed. *Social Justice.* Englewood Cliffs: Prentice-Hall, Inc., 1962.

Morality, Utilitarianism, and Rights. Cambridge: Cambridge University Press, 1992.

Brooks, David.

"The Republican Fausts." *The New York Times.* January 31, 2017.

Buckley, William F., Jr.

God and Man at Yale. Washington: Regnery Gateway, 1986. (Originally published 1951.)

"The Liberal Mind." *Facts Forum News.* June 1955.

"Our Mission Statement." *National Review.* November 19, 1955.

"Why the South Must Prevail." *National Review.* August 24, 1957. (This item was an unsigned editorial widely believed to have been written by W. F. Buckley.)

Up From Liberalism. Whittier: Constructive Action, Inc. 1965.

ed. *Did You Ever See a Dream Walking? American Conservative Thought in the Twentieth Century.* Indianapolis: Bobbs-Merrill Company, Inc., 1970.

Burke, Edmund.

An Appeal from the New to the Old Whigs. Indianapolis: The Bobbs-Merrill Company, Inc., 1962. (Originally published 1791.)

Reflections on the Revolution in France. London: Macmillan and Co., 1890. (There are many editions of this text, including Penguin Books, 1968. Originally published 1790.)

Carter, Stephen L.

The Culture of Disbelief. New York: Anchor Books, 1994.

Case, Anne and Angus Deaton.

"Rising morbidity and mortality in midlife among white non-Hispanic Americans in the 21st century." *Proceedings of the National Academy of Sciences of the United States of America.* Vol. 49. December 8, 2015.

Catholic University of America.

John A. Ryan Papers. Biographical Note. See https://libraries.catholic.edu/special-collections/archives/collections/finding-aids/finding-aids.html?file=ryan.

Collini, Stefan.

Liberalism and Sociology: L. T. Hobhouse and Political Argument in England 1880-1914. Cambridge: Cambridge University Press, 1979.

Coulter, Ann.

In Trump We Trust. New York: Sentinel, 2016.

Croly, Herbert.

The Promise of American Life. The paperback edition used here includes no publishing information. Probably published by CreateSpace Independent Publishing Platform, 2013. (Originally published 1909.)

Curran, Charles E.

American Catholic Social Ethics: Twentieth-Century Approaches. Notre Dame: University of Notre Dame Press, 1982.

Daniels, Norman.

Justice and Justification. Cambridge: Cambridge University Press, 1996.

ed. *Reading Rawls: Critical Studies on Rawls' A Theory of Justice*. Stanford: Stanford University Press, 1989.

De Beauvoir, Simone.

The Ethics of Ambiguity. Translated by Bernard Frechtman. New York: The Citadel Press, 1964.

Dewey, John.

Liberalism and Social Action. New York: Capricorn Books, 1963. (Originally published 1935.)

"The Future of Liberalism." *School and Society*. January 19, 1935.

Dolan, Jay P.

The American Catholic Experience: A History from Colonial Times to the Present. Notre Dame: University of Notre Dame Press, 1992.

Dworkin, Ronald.

Taking Rights Seriously. Cambridge: Harvard University Press, 1978.

Justice for Hedgehogs. Cambridge: Harvard University Press, 2011.

Edin, Kathryn J. and H. Luke Shaefer.

$2.00 a Day: Living on Almost Nothing in America. Boston: Houghton Mifflin Harcourt, 2015.

Ely, Richard T.

Social Aspects of Christianity, and Other Essays. New York: Thomas Y. Crowell & Company, 1889.

"Fundamental Beliefs in My Social Philosophy." *The Forum*, Vol. XVIII, October 1894, p. 173-183.

"Fraternalism vs. Paternalism in Government." *The Century Magazine*, March 1898, p. 780-784.

The World War and Leadership in a Democracy. New York: The MacMillan Company, 1918.

Falwell, Jerry.

Listen, America! New York: Bantam Books, 1981.

Feinberg, Joel.

Social Philosophy. Englewood Cliffs: Prentice-Hall, Inc., 1973.

Flake, Jeff.

Conscience of a Conservative: A Rejection of Destructive Politics and a Return to Principle. New York: Random House, 2017.

Francis (Pope).

Encyclical Letter *Laudato Si'*. The Holy See, 2015.

Frankena, William K.

Ethics. Englewood Cliffs: Prentice-Hall, Inc., 1973.

Friedman, Milton.

Capitalism and Freedom. Chicago: University of Chicago Press, 1962.

Frum, David.

Trumpocracy: The Corruption of the American Republic. New York: HarperCollins Publishers, 2018.

Gauthier, David.

Morals by Agreement. Oxford: Oxford University Press, 1986.

Gewirth, Alan.

Human Rights: Essays on Justification and Applications. Chicago: University of Chicago Press, 1982.

Gilson, Etienne, ed.

The Church Speaks to the Modern World: The Social Teachings of Leo XIII. Garden City: Image Books, 1954.

Goldwater, Barry.

The Conscience of a Conservative. New York: MacFadden Books, 1961. (This book is widely believed to have been ghost written by L. Brent Bozell. Originally published 1960.)

Goodman, Lenn E.

Religious Pluralism and Values in the Public Sphere. New York: Cambridge University Press, 2014.

Gore, Charles. ed.

Property: Its Duties and Rights Historically, Philosophically and Religiously Regarded (second edition). London: Macmillan and Co., 1915.

Gottfried, Paul.

The Conservative Movement. (Revised Edition). New York: Twayne Publishers, 1993.

Green, T. H.

Lectures on the Principles of Political Obligation. London: Longmans, Green, and Co., 1895. (More recent editions of this work include The University of Michigan Press, 1967.)

"Liberal Legislation and Freedom of Contract" in *Works of T. H. Green.* Vol. III. (p. 365-386). Edited by R. L. Nettleship. London: Longmans, Green, and Co., 1888. (This lecture was first delivered in 1881.)

Greenawalt, Kent.

Religious Convictions and Political Choice. New York: Oxford University Press, 1988.

Gremillion, Joseph, ed.

The Gospel of Peace and Justice: Catholic Social Teaching Since Pope John. Maryknoll: Orbis Books, 1976.

Griffin, James.

On Human Rights. Oxford: Oxford University Press, 2008.

Gutiérrez, Gustavo.

A Theology of Liberation. Translated by Sister Caridad Inda and John Eagleson. Maryknoll: Orbis Books, 1973. (Originally published in Spanish 1971.)

"Notes for a Theology of Liberation." *Theological Studies* Volume 31 Issue 2, May 1, 1970, p. 243-261.

Gutmann, Amy and Dennis Thompson.

Democracy and Disagreement. Cambridge: Harvard University Press, 1996.

Haass, Richard.

Foreign Policy Begins at Home. New York: Basic Books, 2013.

Hare, R. M.

Freedom and Reason. Oxford: Oxford University Press, 1963.

Moral Thinking: Its Levels, Method, and Point. Oxford: Oxford University Press, 1981.

"Arguing about Rights" in *Essays on Political Morality.* Oxford: Clarendon Press, 1989.

Hart, H. L. A.

The Concept of Law. London: Oxford University Press, 1961.

Law, Liberty, and Morality. Stanford: Stanford University Press, 1963.

Haworth, Lawrence.

Autonomy: An Essay in Philosophical Psychology and Ethics. New Haven: Yale University Press, 1986.

Hayek, Friedrich.

The Road to Serfdom. Chicago: University of Chicago Press, 1944.

"The Pretense of Knowledge." Nobel Prize lecture, 1974. (Lecture available at https://www.nobelprize.org/prizes/economic sciences/1974/hayek/lecture/.)

Hazlitt, Henry.

Economics in One Lesson. New York: MacFadden, 1961. (Originally published 1946.)

Held, Virginia.

Rights and Goods: Justifying Social Action. Chicago: The University of Chicago Press, 1984.

Feminist Morality: Transforming Culture, Society, and Politics. Chicago: The University of Chicago Press, 1993.

Herskovits, Melville J.

Cultural Relativism: Perspectives in Cultural Pluralism. Edited by Frances Herskovits. New York: Vintage Books, 1973.

Hobhouse, L. T.

Liberalism. London: Williams & Norgate, 1919. (*Liberalism* was first published in 1911 and is available in many later editions including Oxford University Press, 1964.)

Hollenbach, David.

Claims in Conflict: Retrieving and Renewing the Catholic Human Rights Tradition. New York: Paulist Press, 1979.

Holmes, Oliver Wendell, Jr.

"Natural Law." *Harvard Law Review.* Vol. 32 (1918), No. 1, p. 40-44. (Versions of this article vary and some do not include the exact quotation used in this dialogue. The version quoted here is taken from the *Harvard Law Review* archived on JSTOR.org.)

Hume, David.

Enquiries Concerning the Human Understanding and Concerning the Principles of Morals. Edited by L. A. Selby-Bigge. Oxford: Oxford University Press, 1902. (Originally published 1748 and 1751 respectively.)

John XXIII (Pope).

See anthology edited by Gremillion for *Pacem in Terris.*

Judis, John B.

The Populist Explosion: How the Great Recession Transformed American and European Politics. New York: Columbia Global Reports, 2016.

Kazin, Michael.

The Populist Persuasion: An American History. New York: Basic Books, 1995.

Keller, Rev. Edward A.

Christianity and American Capitalism. Chicago: The Heritage Foundation, Inc., 1953.

Kelley, David.

A Life of One's Own: Individual Rights and the Welfare State. Washington: The Cato Institute, 1998.

Keynes, John M.

Essays in Persuasion. New York: W. W. Norton & Company, Inc., 1963.

"An Open Letter to President Roosevelt." 1933. This letter is available on many web sites including http://la.utexas.edu/users/hcleaver/368/368KeynesOpenLetFDRtable.pdf.

King, Martin Luther, Jr.

"Letter from Birmingham Jail." 1963. (This letter is available at many sites on the internet. For example, it can be found at the Martin Luther King, Jr. Research and Education Institute at Stanford University.)

Kirk, Russell.

The Conservative Mind from Burke to Eliot. 7ᵗʰ edition. Washington: Regnery Publishing, Inc., 1986.

Kristol, Irving.

Reflections of a Neoconservative: Looking Back, Looking Forward. New York: Basic Books, Inc., 1983.

Kukathas, Chandran and Philip Pettit.

Rawls: A Theory of Justice and its Critics. Stanford: Stanford University Press, 1990.

Kymlicka, Will.

Contemporary Political Philosophy: An Introduction. 2ⁿᵈ edition. Oxford: Oxford University Press, 2002.

Lay Commission on Catholic Social Teaching and the U.S. Economy.

"Liberty and Justice for All." 1986. This report is available online at *Crisis Magazine* at the following URL: *https://www.crisismagazine.com/1986/special-report-liberty-and-justice-for-all.*

Leo XIII (Pope).

See anthology edited by Gilson for *Rerum Novarum* and other encyclicals by Leo XIII.

Locke, John.

Two Treatises of Government. Edited by Peter Laslett. Cambridge: Cambridge University press, 1960. Issued as a Mentor book by New American Library in 1965. (Originally published 1689.)

Lomasky, Loren E.

Persons, Rights, and the Moral Community. New York: Oxford University Press, 1987.

Mackie, J. L.

Ethics: Inventing Right and Wrong. New York: Penguin Books, 1977.

McLaughlin, Terence, ed.

The Church and the Reconstruction of the Modern World: The Social Encyclicals of Pius XI. Garden City: Image Books, 1957.

Meyer, Frank S.

In Defense of Freedom and Related Essays. Indianapolis: Liberty Fund, Inc., 1996.

Mill, John Stuart.

Utilitarianism. London: Longmans, Green and Co., 1901. (Originally published 1861. Many editions of this work have been published.)

On Liberty. Indianapolis: The Bobbs-Merrill Company, Inc., 1956. (Originally published 1859.)

Mills, Charles W.

"'Ideal Theory' as Ideology." *Hypatia.* Vol. 20, no. 3 (Summer 2005), p. 165-184.

Moore, Stephen and Arthur B. Laffer.

Trumponomics: Inside the America First Plan to Revive Our Economy. New York: St. Martin's Press, 2018.

Narveson, Jan.

The Libertarian Idea. Philadelphia: Temple University Press, 1988.

"The Contractarian Theory of Morals: Frequently Asked Questions." 2003. Available at www.gkpn.de/narveson2.pdf.

National Conference of Catholic Bishops.

Economic Justice for All. Washington: United States Catholic Conference, Inc., 1986.

Neuhaus, Richard John.

The Naked Public Square: Religion and Democracy in America. Grand Rapids: William B. Eerdmans Publishing Company, 1984.

Nielsen, Kai.

Why Be Moral?. Buffalo: Prometheus Books, 1989.

Nisbet, Robert.

Conservatism: Dream and Reality. Minneapolis: University of Minnesota Press, 1986.

Nozick, Robert.

Anarchy, State, and Utopia. New York: Basic Books, Inc., 1974.

Nunez, Ted.

Sustainable Abundance for All: Catholic Social Thought and Action in a Risky, Runaway World. Eugene: Cascade Books, 2018. (The Kindle edition is quoted here. Kindle location numbers are used in place of page numbers.)

Nussbaum, Martha C.

"Capabilities and Human Rights." *Fordham Law Review*. Vol. 66 (1997), p. 273-300.

"Aristotelian Social Democracy" in *Aristotle and Modern Politics*. Edited by Aristide Tessitore. Notre Dame: University of Notre Dame Press, 2002.

Frontiers of Justice: Disability, Nationality, Species Membership. Cambridge: The Belknap Press, 2006.

Creating Capabilities: The Human Development Approach. Cambridge: The Belknap Press, 2011.

Paul, Jeffrey, ed.

Reading Nozick: Essays on Anarchy, State, and Utopia. Totowa: Rowman & Littlefield, 1981.

Paul VI (Pope).

See anthology edited by Gremillion for *Humanae Vitae*. Different English versions of *Humanae Vitae* have different wording for paragraphs 10 and 11. This book uses the version in the Gremillion anthology.

Payne, Stanley G.

Fascism: Comparison and Definition. Madison: University of Wisconsin Press, 1980.

Perry, Michael J.

Love and Power: The Role of Religion and Morality in American Politics. New York: Oxford University Press, 1991.

Pesch, Heinrich, S.J.

Ethics and the National Economy. Translated by Dr. Rupert Ederer. Norfolk: IHS Press, 2004.

Pilon, Roger.

"Ordering Rights Consistently: Or What We Do and Do Not Have Rights To." *Georgia Law Review.* Vol. 13 (1979a), p. 1171-1196.

"A Theory of Rights: Toward Limited Government." Unpublished Dissertation. University of Chicago, 1979b.

Pogge, Thomas.

John Rawls: His Life and Theory of Justice. New York: Oxford University Press, Inc., 2007. (Original German edition, 1994.)

Realizing Rawls. Ithaca: Cornell University Press, 1989.

Rawls, John.

A Theory of Justice. Cambridge: Harvard University Press, 1971.

Political Liberalism. Paperback edition with new introduction. New York: Columbia University Press, 1996.

Justice as Fairness: A Restatement. Edited by E. Kelly. Cambridge: The Belknap Press, 2001.

Reed, Ralph.

Active Faith: How Christians Are Changing the Soul of American Politics. New York: The Free Press, 1996.

Reich, Robert.

"The American Fascist." RobertReich.org. March 8, 2016.

Richter, Melvin.

The Politics of Conscience: T. H. Green and His Age. Cambridge: Harvard University Press, 1964.

Robbins, Harold.

The Sun of Justice: An Essay on the Social Teaching of the Catholic Church. London: Heath Cranton Limited, 1938. (The 2011 Kindle edition is quoted here. Kindle location numbers are used in place of page numbers.)

Robertson, Pat.

The New World Order. Dallas: Word Publishing, 1991.

Roosevelt, Theodore.

"The New Nationalism." Speech given in Osawatomie, Kansas on August 31, 1910. Speech available at https://obamawhitehouse. archives.gov/blog/2011/12/06/archives-president-teddy-roosevelts-newnationalism-speech.

Ryan, John.

"The Bishops' Program of Social Reconstruction." Washington: National Catholic Welfare Conference, 1919.

Economic Justice. Edited by Harlan R. Beckley. (This volume contains selections from *Distributive Justice* and *A Living Wage* by John Ryan.) Louisville: Westminster John Knox Press, 1996.

A Better Economic Order. New York: Harper & Brothers Publishers, 1935.

Letter on Father Charles Coughlin published in *Commonweal*, October 1936. This letter is available online at: http://historymatters.gmu. edu/d/126/.

Sandel, Michael J.

Liberalism and the Limits of Justice. 2nd edition. Cambridge: Cambridge University Press, 1998.

Justice: What's the Right Thing to Do?. New York: Farrar, Straus and Giroux, 2009.

Scanlon, T. M.

What We Owe to Each Other. Cambridge: Harvard University Press, 1998.

Scaramucci, Anthony.

Trump: The Blue-Collar President. New York: Hachette Book Group, Inc., 2018.

Schlafly, Phyllis, Ed Martin, and Brett M. Decker.

The Conservative Case for Trump. Washington: Regnery Publishing, 2016.

Schmiesing, Kevin E.

"Another Social Justice Tradition: Catholic Conservatives." *University of St. Thomas Law Journal*, Vol. 2 (2005), p. 308-325.

Sen, Amartya.

The Idea of Justice. London: Penguin Books, 2010.

Sidgwick, Henry.

The Methods of Ethics. 7th edition. New York: Dover Publications, Inc., 1966. (First edition originally published 1874.)

Singer, Peter.

"A Reply to Martha Nussbaum." *The Tanner Lectures on Human Values*, 2002.

Smith, Adam, LL.D.

An Enquiry Into the Nature and Causes of the Wealth of Nations. Three volumes. Printed for G. Walker and others, 1822. (Originally published 1776. There are many editions of this work, including the Edwin Cannan edition published by Random House, Inc., 1937.)

Spencer, Herbert.

Social Statics: or The Conditions Essential to Human Happiness Specified, and the First of Them Developed. London: John Chapman, 1851.

The Man versus The State. Edited by Donald Macrae. Harmondsworth: Penguin Books, Ltd., 1969. (Originally published 1884.)

Stein, Mark.

"Nussbaum, a Utilitarian Critique." *Boston College Law Review*. Vol. 50, Issue 2 (2009), p. 489-531.

Thomson, Judith Jarvis.

The Realm of Rights. Cambridge: Harvard University Press, 1990.

"Some Ruminations on Rights," in *Reading Nozick: Essays on Anarchy, State, and Utopia*. Edited by Jeffrey Paul. Totowa: Rowman & Littlefield, 1981.

Vallentyne, Peter.

"Left-Libertarianism and Liberty." in *Contemporary Debates in Political Philosophy*. Edited by Thomas Christiano and John Christman. Blackwell Publishing Ltd., 2009a.

"Left-Libertarianism as a Promising Form of Liberal Egalitarianism." *Philosophic Exchange*, Vol. 39 (2009b), No. 1, Art. 1.

Vallentyne, Peter and Hillel Steiner, ed.

Left-Libertarianism and its Critics: The Contemporary Debate. New York: Palgrave Macmillan, 2001. (This anthology includes Vallentyne's article "Left-Libertarianism: A Primer.")

Viereck, Peter.

Conservatism Revisited. Revised and enlarged Edition. New York: The Free Press, 1962.

Conservatism: From John Adams to Churchill. Princeton: D. Van Nostrand Company, Inc., 1956.

Vlastos, Gregory.

"Justice and Equality." in *Social Justice*. Edited by Richard B. Brandt. Englewood Cliffs: Prentice-Hall, 1962.

Waldron, Jeremy.

The Right to Private Property. Oxford: Clarendon Press, 1988.

Weiler, Peter.

The New Liberalism: Liberal Social Theory in Great Britain 1889-1914. New York: Garland Publishing, Inc., 1982.

White, Alan.

"If You Can Understand This Essay, Then You Have Moral Rights and Moral Duties." *Open Philosophy*. Vol. 3 (2020), 28 May, p. 161-174. (This article is available at https://www.degruyter.com/view/journals/opphil/3/1/article-p161.xml.)

Will, George F.

Statecraft as Soulcraft: What Government Does. New York: Simon & Shuster, Inc., 1983.

The Conservative Sensibility. New York: Hachette Books, 2019.

Wolff, Michael.

Fire and Fury: Inside the Trump White House. London: Little, Brown, 2018.

Woodward, Bob.

Fear: Trump in the White House. New York: Simon & Shuster, 2018.

Young Americans for Freedom.

"Sharon Statement." 1960. The Sharon Statement is available from many sources on the World Wide Web.

Attributions, Permissions, and Licenses

Photo attributions for characters in the dialogue (source: Unsplash.com)

Professor Sidgwick – photo by Chris Blonk
Ann – photo by Sean Kong
Ayesha – photo by Mike Von
Dee – photo by Alex Gagareen
Diego – photo by Damon Hall
Elijah – photo by Mubariz Mehdizadeh
Fred – photo by Rubén Visuals
John – photo by Norbert Kundrak
Mike – photo by Gregory Hayes
Vera – photo by Allison Griffith

Photo attributions and licenses for figures other than characters in the dialogue. All images have been cropped to fit the layout of this book.

Buckley, William F.

This image was downloaded from Wikimedia Commons. Wikimedia Commons indicates that this work is the work of a federal government employee and is in the public domain in the United States.

Burke, Edmund

This image was downloaded from Wikimedia Commons. It is a photographic reproduction of a painting by Joshua Reynolds. The Wikimedia Foundation identifies this image as in the public domain in the United States because it is a faithful photographic reproduction of a work of art in the public domain. {{PD-Art|PD-US}}

Dewey, John

This image was downloaded from Wikimedia Commons and is identified as being in the public domain. The photo is attributed to Underwood & Underwood. Wikimedia Commons indicates that this work is from the Library of Congress and that according to the library there are no known copyright restrictions on the use of this work.

Falwell, Jerry

This image was downloaded from Wikimedia Commons. The photo is attributed to Liberty University. The Wikimedia Foundation indicates that the image may be used by anyone for any purpose. A GNU free documentation license version 1.2 or later applies. The license may be found at: https://commons.wikimedia.org/wiki/Commons:GNU_Free_Documentation_License,_version_1.2. A Creative Commons CC BY-SA 3.0 license applies.

Pope Francis

This image was downloaded from Wikimedia Commons. It is attributed to the Casa Rosada (Argentina). A Creative Commons CC BY-SA 2.0 license applies.

Goldwater, Barry

This image was downloaded from Creative Commons and is marked as being in the public domain. The photo is attributed to Nominay. A Creative Commons CC PDM 1.0 license applies.

Green, Thomas Hill

This image was downloaded from Wikimedia Commons. A Creative Commons CC BY-SA 4.0 license applies.

Hobhouse, L. T.

This image was downloaded from Wikimedia Commons and is identified as having no known copyright restrictions. The photo is attributed to the Library of the London School of Economics and Political Science.

Hollenbach, David

This photo was provided by Father David Hollenbach, S.J. No formal license applies.

Jefferson, Thomas

This image was downloaded from Wikimedia Commons. It is a photographic reproduction of a painting by Rembrandt Peale. The Wikimedia Foundation identifies this image as in the public domain in the United States because it is a faithful photographic reproduction of a work of art in the public domain. {{PD-Art|PD-US}}

Reed, Ralph

This image was downloaded from Wikimedia Commons. The photo is attributed to Gage Skidmore. A Creative Commons CC BY-SA 2.0 license applies.

Roosevelt, Theodore

This image was downloaded from Wikimedia Commons and is identified as being in the public domain.

Ryan, John A.

This image was downloaded from Wikimedia Commons. It is attributed to the Harris & Ewing collection at the Library of Congress. According to the library, there are no known copyright restrictions on the photograph.

Smith, Adam

This image was downloaded from Wikimedia Commons. It is photographic reproduction of a medallion made by James Tassie. The Wikimedia Foundation identifies this image as in the public domain in the United States because it is a faithful photographic reproduction of a work of art in the public domain. {{PD-Art|PD-US}}

Vallentyne, Peter

This photo was provided by philosopher Peter Vallentyne. No formal license applies.

Links to Creative Commons Licenses Referred to Above

Creative Commons CC PDM 1.0. The license is available at https://creativecommons.org/publicdomain/mark/1.0/?ref=ccsearch&atype=rich.

Creative Commons CC BY 2.0. The license can be found at https://creativecommons.org/licenses/by/2.0/?ref=ccsearch&atype=rich.

Creative Commons CC BY-SA 2.0. The license is available at https://creativecommons.org/licenses/by-sa/2.0/.

Creative Commons CC BY 3.0. The license can be found at https://creativecommons.org/licenses/by/3.0/.

Permissions for Quotations
*Grateful acknowledgement is made for permission to quote
from the following material in copyright.*

Anarchy, State, and Utopia by Robert Nozick, Copyright © 1974. Reprinted by
permission of Basic Books, an imprint of Hachette Book Group, Inc.

The Concept of Law, by H. L. A. Hart. Copyright © 1961 Oxford University
Press. Reproduced with permission of the Licensor through PLSclear.

The Conservative Case for Trump, Copyright © 2016 Regnery Publishing.
Reprinted with permission of the publisher.

Frontiers of Justice: Disability, Nationality, Species Membership, by Martha
C. Nussbaum, Cambridge, Mass.: The Belknap Press of Harvard University
Press, Copyright ©2006 by the President and Fellows of Harvard College.
Reproduced by permission.

Listen, America! by Jerry Falwell. Copyright © 1981 by Bantam Books.
Reprinted by permission.

*Sustainable Abundance for All: Catholic Social Thought and Action in a Risky,
Runaway World*, by Ted Nunez, Copyright © 2018 by Cascade Books. Used by
permission of Wipf and Stock Publishers.

A Theory of Justice, by John Rawls, Cambridge, Mass.: The Belknap Press of
Harvard University Press, Copyright ©1971 by the President and Fellows of
Harvard College. Reproduced by permission.

ACKNOWLEDGEMENTS

I would like to acknowledge the help I received from several people in writing and publishing these dialogues. Audrey Hoisington edited an early version of the manuscript. Linda Lögdberg edited a later version. Both added many improvements in clarity and consistency. Lisa Daly designed the layout for the dialogues, providing visual elements that help the reader to understand the movement of a semi-linear text. Alison DeLuca provided knowledge of the entire process of publishing a book at Amazon.com. Finally, my friend Peggy Morrison read the manuscript, offered many suggestions, and put up with me while I was writing. The remaining errors and limitations are entirely my own.

Made in the USA
Monee, IL
17 September 2021

78034003R10208